STER

C

D1340347

IMAGINE THERE'S NO WOMAN ■■■■■■

THE MIT PRESS · CAMBRIDGE, MASSACHUSETTS · LONDON, ENGLAND

IMAGINE THERE'S NO WOMAN ▄▄▄

Ethics and Sublimation

Joan Copjec

This book was set in Berthold Akzidenz Grotesk and Emigre Mrs. Eaves by Graphic Composition Inc. and was printed and bound in the United States of America.

Library of Congress Cataloging-in-Publication Data

Copjec, Joan.

Imagine there's no woman : ethics and sublimation / Joan Copjec.

p.   cm.

Includes bibliographical references and index.

ISBN 0-262-03299-6 (hc : alk. paper)

1. Ethics. 2. Feminist ethics. I. Title.

BJ1012.C68   2002

170—dc21   2002023070

It is as *figlia di Anna*, a name by which I am proudly known, that I wrote this book, which I now dedicate to the memory of my mother, Ann Armento Copjec, and to that of my brother, John Peter Copjec. To say more about either would be to say too little.

ACKNOWLEDGMENTS

This book has benefited from the fellowship of colleagues at three institutions from which I received grants in the last several years and which I would like warmly to thank for their support: the Society for the Humanities, Cornell University (1995–1996); the Center for the Critical Analysis of Contemporary Culture, Rutgers University (1997–1998); and the "Antinomies of Postmodern Reason" research group at the Kulturwissenschaftliches Institut, Essen, Gemany (2000–2002).

Roger Conover was an active and engaged editor; I thank him for his many creative suggestions, and Judy Feldmann for her careful attention to the final manuscript. Carol Paulino and Robert Copjec were critical to keeping the project going. Their generosity and steadfastness saw me through the toughest moments. Michael Sorkin, whose resources of personality are mysterious and ramifying, invented distractions, doled out encouragement, and ignored my fits of moodiness—as needed. This book owes much to his flexible good nature.

INTRODUCTION: IMAGINE THERE'S NO WOMAN

As questions of ethics once again begin to top the theoretical agenda, everyone, it seems—including those who want for the most part to reinstate his authority—has a stone or two to throw at Kant. But the one thrown by Jacques Lacan is uniquely effective in driving a hole through the architecture of Kant's thought. The nugget with which Lacan takes aim—"Long live Poland, for without Poland there would be no Poles!"—is immediately recognizable as a found object, lifted from the text of Alfred Jarry's *Ubu roi*.[1] A blunt, even childish instrument, one might say. And yet the inane truism it spouts *is* effective—not because it taunts Kant for relying on tautologies but because it is *untrue*. For, although it may seem to go without saying that the very existence of individuals calling themselves Poles depends fundamentally on the existence of a Poland under whose logical harbor they are necessarily subsumed, history has not borne out this elementary logic. Indeed, what has distinguished Poles—as well as Jews, Armenians, Latvians, Chechens, Kosovards, native Americans (the list reads like a "cheat sheet" for some of the major political struggles of the modern era)—is their ability to resist obliteration despite their lack of a sheltering homeland. Lacan's irreverent claim is that Kant, like père Ubu, is too fond of analytic judgment—which can only unfold a knowledge we already have but not materially add to it—for his own good. Propping up his thesis about the universalizability of moral law on the law of noncontradiction, Kant pays short shrift to those sorts of synthetic, historical judgments that would, for example, permit him to refute Ubu's unworldly illogic.

Although this charge is eminently important, one is obliged to admit that it is not new. Far from being an uncommon criticism, it is the same stone thrown at Kant by countless others: he neglected the sensible intuition of empirical circumstances in favor of universal ideas. What interests me in Lacan's reformulation of the standard criticism is its mischievous—though nontrivial—design to *place the opponents of Kant off balance* by torturing that very intuition with which they seek either to invalidate or rectify his ethical theory. Rather than renouncing Kant's formalism, Lacan aims here at shoring it up. For, while noting that père Ubu's self-enclosed statement is refuted by history, he is not merely critiquing formalism but reposing the question of how human forms materially contribute to the emergence of history.

One should not fail to notice that the maxim chosen as taunt is one that asks to be translated into set theoretical terms. It turns on the question of whether there can be a predicate—here, Poles—without any extension, or to which no set, or whole—here, Poland—corresponds. The historically attested answer is, as we have just stated, an emphatic "yes." But this answer will too easily, too automatically, be assumed to respond to Foucault's frugal advice that some nominalism is always necessary. Much of cultural theory has, in my opinion, helped itself to an overdose of nominalism and would thus be quick to find in Lacan's example confirmation of its position: *there are only particular persons and things,* despite the fact that culture continually builds and unbuilds—while mistaking them for givens—series of arbitrary and alterable universals, whether these be nations, institutions, identities, or moral laws. Universals are seen by nominalists simply as illusions to be deconstructed and dispersed.

If the lesson set theory had eventually to absorb—namely, we *cannot* form a set, a whole, from every predicate, every property ascribable to a person or thing—were taken seriously, however, the position of nominalism, or what we are now calling "particularism," would be sternly rebuked. By way of explanation let me briefly review the genesis of this central and yet traumatic tenet of set theory. Gottlob Frege, curious about "aggregative thought"—that is, about what it is we do when we add things to each other in order to accomplish ordinary tasks, such as taking a census of citizens residing in a country—believed he could establish the laws of arithmetic on a purely logical basis and could thereby eliminate other, "psychological methods of argument" to which he expressed an appropriate aversion.[2] After condemning the historicism to which these other methods perforce give rise, he attempted to develop the laws of counting on surer ground by defining number as dependent on the procedure by which we subsume empirical objects under concepts to form sets (for example: concrete persons under the concept or predicate "Polish" to form the set of a distinct number of Poles). In other words, we do not merely count things, we count things falling under concepts. But this procedure did not turn out to be as solidly grounded as Frege thought it was. A single letter from Bertrand Russell was enough to unsettle Frege's theory to such a degree that the several attempts made to restore it have all been shown to be flimsy and makeshift. In his momentous letter, Russell proposed a concept (or predicate or condition) from which it was impossible to form a set. That concept was "a set that does not include itself."

Far from being a logical freak, this concept describes the most common of sets. If one were to teach a course on the films of Alfred Hitchcock, for example, one would operate with a set of this sort. In preparing a syllabus, one would easily determine that *The Birds* and *The Paradine Case,* however different they might seem, were both identical to the concept "films made by Hitchcock" and thus proper candidates for inclusion in the course, while Claude Chabrol's *Le Boucher* would be excluded on the grounds that it was not identical to the concept "films made by Hitchcock" even though, influenced by Hitchcock, it was similar in recognizable ways to his films. One could just as easily determine that "the set of films made by Hitchcock" would itself be excluded, on the grounds this time that the course was about *films* and not about *sets* or *set theory.* In other words, the "set of films made by Hitchcock," is *not* a member of itself, is not a member of the set of films made by Hitchcock, and there is no difficulty in understanding why this is so. It is evident, too, that the concept is a pertinent one inasmuch as there are sets that would *not* fall under its description. The "set of things that are not Hitchcock films," for instance, *would* include itself (and would therefore not constitute a set that does not include itself). A problem arises only when one asks whether one can form *a set* from the concept "a set that does not include itself," a set of all sets answering to this condition. For, this perfectly ordinary condition (as we have just seen) cannot, without producing a formal contradiction, yield an extension, a set. There cannot be a set of sets that do not include themselves because such a set would be an indisputable contradiction in terms.

Now, this notorious demonstration of our inability to move automatically from a concept to the existence of a numerable set, an all or whole, may appear to confirm positions that are themselves opposed. On the one hand, it might be pressed into service to support the nominalist position that there *are* no sets, classes, or universals of any kind. With Russell's paradox we can seem to be witnessing the comeuppance of abstract thought, which here becomes entangled in its own snares while trying to introduce categories, sets and classes, that have no existence in reality. On the other hand, the paradox might be taken to exemplify Kant's transcendental position that being is not a predicate, that being as such transcends and thus makes fail every concept or the very reason that tries to grasp it. The paradox would confirm in the first case the nonexistence, and in the second the existence of the being that is in question; but in each case it would be a certain impotence of thought that would be laid bare. Alain Badiou, militant mathematician and highly independent disciple of Lacan, has comprehensively argued, however, that the paradox exposes not the confused relation of thought to itself, but the power of thought, of the concept, to capture being, to effect existence. He draws from the paradox its *ontological* import, describing Russell's concept as "a *materialist* argument [which] demonstrates that multiple-being is anterior to the statements that affect it."[3] One could restate Badiou's conclusion thus: if we cannot proceed without hitch from a concept to the existence of its extension or to the existence of the totality of what it predicates, as Frege wanted to believe we could, this is not because at some point thought falters in its attempt to think being, but because *being is not-all, being itself never forms a totality. Moreover, it is thought that makes an all of being impossible. It is thought that makes this impossibility of constituting an all a property (not of thought, but) of being.* Russell demonstrated (which is not to say he *argued,* for indeed he resisted and continuously tried to undo what he had inadvertantly shown) not that we cannot *think* the all of being, but that there *is* none. There is no whole of being, no "all there is," there are only appearances in their particularity.

In attempting to distance itself from the nominalist position, does this one not end up running headlong into it? Or, what is the difference between the position adopted by Badiou, after Lacan, and nominalism? Lacan does not argue that there are no universals, only particular things; rather, he maintains that *universals are real.* To limit one's observation only to appearances, to particular things, is to overlook the existence of the real, which is precisely what makes an all of being impossible. In other words, if there are only appearances in their particularity, this is due to the fact that the real, a by-product or residue of thought, detaches itself from thought to form its internal limit. This limit has both a synthesizing function that universalizes by causing thought to revolve around it *and* a detotalizing function, since it subtracts itself from thought. This subtraction, in turn, "establishes a fracture, a bi-partition, a splitting" in the order of being as appearance.[4]

Let us return to the scene of stone throwing I invoked earlier. With what does Lacan hit Kant? With history, we said. Fredric Jameson is therefore right;

history is what hurts, in this case because it gives the lie to a purely logical, analytical claim. But Lacan approaches history by opposing Kant's logic with a logic of a different sort: that of set theory.[5] In so doing he does not deconstruct or disperse the universal; rather he redefines it as that which disperses being. But what is the point—for ethics—of toying with père Ubu's silly maxim? I would claim that Lacan is recommending a new ethical imperative: "Imagine there's no Poland!" Jacques-Alain Miller has pointed out that the relation between Poles and Poland mimics that between deposits and depositaries in the example Kant gives in his second *Critique* to support the imperative, "Act as if the maxim of your action could be taken as a maxim for all."[6] Kant asks us to imagine a greedy depositary who receives a deposit from someone who then dies without leaving a record of the transaction. Though this individual depositary might deny receipt of the deposit, his action could not be elevated into a universal maxim, a maxim for all, for this would only end up sabotaging the very system of deposits. The basic act of depositing money requires a depositary to be "equal to his charge."[7] Deposits are to Poles, then, as depositaries are to Poland; the former depend for their continued existence on the safeguard of the latter. The obvious target of Lacan's mockery is Kant's belief that one could come up with a logical formula for determining whether an act was ethical or not, as if there could exist an external gurantee for the rightness of an act.

But the imperative "Imagine there's no Poland!" does more than this; it draws Kant's ontology into the target area. For, to say there is no "Poland" is to say there are no noumena beyond phenomena, that there is nothing beyond appearances. Lacan's attack on "Poland" is a radical one, it is an attack on the transcendental categories and the assurances they provide us: "When I am presented with a representation, I assure myself as a consciousness that knows that it is only representation, and that there is, beyond the thing, the thing itself. Behind the phenomenon, there is the noumenon."[8] In sum, the stone Lacan lobs at Kant is the hard stone of the real, which "takes out" the transcendental categories and drives a hole through phenomena. Or: the real displaces transcendence.

At the beginning of his seminar on feminine sexuality, Lacan suggests that in addressing the subject of woman he will also in effect be rewriting his *Ethics* seminar. Now, although it is true that *The Ethics of Psychoanalysis* did showcase the act of a woman, namely Antigone, in the process of elaborating a theory of ethics, Lacan's suggestion that ethics *as such* might have a significant relation to feminine sexuality is initially puzzling, to say the least. Insofar as it hints at "Lysenkoism," that is, insofar as it seems to parallel the absurd claim once made for the legitimacy, even superiority, of a proletarian science, the proposal is more than that; it is worrisome. The consequences of the notion of a feminine ethics would be no less disastrous for ethics than that of a proletarian science was for the Soviet economy; ethics, like science, must be universal if it is to be worthy of its name. The proposal is, moreover, counterintuitive in psychoanalytic terms, in that from Freud on woman has been predominantly conceived as constitutionally less likely than a man to develop an ethical consciousness. Additional reservations arise from the arguments Lacan makes himself in the very seminars he is attempting to link. In his earlier work he insisted that his ethics was "rigorously atheistic," and yet in the later seminar he speaks in the same breath of feminine sexuality and God and expounds on the ecstatic jouissance of St. Theresa, the mystic represented by the Bernini statue.

To make sense of the opening suggestion, which is repeated throughout the seminar, that *Encore* is an encore presentation or rewriting of *The Ethics of Psychoanalysis,* one would do well to pass through "Kant with Sade," the essay-resume of the ethics seminar in which the père Ubu quotation plays its strategic role. For what *Encore* again does is offer an imperative to counter Ubu's, but now rephrased in this way, "Imagine there's no Woman!" In considering feminine sexuality, Lacan returns to the problematic of ethics by returning to and now foregrounding the question of being that remained in the background in the earlier seminar. The famous formulation of a feminine "not-all," that is, the proposal that there is no whole, no "all" of woman, or that she is not One, is fundamentally an answer not just to the question of feminine being, but to being as such. It is not only feminine being, but being in general that resists being assembled into a whole. Lacan leaves little room for ambiguity on this point when in the midst of making his argument about femininity, he pauses to remark, "Everything that has been said about being assumes that one can refuse the predicate and say 'Man is,' for example, without saying what. The status of being is closely related to this lopping off of the predicate."[9]

Lacan is unhappy with this account of being, which for him, as a psychoanalyst, smacks too much of philosophy. When philosophers claim that being has no predicate, that we cannot say anything about it other than that it is, they mean that being is what is common to everyone. Being is common to all men, regardless of whether they are short or tall, Arabs or Jews, as rich as Bill Gates or as poor as a migrant worker. The being of philosophers is vast and shareable by all who exist. For psychoanalysis it is a different matter, since there one speaks only of "sexed being," being which concerns jouissance. What does Lacan substitute for the vast and shareable being of the philosophers? Object a, or jouissance as that bit of nonbeing at the subject's core. Lacan does not invent this; the idea comes straight from Freud, as I will show in the first chapter. In *Beyond the Pleasure Principle,* Freud explicitly states that satisfaction, the object of the drive, *replaces* the conceptual categories that define being, for example, in Kant. We are obliged to note that the theory of the drive substitutes for an ontology in Freud.

Of this bit of nonbeing—satisfaction, the object of the drive—it is also impossible to predicate anything, this time, however, not because it is common to all, but because it is singular. Support of the subject in his or her singularity, this being does not preexist the subject but comes about as a result of some "corporeal contingency" (SXX: 93). Jouissance, the experience of the body, is produced in a purely contingent manner; it simply happens to the subject. Moreover, if jouissance functions as support of the subject, it is in a way quite different from the being of the philosophers. Jouissance is an unsupportable support, unbearable to the subject who defends against it through the production of a fundamental fantasy. The whole and shareable being of the philosophers has, then, no place in Lacan, who thinks rather of nonbeing as partial objects of the drive, partial objects of satisfaction; that are unique to the subject, who must now be approached in a finite way, that is to say, *one by one.* You will notice, however, that this discussion, which has followed the thread of Lacan's own argument, has moved from a specific claim about feminine being to a general claim about "sexed being" as such.

For this reason Lacan must be understood to be making a claim about ethics in general in his *Encore* seminar, rather than proposing a separate ethics of the feminine. His ethics takes off from the proposal that being is not-all or there is no whole of being. And yet if it is woman who is privileged in Lacan's analysis this is because she remains closer to the truth of being, while man obfuscates this truth through a nostalgic, secondary operation that allows him to maintain a belief in the plenitude of being to come. This is not to say that every woman acts ethically or that no man can ("There are men who are just as good as women. It happens" [SXX: 76]) only that the ethical act is in itself feminine in Lacan's terms. It is woman who is guardian of the not-all of being. I propose this phrase as a way of marking a trail that leads from the ethics seminar, in which Antigone is described as "the guardian of criminal being," to *Encore*, where Lacan defines being as not-all. That which Lacan first designated as criminal being becomes in the later work sexual being.

Part of the reason the relation between femininity and ethics was obscured previously in psychoanalysis is that the superego was often mistaken for a measure of morality. Critiquing this error and turning instead to sublimation—a category whose underdevelopment by Freud significantly matches and only marginally exceeds his underdevelopment of the concept of woman—for a means to connect the not-all of being to an ethics of the act, the first half of this book explores the logic of Antigone's disobedience of an edict of the State; the controversial silhouettes of the young black artist, Kara Walker; the *Untitled Film Stills* of Cindy Sherman; and the final gesture of the mother toward her daughter in the well-known melodrama, *Stella Dallas*.

That the concept of sublimation is so poorly developed in the writings of Freud is due in part to the "epistemological obstacle" of his conservative taste in art. It is an irony of history that at the same time Freud was formulating his theory of aesthetic pleasure, which conceived the latter as a "mild narcosis,"[10] Duchamp was gaining attention for his condemnation of the "habit-forming drug of taste," which he faulted as the cause of the bourgeois connoisseur's distaste for the unsettling practices and pleasures of avant-garde art. Freud associated art with a weak, "compensatory" pleasure and conceived it as a temporary means of stopping up life's little lacks or as a salve to its minor disappointments; this of course entered into his conception of sublimation as productive of a pleasure purified of any sensuous or corporeal support, a contemplative pleasure that could do without any actually existing object. It is unfortunate, to put it mildly, that in 1930, the date of *Civilization and Its Discontents*, Freud would there characterize art in such a way as completely to ignore the work of "Picasso, Brancusi, Schwitters, Tatlin and Lissitzky, among others," which would in a few short years be yanked from museums and, in some cases, destroyed by fascist demagogues, who would denigrate it as "the product of deviance, madness, hubris, and venereal disease, and as a threat to the 'pure' culture of the Aryan race."[11] Lacan, who had a different understanding of art and a close association with the surrealist avant-garde, obliges us to take another look at the relation of sublimation to purification. Everything depends on what we believe art to be purified of. Where Freud thought it was "primitive sensations" or "sensuous enjoyment," Lacan claimed it was "fear and pity" instead. That is, he named those emotions that facilitate our subservience to the superego and the imaginary ideals it sets up in order to berate us with our shortcomings. Insofar, then, as sublimation can be claimed to result in a tempering of passions, these are nevertheless not the passions Kant referred to as belonging to the "rabble of the senses," but those of the cruel superego. Sublimation mitigates moralistic frenzy, however, by marshalling a force no less terrible, no less inhuman, than that of any absolutely moral(istic) agent, and we will witness the terrible impersonality of that force in the examples we take up below.

Lacan's notorious proposition, "Woman does not exist," has sacrificed its meaning to a certain shock value. The proposition's notoreity has blocked serious efforts to understand what is actually shocking about it: its reliance on a definition of being as plural and partial, as small objects of the drive. The imperative motivating this book was to take this proposition seriously by imagining there's no Woman, imaging what the consequences are—for ethics—of the notion of being it implies. The ethics of psychoanalysis follows from its fundamental critique of ontology, from the theory of the drive and sublimation by which it displaces philosophical inquiries into the ontology of the subject. This ethics concerns the subject's relation to these small pieces of being, not primarily its relation to other people or to the Other.

One does not know if Lacan had Levinas in mind when at the beginning of *Encore* he refers to the interval between his writing of *the Ethics of Psychoanalysis* and the writing of the current seminar as the time of the "after you." One suspects there are ironic nods in Levinas's direction at various places in the seminar, but the attempt to establish parallels between Lacan and Levinas seems to me undermotivated. In this regard, it is necessary to take Lacan's references to God in *Encore* as fully compatible with his earlier statement that his is a "rigorously atheistic" ethics. The jouissance of the woman of which Lacan speaks has nothing to do with her capacity to transcend the symbolic or exist outside language. In fact, if woman has easier access than man to the God of jouissance, this is because she is less susceptible than he is to the lure of transcendence.

In the second part of the book I depart from this focus on woman to examine the superegoic underside of ethics: the concept of radical evil originally proposed by Kant; the manner in which envy corrupts liberal demands for equality and justice; and the differences between sublimation and perversion. In keeping with the focus on artistic sublimation in the first half, the second relates its arguments where it can to artistic texts, including Pasolini's *Salò*; the film noir classic, *Laura*; and the Zapruder film of the Kennedy assassination, while discussing Kant's *Religion within the Limits of Reason Alone*; John Rawls's *Theory of Justice*; Elaine Scarry's *On Beauty and Being Just*; Jonathan Crary's *Techniques of the Observer*; and Jean-Paul Sartre's *Being and Nothingness*.

To approach the question of ethics from the perspective of psychoanalysis may strike some as a narrowing of the issue and a needless confinement of the debate to the terms of a special language. My arguments here are premised on the belief that psychoanalysis is the mother tongue of our modernity and that the important issues of our time are scarcely articulable outside the concepts it has forged. While some blasé souls argue that we are already beyond psychoanalysis, the truth is that we have not yet caught up with its most revolutionary insights.

THE FEMININE ACT OF SUBLIMATION ▬▬▬▬▬▬▬

I

The Tomb of

Perseverance:

On *Antigone*

Greek tragedy is the term we commonly use to refer to it, but it would be more accurate to say *Attic* or *Athenian tragedy,* since it was only in the city-state of Athens that this aesthetic form was nourished and thrived. Yet not even this correction sufficiently discloses the intimate relation that bound this particular city to this particular form, for tragedy was not simply founded in Athens (between 534 and 530 B.C.) and there declared dead (by Aristotle, in 414 B.C.), it also helped invent the very city that invented it.[1] As Jean-Pierre Vernant has argued:

> [Athenian] tragedy is contemporary with the City [Athens] and with its legal system. . . . [W]hat tragedy is talking about is itself and the problems of law it is encountering. What is talking and what is talked about is the audience on the benches, but first of all it is the City . . . which puts itself on the stage and plays itself. . . . Not only does the tragedy enact itself on stage . . . it enacts its own problematics. It puts in question its own internal contradictions, revealing . . . that the true subject matter of tragedy is social thought . . . in the very process of elaboration. [2]

That is, not only did the Athenians insert themselves into their tragic dramas—as Chorus members, who judged the actions of the protagonists in the same way as the tribunal of citizens in the audience was judging the unfolding tragedy against others performed for the same contest—they also posed, through their tragedies, the juridical and ethical questions they were currently confronting in actuality.

But if the form of Athenian tragedy is so local, tied not only to a specific place, a particular and precisely datable time, and a unique set of social problems, it would seem, then, according to the historicist-relativist thinking of our day, to offer nothing that might help us think through the juridical and ethical issues raised by the modern city. In fact, to begin a consideration of contemporary urban issues with a reference to Athenian tragedy is automatically to brand oneself with the sin of anachronism. I propose, however, that the question should not always be "How can we rid ourselves of anachronism?"—for it is sometimes more relevant to ask "What is the significance of anachronism?" How can we account for the temporal nomadism of figures from the past? And, in this context, how is it possible that the drama of Antigone still concerns us?[3]

The simplest initial response would be to point out that German Idealism *resurrected* Antigone at the beginning of our own era and refashioned her as the paradigmatic figure of *modern* ethics. Hegel, Schelling, Hölderlin all wrote with deep fascination about this young Athenian woman, and it is their fascination that commands contemporary interest in her.[4] Voicing, undoubtedly, the sentiments of his colleagues in addition to his own, Hegel proclaimed *Antigone* "one of the most sublime, and in every respect most consummate works of human effort ever brought forth."[5] Despite this transhistorical judgment, however, before the intervention of German Idealism, the play had not received any special attention and had, in fact, been relatively neglected. It was only after paeans such as Hegel's began to revive the play that it became a major reference point of ethical speculation, including that of Kierkegaard, Brecht, Anouilh, Irigaray, Derrida, and, of course, Lacan. In 1978 *Germany in Autumn,* a compilation film produced by nine New German Cinema directors, was released. Focusing on questions of a family's right to bury its dead and the right of citizens to rebel against their government, the film loosely associated actions taken by the Red Army Faction and the Baader-Meinhof terrorists against the German state with Antigone and Polynices' rebellion against Creon and the city-state of Thebes. More recently, Jean-Marie Straub and Danièle Huillet's 1992 release of their film version of Brecht's adaptation of Holderlin's translation of Sophocles' *Antigone* has demonstrated that the legacy of German Idealism's retrieval of Antigone lives on. If our interest in her is an archaism, then it is a peculiarly modern one. What will concern me in the following analysis is less the historical conditions that reawakened interest in *Antigone* (the Hellenistic bent of German Idealism has been amply explored) than the play's own susceptibility to a rereading in the modern context (how is it possible to resurrect such an old drama?); for this issue is closely linked to the ethical issues raised in the play.

My approach to these issues begins with a single rereading of *Antigone,* or, more accurately, a rereading of a prior rereading: Lacan, in *The Ethics of Psychoanalysis,* reinterprets Sophocles' play by challenging Hegel's interpretation in *The Phenomenology of Spirit.* Although later, in the *Philosophy of Right,* Hegel would read the play straightforwardly as a modern drama of ethical action, in the *Phenomenology* he reads it as a tragedy belonging to an earlier moment that he describes (perhaps metaphorically) as that of the Greek city-state; at this moment the opposition between the universal and the particular, the state and the family, human and divine law, man and woman could not be practically overcome. Hegel argues that classical Greek society held the two poles of these oppositions together, in a precarious equilibrium, through *custom,* which provided the community with a concrete unity. But when any decisive action was taken, this equilibrium collapsed into real and irresolvable conflict. Through the ethical *act,* the ethical *community* was dissolved, for the act "initiates the division of itself into itself as the active principle and into the reality over against it, a reality which, for it, is negative. By the deed, therefore, it becomes guilt. . . . And the guilt also acquires the meaning of *crime,* for as simple, ethical consciousness, it has turned towards one law, but turned its back on the other and violates the latter by its deed." [6] Only *inaction,* then, can remain innocent in the Greek polis; every *act,* insofar as it decisively chooses one pole of the opposition, one law, over the other, renders the actor guilty. This inevitable and tragic result is, according to Hegel, the very point of these dramas in general and of *Antigone* in particular, for there each protagonist, each ethical consciousness "sees right only on one side and wrong on the other, that consciousness which belongs to the divine law sees in the other side only the violence of human caprice, while that which holds to human law sees in the other only the self-will and disobedience of the individual who insists on being his own authority" (para. 466).

Hegel here effectively argues that Antigone ("that consciousness which belongs to the divine law") and Creon ("that which holds to human law") are, in their very decisiveness and intransigence, *both* guilty, both in the wrong, insofar as they both abandon or alienate one principle through the very act of embracing its opposite. Acting on behalf of a particular individual, her brother, Antigone betrays the community and terrorizes the state, while Creon acts on behalf of the city-state and thus sacrifices Polynices and the values of the family.

Lacan attacks the deep undecidability of this reading in order decisively to side with Antigone, praising hers as the only real, ethical act in the play and condemning the actions of Creon as crimes. In this reading it is *only* Creon who, through his actions, renders himself guilty. This is not to say that Antigone's implacability goes unnoticed by Lacan; he is as strict as Hegel is in observing the raw, untamed, and uncompromising nature of Oedipus's daughter's rebellion. "The nature of the girl is savage, like her father's, and she does not know how to bend before her troubles," is what the Chorus says of her, and Lacan is quick to agree.[7] But as a psychoanalyst—and here we catch a glimpse of the difference between psychoanalysis and philosophy or psychology—he does not read the *behavior* of each of the protagonists, he defines the *structure* through which their acts must be read. Thus, although Antigone and Creon may be equally stubborn in the performance of their duties, this stubborness, according to which fantasy structure it enters, admits of a fundamental distinction that Lacan will use to ruin the symmetry Hegel so carefully constructs.

In *Three Essays on the Theory of Sexuality*, Freud warns us not to conflate *Fixierarbeit*, which is an inexplicable fixation that persists despite every external attempt to dislodge it, with *Haftbarkeit*, "which is perhaps best translated by 'perseverance' but has a curious resonance in German, since it means also 'responsibility,' 'commitment'"[8] It is this distinction introduced by Freud that lies behind and undergirds Lacan's insistence that Antigone, and she alone, is the heroine of Sophocles' play; her *perseverance* in carrying out the burial of her brother is ethically different from Creon's *fixation* on enforcing the statist prohibition against his burial.

How Freud is able to distinguish between these two kinds of act is what we will have to determine, but Lacan gives us a clue when he refers to them as separate effects of "the individual libidinal adventure" (SVII: 88). Whatever else needs to be said about the distinction, it is clear from this that it cannot be drawn without taking into account the *sexual* being of the subject who acts. The reason Hegel's reading has received so much feminist attention is precisely because it seems to be attentive to this issue insofar as it foregrounds the sexual difference that separates the play's main protagonists. But this difference turns out to be, in his reading, only a gender or biological difference, not a sexual one; that is, Antigone and Creon enact a division of labor that is defined sociologically, according to the spaces they are allowed to inhabit and the roles they are encouraged to assume, given their biology. In fact, Hegel consciously aims to *avoid* sex as far as possible, which is why he chooses to focus not on the husband/wife, but on the brother/sister relation. This relation, he says, provides a truer or "unmixed" picture of the difference between the sexes insofar as it excludes sexual desire. This positing of a family relation free of libido is problematic to begin with—both Freud and Foucault, in different and definitive ways, have exposed the family as a hotbed of desiring relations—but it is absolutely stupefying in light of the fact that the family in question here is Oedipus's and no stranger, then, to the taint of incest. The Greek text, which loads Antigone's references to her brother with libidinal overtones, never lets us forget the fact that the tragedy that plays itself out before our eyes is in some sense a consequence of the incestuous union between Oedipus and his mother. It is necessary to conclude, then, that there is in this section of *The Phenomenology* no sex and no sexual difference, properly speaking. This has the effect of leaving the notions of work and act undisturbed or unproblematized by sexual enjoyment.

According to Freud, however, between sex or libidinal satisfaction and work there is a permanent antagonism that threatens work (or the act) with extinction. As he notes in *Civilization and Its Discontents,* "No other technique for the conduct of work attaches the individual so firmly to reality as laying emphasis on work . . . [which is] indispensible to the preservation and justification of existence in society. . . . And yet . . . work is not prized by men. They do not strive after it as they do after other possibilities of satisfaction."[9] By rethinking the notion of work through that of pleasure, Freud opens Aristotle's distinction between the *act,* in all its rarity, and mere *action* to a redefinition in which what matters is the kind of relation each maintains toward sexual enjoyment. If the avowed ambition of the *Ethics* seminar is to remove the discussion of ethics from "the starry sky" and place it where it belongs, "in our bodies, and nowhere else," that is, if its ambition is to define an ethics of the *embodied* subject, then its crucial first step is to foreground the relation between work and the body as the site of pleasure, in order to distinguish the act of Antigone from the action of Creon on this ground.

Before embarking on an analysis of these relations, it will be useful to take a look at Hegel's reading from a different perspective, one that will eventually complicate the notion of pleasure. What makes Antigone and Creon equally guilty, in Hegel's eyes, is the fact that in choosing one course of action they thereby lose something that is not merely expendable, but that sustains, or is the necessary condition of, the very thing they choose. Antigone and Creon act on behalf of the particular and the universal, respectively, but since there is no particular without the universal, and vice versa, each choice ends in a betrayal of that in the name of which it is made. Thinking, of course, of Hegel, Lacan termed the either/or structure of such choices the "*vel* of alienation" and cited the mugger's offer, "Your money or your life," as illustration of its lose/lose possibilities.[10] Once the choice is offered, you're done for—no matter which alternative you take. Between these terms, clearly the only real choice is life, but from the moment of your decision, yours will be a life severely limited by the loss of your wealth.

Now, it would seem that the revolutionary slogan, "Freedom or death," offers a choice with the same alienating structure. If you choose freedom and thereby invalidate the threat of death, you have no way of demonstrating your independence of the life situation, as Hegel argued in his essay on "Natural Law"; that is, you have no way of demonstrating that your choice is free. So, in this case the only real choice is death, since it alone proves that your choice has been freely made. Yet once this decision is taken, you lose all freedom but the freedom to die. This is what Hegel called the "freedom of the slave."

If you attend closely, however, you will notice that the second or *ethical* choice between freedom and death does *not* conform to the first. The description of the first choice as a mugging is meant to underscore what is at stake here; it suggests that this particular choice is a game played entirely in the Other's court. Stumbling into its preprogrammed scenario, you, its victim, might have been anyone at all, and you must react, if you are rational, in a purely formal way, by making an *analytical* judgment and surrendering your purse. Kant's moral law, "Act in such a way that the maxim of your action may be accepted as a universal maxim," would be sufficient to get you through this urban dilemma; it would prescribe the correct choice. But this only underscores the problem with this statement of the moral law: it still imagines a choice prescribed by law, however formal it may be, and reduces the notion of the *universal* to that of the *common* (SVII: 77). In this case, everyone must act in the same way, but *must* loses its ethical connotation, since it is now guided by, rather than independent of, external sanction.

In the second example, however, by choosing one does *not* automatically lose what is not chosen, but instead *wins* some of it. Lacan attributes the difference between the two examples to the appearance of death in the second. It is through the introduction of the "lethal factor," as he puts it, that the revolutionary choice opens the possibility of an act about which it is improper to say that it sacrifices freedom, that it loses it to the structure of alienation. The choice of death gains freedom. This point is utterly incomprehensible unless one assumes that the death one opts for in the second example is not the same one that is avoided in the first. That is, at the point at which death intersects freedom—which is to say, at the point at which it intersects the *subject*—it ceases to be conceivable in literal or biological terms. The authority for this observation is, again, Freud, who argued that death is for the subject only "an abstract concept, with a negative content."[11] For this reason it does not enter psychoanalysis as such, but only in the form of the death drive. We must assume, then, if we are speaking of the embodied rather than the abstract subject, that what is at issue in the intersection of freedom and death is not biological death, but the death drive. It is to the latter that we owe the possibility of an ethical act that does not alienate freedom or incur additional guilt. More specifically, it is to *sublimation,* which is strictly aligned with the drive as such in Lacan's account, that we owe this possibility.

My argument, in sum, is that Lacan attacks Hegel's argument by (1) sexualizing work or, better, the act and (2) debiologizing death in an effort, in both cases, to corporealize the ethical subject. I understand that this appears to give rise to a contradiction: to declare ethical action, as such, a sublimation would seem to purify action of all reference to the body and pleasure. But this apparent contradiction arises from a common yet faulty definition of sublimation. If one were successfully to show that "sublimation is not, in fact, what the foolish crowd thinks . . . [it] doesn't necessarily make the sexual object disappear—far from it" (SVII: 161), then the contradiction would be dissolved.

IMMORTALITY IN THE MODERN AGE

Let us focus our attention, finally, on the act of Antigone. What precisely does she do? Hegel's version is the following: she buries her brother, Polynices, in order to elevate him to the status of "imperishable individuality"; she makes him "a member of the community which prevails over . . . the forces of particular material elements . . . which sought to . . . destroy him" (para. 452). This is Lacan's version: "Antigone chooses to be . . . the guardian of the criminal as such. . . . [B]ecause the community refuses to [bury Polynices, she] is required . . . to maintain that essential being which is the family *Até,* and and that is the theme or true axis on which the whole tragedy turns. Antigone perpetuates, eternalizes, immortalizes that *Até*" (SVII: 283). The two versions may appear to be roughly equivalent, but a striking difference (and one that will lead us to observe others) occurs in Lacan's introduction of a word that draws attention to a notion which not only Hegel but the entire modern period is loath to look at too directly or closely, a notion that has, since the Enlightenment, become more obscene even than death; this is the notion of immortality. What does it mean to "immortalize *Até*"? In modern times, it is not only the Greek word *até,* but also *immortalize* that strikes us as anachronistic.

Yet, although one might have expected the notion of immortality to perish completely, to become a casualty of the Enlightenment's secularization of reason and its dissolution of the links to its past, the truth turns out to be more complex. For, while officially we moderns are committed to the notion of our own mortality, we nevertheless harbor the secret, inarticulable conviction that we are *not* mortal. Indeed, as Hans Blumenberg announces in his monumental book, *The Legitimacy of the Modern Age,* not only does the idea of immortality not disappear, it is even "pushed forward by Lessing, Kant, and Herder to the point of the idea of reincarnation."[12] And in his essay, "The Death of Immortality?" Claude Lefort similarly exposes the insistence of the notion of immortality within the modern period, remarking that "after the Bonapartist coup d'etat in the middle of the last century . . . the question of immortality [took on] . . . a political import. Astonishing as it may seem to us, in order to be a true republican, a true democrat, or a true socialist, one either had to deny or affirm a belief in immortality."[13] Blumenberg and Lefort both stress that this notion is not a simple hold-out from a superceded past, the survival in the present of an old religious idea; it is, rather, a new product of the break from our religious past. But though they concur generally on the need to differentiate the classical from the modern notion of immortality, they are at odds on the question of how the distinction should be made.

According to Lefort's account, the classical notion named a kind of mortal ambition to participate in everlastingness through the accomplishment of great works or deeds, although the deed itself was not thought to have any chance of enduring, ultimately. Since every human effort was conceived as time-bound, none could hope to elevate itself above the temporal flux in order to install itself within the timeless realm of eternity. Thus, although the deed could win for its doer some measure of glory or *immortality,* it could not win *eternity,* which meant that it was worth relatively little. The modern notion of immortality benefits from the collapse of our belief in an eternal realm. Where formerly every deed (and the active life, in general) was thought to fail insofar as it was unable to elevate itself *out of time,* into eternity, in modernity the deed was reconceived as affording one the possibility of transcending historical time *within* time. This is what is new: this idea that the act could raise itself out of impotence, or out of the immanence of its historical conditions, without raising itself out of time. It is at this point that the act—or work in this specific sense—took on a value it could not have had in the classical era. The valorization of the act helped to forge, Lefort argues, a new link between immortality and "a sense of posterity" (L, 267). The great social revolutions at the end of the eighteenth century may have severed all ties with the past, but they did so, paradoxically, in order to establish a permanence in time, a durability of human deeds that was not possible previously. The difference arises because the "sense of posterity" now took place across a historical *break*; what was thus brought forth was "the idea of a conjunction between something that no longer exists and something that does not yet exist" (L, 270).

In the argument presented by Blumenberg, the notion of posterity is not linked to that of immortality, but instead opposes or replaces it. This argument is imbedded in a larger one, which states that the attainment of complete knowledge by any individual has in the modern age been rendered strictly inconceivable. Within modernity, knowledge is objectified through scientific *method,* which means that it ceases to be a matter of individual *intuition*; that is, methods of objectification transform the process of acquiring knowledge into one that extends infinitely beyond the cognitive compass, and even ambition, of any single enquirer. Along with this objectification, the sheer speed with which knowledge comes into being is superseded, and discarded as useless, threatens to turn the curious into functionaries of the process of knowledge and to render the possession of knowledge irredeemably fleeting and incomplete. For these reasons, no individual, only a generational series of them, can become the subject of modern knowledge.

It is in order to clinch this argument that Blumenberg introduces Ludwig Feuerbach's notion of immortality into the discussion. According to Blumenberg's summary, Feuerbach "extracted the anthropological core" hidden within our modern notion of immortality, to produce the following definition: "immortality extrapolated as the fulfillment of theory is the product of the difference . . . between the 'knowledge drive,' which relates to species man, and its unsatisfied actual state in the individual man" (B, 441)—as we will see, this will form the basis of Freud's understanding of the superego. In other words, once the rapid and conspicuous progress of modern knowledge makes the individual's limited share in this progress unbearable, the notion of immortality arises as a way of healing the wound between the species and the individual, of assuaging the structural dissatisfaction that emerges from their difference. A kind of error of prolepsis, immortality negates history in order to posit a *spatial* beyond where the future is already waiting to bestow itself on the individual. This error is *modern* because its anticipation of reward is based on the perception of the actual, temporal progress of man rather than on the presumed munificence of an eternal being; it is *mistaken* in that it unjustifiably converts some as-yet-unrealized temporal progress into a spatial paradise.

To correct this mystification, Feuerbach argues, man needs to *surrender* the notion of immortality and confront the finality of his own death. This will allow man, unimpeded by otherworldly distractions, to concentrate his energies into the pursuit of his "knowledge drive [*Wissenstrieb*]," which is, for him, a *biologized* curiosity, through which "the interests of the species are imposed on the individual as an obligation, but through which at the same time the individual lays claim to a counterinterest" in his own happiness (B, 444). What this says, in brief, is that only the species is able to accomplish the destiny of man, and this destiny is man's happiness on earth. The knowledge drive—which Feuerbach also calls the "happiness drive"—aims at happiness by seeking to know not the answers to metaphysical questions, but only those truths that will help satisfy the material needs of man; it thus places man within the cooperative machinery of the human pursuit of knowledge without reducing him to a mere cog, since this machine is specifically designed for *his* earthly benefit, for the benefit of his mortal existence.

　　While these conclusions are Feuerbach's, one looks in vain in the discussions of Kant and Freud that precede and follow this one in *The Legitimacy of the Modern Age* for some word of dissent from Blumenberg. One encounters instead the dubious implication that there is a *continuity* among these thinkers on the notion of the knowledge drive. If anything, Feuerbach is shown slightly to improve on Kant, for the former not only takes over the latter's position—that there are certain suprasensible ideas which are unsuited to human reason, which we cannot and should not strive to know—he also removes the last vestiges of the spatial metaphor of limits still discernible in Kant. Feuerbach thus allows us to view reason's limits as purely temporal; he teaches us finally that man has no "supernatural knowledge drive" (B, 442). And though Freud's notion of a knowledge drive (*Wissentreib*) is presented as similar to Feuerbach's in many respects, we are warned that in the study of Leonardo da Vinci, Freud does not pay sufficient attention to "the historical conditions affecting [Leonardo's] individual biography" (B, 452).

　　The distortions this continuity thesis precipitates are considerable; I will cite only the most basic. Kant's solution does not, as Blumenberg alleges, wipe out the tension between self-knowledge and salvation, or the immanent and transcendent destinies of the subject; quite the reverse. In Kant, the suprasensible is not simply eliminated from the realm of knowledge and thought, as it is in Feuerbach; it is instead retained as the very condition of thought. That is: no thought *without* the suprasensible. As far as the criticism of Freud is concerned, that he does not dwell excessively on Leonardo's historical conditions is indication not of a weakness in his theory, but of its positive contribution. For Freud, the knowledge drive is bound up with the solution of sublimation, the problem being to explain how thought manages to escape compulsion and inhibition, or to explain how it escapes being a mere symptom of its historical conditions.

So far I have argued that the difference between Lefort and Blumenberg (or Feuerbach, since on this matter no discernible distance separates the commentator from the author on whom he comments) hinges on the fact that Lefort links immortality and posterity while Blumenberg opposes them. But there is another crucial difference that affects their respective notions of posterity, which also turn out to be dissimilar. The conjunction of immortality with posterity, in Lefort, takes place through a notion of singularity, which is absent in Blumenberg.[14] Here is Lefort's most concise statement: "The sense of immortality proves to be bound up with the conquest of a place *which cannot be taken,* which is invulnerable, because it is the place of someone . . . who, by accepting all that is most singular in his life, refuses to submit to the coordinates of space and time and who . . . for us . . . is not dead" (L, 279).

Someone dies and leaves behind his place, which outlives him and is unfillable by anyone else. This idea constructs a specific notion of the social, wherein it is conceived to consist not only *of* particular individuals and their relations to each other, but also *as* a relation to these unoccupiable places. The social is composed, then, not just of those things that will pass, but also of relations to empty places that will not. This gives society an existence, a durability, despite the rapid and relentless alterations modernity institutes. If, with the collapse of eternity, the modern world is not decimated by historical time, it is because this unoccupiable place, this sense of singularity, somehow knots it together in time. Singularity itself, that which appears most to disperse society, is here posited as essential rather than antagonistic to a certain modern social bond. Not only this, but another paradox seems to define this bond; singularity is described both as that which is "localized in space and time" (L, 270) and as *universal,* as that which refuses the coordinates of space and time, which is unsituatable within time. (Clearly, *singularity* is distinct from *particularity,* which is also localized, but which we commonly and rightly associate with things that fade with time and distance, with the ephemeral, things that do not endure.)

This notion of singularity, which is tied to the *act* of a subject, is defined as *modern* because it depends on the denigration of any notion of a prior or superior instance that might prescribe or guarantee the act. *Soul, eternity, absolute* or *patriarchal power,* all these notions have to be destroyed before an act can be viewed as unique and as capable of stamping itself with its own necessity. One calls *singular* that which, "once it has come into being, bears the strange hallmark of something that *must be,*" and therefore cannot die (L, 279). Significantly, this notion of singularity, which gives rise to our obscure, one might even say *unconscious* sense of immortality, is associated by Lefort with the writer, that is, with sublimation.[15] For it is through the psychoanalytic concept of sublimation that we will be able to clarify exactly how singularity is able to figure and not be effaced by the social bond.

However incomplete the notion of sublimation remains at this point, it is nevertheless clear that it is *meant* to bridge the gap between singularity and sociality. So, the immediate question becomes: what allows Feuerbach to do without it? Or: what *blocks* the emergence of any sense of singularity or temporal immortality in his theory? Recall that Feuerbach entertained (and rightfully rejected) only a *spatial* concept of immortality; no temporal version of the notion (whereby one could conceivably transcend time *within* time) presented itself to him as it does to Lefort. Why not? What Feuerbach sets out to do is to eliminate every trace of transcendence by incarnating the notion of eternity in the finite and forward movement of time, that is: in progress. Yet, as we have already suggested, the elimination of eternity presents a unique problem for the modern age; it risks the dissolution of society in a temporal vat. Something has to endure, it would seem, for progress to be conceivable. In fact, Kant made this very argument: "[I]nfinite progress is possible . . . only under the presupposition of an infinitely enduring existence . . . of . . . rational being."[16] But whereas he offered this argument in defense of the postulate of the immortality of the *soul,* commentators have pointed out that his argument actually requires, if it is to make any sense, an immortal *body.*[17] Feuerbach tacitly acknowledges the problem, as well as the corporeal requirement for its solution, in his proposed notion of posterity as an infinite *succession* of bodies seeking happiness—which nicely avoids the seemingly self-contradictory notion of an immortal *individual* body.

The nub of this solution is sheer and continuous succession. None of the bodies by itself possesses or actualizes immortality in the way the body of the Monarch was thought to do during the ancien régime, for example. Succession alone allows the individual enquirer to be taken up and included within the whole without limits of humanity, and it alone saves society from the pulverization of time. This solution also soothes the structural insatisfaction, the unbearable gap, between the individual, whose share of progress is minuscule, and posterity, which "possesses in abundance" the happiness the individual seeks. Finally, this

solution allows one to argue that the limits of human knowledge are merely temporal and thus capable of being gradually eliminated.

THE DEATH DRIVE: FREUD'S THESIS ON FEUERBACH

Feuerbach is right to want to snatch life back from eternity in order to insert it
into historical time. The problem is, however, that for him, this insertion means
that life is conceivable only in biological terms, that is, as *finite*, or as defined by its
temporal limit, death. His description of the relation between the human individual and his or her posterity attempts to offer an alternative to Aristotle's description of an animal's relation to its species, which relation, Aristotle argues,
renders the animal eternal, a part of ever-recurring life: "Nature guarantees to
the species their being forever through recurrence [*periodos*], but cannot guarantee such being forever to the individual."[18] But if his *biological definition of human life*
nevertheless risks reducing the individual subject to its "animal dimension," this
is because it shares too much not with Aristotle, but with a modern and problematic definition of life.

To which conception do we refer and why is it problematic? At the end
of his essay, "Critique of Violence," Walter Benjamin isolates this conception
when he mentions with disdain the familiar proposition that "higher even than
the happiness and justice of existence stands existence itself." Judging this belief
in the sacredness of life itself, that is, in the sacredness of "bodily life vulnerable
to injury by [our] fellow men," to be "false and ignominious," he speculates that
it is probably of recent origin, "the last mistaken attempt of the weakened West-
ern tradition to seek the saint it has lost in cosmological impenetrability."[19]

In *Homo Sacer: Sovereign Power and Bare Life,* Giorgio Agamben follows up on
Benjamin's suggestion by tracking the emergence of this dogma, wherein *bare* life,
or life itself denuded of any political form or "protective covering," is deemed sacred. Whereas in classical Greece, *bios* (a *form of life,* or way of living, defined within
the political sphere) could be, and systematically was, distinguished from *zoe* (the
simple *fact of life,* common to animals, men, and gods), in modern society, he argues, *bios* and *zoe* became conflated, making bare, biological life the very matter of
modern politics. Agamben thus adopts Foucault's thesis that in the middle of the
nineteenth century—or, at the "threshold of biological modernity"—natural life
became the primary concern of the State and, as a result, politics was transformed
into *biopolitics.* With the development of the "life sciences," the old "territorial

State" (in which power asserted itself through the possession and control of geographical territory) gave way to the "State of population" (in which power reigns less over land than over life itself): "the species and the individual as a simple living body become what is at stake in a society's political strategies."[20] It is against this backdrop that Feuerbach's notion of the biologically based "happiness drive" must be understood; it is in this context that its political profile assumes its ominous shape.

If modern political power becomes coextensive or *conflated with,* as was said a moment ago, the life over which it assumes sovereignty, it does so paradoxically by declaring bare life to be *separable from* forms of life, that is, from the political sphere wherein the living individual is accorded certain rights and powers. That is to say, it is only by declaring a (permanent) state of emergency, triggered by the emergency bare life poses, that modern power is able to suspend its self-limiting laws and assume absolute power over that same denuded (or, now, politically vulnerable) life. But if bare life in this way becomes barely distinguishable from the political power that invents it as simultaneously excluded from its sphere and as the very territory over which it reigns, *Homo Sacer* remains more interested in exploring the strategies of power than the notion of bare life they construct. The book's references to Foucault are therefore limited to *The History of Sexuality* and *Dits et écrits,* where the focus is primarily on these strategies, rather than on the emergence of the biological definition of human life or, as Foucault puts it, the conceptual "bestialization of man." When Agamben faults Foucault, then, for failing to demonstrate how political techniques and technologies of the self ("by which processes of subjectivization bring the individual to bind himself to his own identity and consciousness and, at the same time, to an external power")[21] converge to produce that form of "involuntary servitude" which characterizes the modern subject, we recognize a need to know more about the biological definition of life if we are ever going to be able to explain how modern power is able to sink its roots so thoroughly—so *inexhaustibly*—into bare life. What is it about this definition of life that allows power to assume such an extensive, even capillary hold over it?

Though not a response to this question, *The Birth of the Clinic,* particularly the chapter "Open Up a Few Corpses," in which Foucault fittingly characterizes biological modernism as a "mortalism," might begin to provide an answer. Placing the French physiologist Bichat in the conceptual vanguard of this modernism, Foucault describes the former's innovation thus:

[I]n trying to circumscribe the special character of the living phenomenon Bichat linked to its specificity the risk of . . . death—of the death
which life, by definition, resists. Bichat relativized the concept of death,
bringing it down from the absolute in which it appeared as an indivisible,
decisive, irrecoverable event: he volatilized it, distributed it throughout
life in the form of separate, partial, progressive deaths, deaths that are so
slow in occurring that they extend even beyond death itself.[22]

The "medical gaze" of which Foucault speaks throughout *The Birth of the Clinic,* the
gaze, in Agamben's terms, of sovereign power, is an eye that sees death everywhere
immanent in life, sees everywhere this threat to life, and finds in this very ubiq-
uity the excuse for its own insidious and equally ubiquitous control. To the exact
extent that life becomes defined by death, is permeated by death, it becomes permeated by power.

　　　　To return to Benjamin's formulation, from the nineteenth century on,
"*bodily life*" is defined essentially as *that which is "vulnerable to injury,"* by processes of disease as well as by our fellow men. To measure the novelty of this notion, Benjamin
asks his readers to reflect on the fact that this essential vulnerability, which we now
choose to label *sacred,* bore in antiquity the mark of *guilt,* that is, it was a sign of ab-
jection.[23] Human life has always been known to be vulnerable to disease and
death, of course, but only in the nineteenth century did this vulnerability become
sacralized, by the discourses of power, as its essential aspect. Agamben, however,
departs from Foucault and Benjamin by seeing this notion of bare life not simply
as a rupture with previous thought but as the culmination of a gradual solidifi-
cation, throughout history, of the link between nude or bare life and sovereign
power. Thus, when he declares, for example, that "*Not simple natural life, but life exposed
to death (bare life or sacred life) is the originary political element,*" it is in the midst of a discussion of Roman law, which is in this sense not so different from that of the mod-
ern legal-juridical order.[24]

　　　　"Politicizing Death," the penultimate chapter of *Homo Sacer,* opens with
a reference to a 1959 study of what two French neurophysiologists termed *coma de-
passé* (overcoma), a degree of coma, or of death's incursion into life, involving a
much greater loss of vital functioning than that which had previously been allowed
to pass for life. The argument of the chapter is that advances in life-support tech-
nology have led medical science to redefine death by pushing its limits beyond
those set by earlier standards. And as the limits of death are extended, so too are

the reaches of sovereign power, which now begins to decide on the fate of a new class of citizens, the "neomorts," or *faux vivants,* that is, the new "living dead," over which power assumes a unique sort of control. What Agamben asks us to bear witness to is the fact that this recent extension of life beyond the cessation of its vital functions and the consequent increase of State power were enabled by the emergence of the life sciences in the nineteenth century wherein death was conceived not as an absolute and unique event, but as a multiple phenomenon, immanent in life, dispersed through time, and extending "beyond death itself." Yet one of the most original aspects of Agamben's argument, as hinted, is the linkage of the historical account with a metaphysical one. It is, in the end, a certain metaphysical tradition that Agamben wishes to indict for the high crimes of biopolitics (in his narrative, the Nazi concentration camp comes to replace the city as the paradigmatic sociopolitical unit of this politics) because, he argues: by the way in which it isolates its proper element—bare life—biopolitics reveals its fundamental collusion with the metaphysical tradition. That is to say, he views the positing of *bare life* as strictly equivalent to the positing of *pure Being* insofar as both issue as responses to the encounter with an "unthinkable limit" beyond which these elements are then supposed to dwell, "indeterminate and impenetrable."[25] According to this analysis, a logic of exception has been in place *ab urbe condita,* positing a limit and a beyond to the order of political life; this logic eventually provided support for the notion and construction of the camps. Thus, while divisions may have flickered momentarily in the classical City, Antigone may once have rebelled against Creon, these divisions and that rebellion were always placed at risk by the logic of exception that nourished sovereign power. And now, "we no longer know anything of the classical distinction between *zoe* and *bios,* between private life and political existence, between man as a simple living being at home in the house and man's political existence in the city."[26] Moreover, the current models, by which the "social sciences, sociology, urban studies, and architecture . . . are trying to conceive and organize the public space of the world's cities without any clear awareness that at their very center lies the same bare life . . . that defined the biopolitics of the great totalitarian states of the twentieth century," are in danger of simply *perpetuating* this politics of bare, bodily—or bestial—life.[27]

In fact, it is almost impossible to imagine—not only for the reader but, one suspects, for Agamben himself, whose final pronouncements are irredeemably bleak—a model that would *not* risk perpetuating this politics. Ironically, the persuasiveness of *Homo Sacer*'s analysis adds another hurdle to the already difficult task of formulating an alternative. For, by focusing, however productively, on historical continuities, Agamben is led to downplay the rupture the nineteenth-century "life sciences" represented, and it is precisely the notion of rupture, of a thought or act that would be able to break from its immanent conditions, that is needed to restore power to life. The most insidious difficulty confronting us, however, is the fact that we ourselves remain dupes of the dogma that death is imbedded in life; that is, we remain victims of the theme of bodily finitude, or of bare life, that these sciences cultivate. Alain Badiou, in an interview in *Artforum,* makes this important point: "The real romantic heritage—which is still with us today—is the theme of finitude. The idea that an apprehension of the human condition occurs primordially in the understanding of its finitude maintains infinity at a distance that's both evanescent and *sacred.* . . . That's why I think the only really contemporary requirement for philosophy since Nietzsche is the *secularization of infinity*" (my emphasis).[28]

Stated thus and affixed to Benjamin and Foucault's disparaging analyses of the modern sanctification of bestial life, this statement strikes one as a long overdue correction of certain contemporary commonplaces. Yet its judgment will remain incomprehensible to cultural theorists who continue to misrecognize bodily finitude as the sobering fact that *confounds* our Romantic pretensions. For these theorists—for whom limits are almost always celebrated, insofar as they are supposed to restrict the expansionism of political modernism and its notions of universalism and will (this is only slightly a caricature)—the body is the limit, par excellence, that which puts an end to any claim to transcendence. What Badiou is here proposing, however, is that our idea of bodily finitude assumes a point of transcendence. Like Agamben, Badiou argues that death becomes immanentized in the body only on condition that we presuppose a beyond.

What is needed, in this case, is not an abandonment of current interest in the body, but a rethinking of it. This rethinking would not have to entail a radical reinvention, for, in truth, another notion of the body has already been proposed, precisely as a challenge to the one offered by the (bare) life sciences. The notion to which I refer is the one suggested by psychoanalysis, where the body is conceived not "biopolitically" as the seat of *death* but, rather, as the seat of *sex.* Contrary to what Foucault has claimed, the sexualization of the body by psychoanalysis does not participate in the regime of biopolitics; it opposes it. Borrowing Badiou's phrase, one could put it this way: through its definition of the sexualized body, psychoanalysis provided the world with a secularized notion of infinity. Or: the concept of an immortal individual body, which Kant could not quite bring himself to articulate, is finally thinkable in Freud.

Yet notoriously, Freud's conclusion, stated in *Beyond the Pleasure Principle,* that *the aim of life is death*—seems on its face to contradict my assertion. Limited to this statement alone, Freud's theory would appear to be in harmony with the bio-theory of his day, insofar as his theory places the death drive at the very core of life and its various ambitions. Not flinching from this conclusion, even buttressing it by arguing that for Freud there are no life drives, that *all* the drives are death drives, Lacan nevertheless calls into question that simplistic interpretation of the death drive which perceives it to be nothing more than an explanation for the fact that a subject often chooses death or unhappiness rather that her own well-being. Why do people commit suicide or act against their own interests? Because of the death drive. If this were all there were to it, the drive would not have met Freud's own standards for conceptual validity. Faced with the proliferation of drives invented to account for almost every definable activity ("the drive to collect," "the drive to shop," and so on), a querulous Freud insisted that a concept which did nothing more than assign a substantialized cause to a specific, known effect, without adding anything new to our knowledge, was empty and useless. Although one of the effects of the death drive may be the free choice of death, this is by no means the drive's only or even assured result.

The paradoxical Freudian claim that the death drive is a speculative concept designed to help explain why life aims at death, in fact, tells only half the story; the other half is revealed by a second paradox: the death drive achieves its satisfaction by *not* achieving its aim. Moreover, the *inhibition* that prevents the drive from achieving its aim is not understood within Freudian theory to be due to an extrinsic or exterior *obstacle,* but rather as part of the very *activity* of the drive itself. The full paradox of the death drive, then, is this: while the *aim (Ziel)* of the drive is death, the *proper and positive activity* of the drive is to inhibit the attainment of its aim; the drive, *as such,* is *zielgehemnt,* that is, it is inhibited as to its aim, or sublimated, "the satisfaction of the drive through the inhibition of its aim" being the very definition of sublimation. Contrary to the vulgar understanding of it, then, sublimation is not something that happens to the drive under special circumstances; it is the proper destiny of the drive. This alignment of the drive with sublimation clarifies a commonplace misconception about sublimation, namely, that it substitutes a more socially respectable or refined pleasure for a cruder, carnal one. Lacan summarizes his complex argument about the death drive by referring to it several times in the *Ethics* seminar as a "creationist sublimation." Significantly, in *The Four Fundamental Concepts,* in the midst of his discussion of the drive, Lacan quotes the following Heraclitean fragment, appropriating it for psychoanalysis: "To the bow (*Biós*) is given the name of life (*Bíos*) and its work is death" (SXI:177). The Greek pun is emphasized in order to place the proper accent on life, as it were—specifically, on the form of life. Life may be joined here to death, but not, we will soon see, in the same way it is in biopolitics.

Historically situated at the very "threshold of biological modernity," as a contemporary of Bichat and the rest, Hegel considered Antigone's act from the point of death. Her deed, he argued, concerns not the living, but the dead, "the individual who, after a long succession of separate disconnected experiences, concentrates himself into a single completed shape, and has raised himself out of the unrest of the accidents of life into the calm of simple universality" (para. 452). That is, Antigone's act may be considered ethical, in Hegel's terms, inasmuch as it involves universal being rather than a particular aspect of it, and it concerns universal being inasmuch as it is undertaken on behalf of a dead and therefore completed being. A problem arises, however, because the universality, or completeness, brought by death is merely *abstract:* it is the product of a natural, biological process, not of a self-conscious subject. Antigone's task, then, is to redeem her brother from this first, biological death and this abstract universality by consciously performing a "second death" through her act of *burial.* She must complete for her brother the reflexive circuit of self-conscious life that he, whose life has been finally shaped by death, can no longer accomplish himself. But what is she able to reflect back to him except his own particularity, his own corporeal finitude, now *consecrated* by her act, raised to the dignity of "universal individuality," which can only mean here a communally recognized individuality? Polynices is by this forever entombed in his own "imperishable individuality," his own imperishable finitude. In this way bare, bestial life has been dignified, rendered sacred.

For Hegel, the fault—the reason Antigone's act is ultimately as compromised as Creon's and results in the sacrifice of universality for the sake of particularity—lies with death. It sunders the journey out from the journey back, divides the circuit of self-reflexivity into mere biological or bodily life (a "mere existent," in his vocabulary), represented by the *corpse* of Polynices, and a bodiless act, purged of desire; the body, divorced from the deed, appears, in Hegel's discussion, only as dead. And the act is powerless to do anything more than enshrine corporeal finitude. In Lacan's estimation, the fault lies with Hegel's ceding too much, at least at this point, to biological death—even if the whole of *The Phenome-nology* is structured as a successive series of attempts to master bodily finitude and death, which has at this historical moment, according to Philippe Aries's massive study, been newly rendered obscene.[29]

Lacan's interpretation turns on his recognition that the body is, rather, the site of a different obscenity, a jouissance that opens a new dimension of infi-nity, immortality. Thus will Lacan be led to describe Antigone's deed not as a be-stowal of "imperishable individuality" on her brother, but as an "immortalization of the family *Até.*" But what does this difference signify in regard to Antigone's re-lation to the dead, to her familial past, or to the city? And what does it signify, to return to the terms of an earlier discussion, in regard to the relation between the *"individual organism,"* which may be looked at, as Freud put it, "as a transitory and perishable appendage to the quasi-immortal germ plasm bequeathed to him by his race," and the *species?*[30] Finally, how can our argument—that Lacan reconnects body and act, the very terms Hegel's analysis sunders—be reconciled with Freud's contention that sublimation pries the act, whether it be a physical act or the act of thinking, from the body's grip?

Let us begin at the most basic level: death, and only death, is the aim of every drive; this is the Freudian proposition. Where the aim of the sexual *instinct* (which is to be found only among animals) is sexual reproduction, the aim of the *drives* (which Freud sometimes calls the *libidinal drives*) is death.[31] This means not only that there is *no original life instinct* directing the subject outward toward another of the species for purposes of copulation, but also that there is nothing directing her toward the outside world for reasons of simple curiosity, as Feuerbach be-lieved, for example. There is no drive impelling the subject toward any sort of fu-sion with others, toward "vital association," which would allow "the community of [subjects to] survive even if individual [subjects] have to die"; a notion Freud dis-misses as the "Eros of the poets and philosophers."[32] Freud claims categorically that *"there is unquestionably no universal instinct toward higher development"*; we must, then, definitively reject the "benevolent illusion" that there is among men a drive to-ward perfection or progress (SE 18: 41; my emphasis). Drive pushes away from or against the stabilization of unities or the dumb progress of developments. But be-fore thoughts of Schopenhauer's philosophy ("death is the 'true result and to that extent the purpose of life'") spring to mind and lead us astray, we must recall that the involuted death drives are described by Freud as working *against* the teleology of a system such as Schopenhauer's and as working instead toward winning for the subject "what we can only regard as potential immortality" (SE 18: 40). How so?

Directed not outward toward the constituted world, but away from it, the death drive aims at the past, at a time *before* the subject found itself where it is now, imbedded in time and moving toward death. What, if anything, does this backward trajectory, this flight from the consituted world and biological death, discover? It will surprise many to learn that Freud does not answer this question negatively by designating the nothing of death or destruction as the actual terminal point of drive, but argues instead that drive discovers along its path something positive, certain "'necessary forms of thought' . . . that time does not change . . . in any way and [to which] the idea of time cannot be applied" (SE 18: 28). Freud rather surprisingly, but explicitly, quotes Kant in this passage. Why? Is it to bolster the philosopher's thesis regarding the conditions of the possibility of thought, which are not subject to temporal alteration or decay and cannot be absorbed within the temporality of thought itself? Not at all. Freud does conceive his notion of drive as an intervention in Kant's philosophy, but the drive does not lend credence to the "Kantian theorem that time and space are 'necessary forms of thought,'" not thinkable in themselves; rather, it significantly revises that theorem. As we shall see, the psychoanalytic theory of Freud replaces the transcendental forms with empty, nonobjectifiable objects, the objects of the drive.

The aim of the drive, we have already said it, is death—or, as Freud alternatively puts it: "the restoration of an earlier state of things," a state of inanimation or inertia (SE 18: 37). Now, this state exists, according to the theory, only as a retrospective illusion, never as an actual state; but its purely mythical status does not prevent it from having had a long history. Plato's *Timaeus,* for example, depicted centuries earlier a similar inanimate past when the Earth, created as a globe and containing all things, had no need of sense organs or, indeed, of organs of any kind: "[T]here would not have been any use of organs by the help of which he might receive his food or get rid of what he digested, since there was nothing that went from him or came into him, for there was nothing besides him."[33] Psychoanalysis rewrites this mythical state as the primordial mother-child dyad, which supposedly contained all things and every happiness and to which the subject strives throughout his life to return.

If this were the end of it (and, unfortunately, too many think it is), the death drive would be a pure will to destruction or a "will to nothingness," in

Nietzsche's sense of the term. For, since this original state is mythical, the search for it is vain, and the endless and unsatisfiable pursuit of it would result in the annihilation of heaven and earth; the death drive would always inevitably end in death, in suicide and devastation. But this error ignores two essential facts: (1) that there is no single, complete drive, only partial drives, and thus *no realizable will to destruction*; and (2) the second paradox of the drive, which states that the drive inhibits, as part of its very activity, the achievement of its aim. Some inherent obstacle—the *object* of the drive— simultaneously *brakes* the drive and *breaks it up*, curbs it, thus preventing it from reaching its aim, and divides it into partial drives. Rather than pursuing the Nothing of annihilating dissatisfaction, the now partial drives content themselves with these small nothings, these objects that satisfy them. Lacan gives to them the name *objects a*; they are, as it were, simulacra of the lost (maternal) object, or as Freud and Lacan both refer to it, of *das Ding. Object a* is, however, the general term, Lacan designates several specific objects: *gaze, voice, breast, phallus.* In other words, he gives them the names of bodily organs. Let us clarify why the objects are given these names and how they displace Kant's "necessary forms of thought."

The first thing to note is that Freud's analysis of the subjective constitution of knowledge of reality is concentrated on a genetic account of what takes place, whereas Kant's is more concentrated, at least in the first two *Critiques,* on a description of the conditions of thought.[34] It is in part due to his genetic orientation that the mother-child dyad is privileged in Freud from the beginning. In the 1895 *Project for a Scientific Psychology,* specifically in the section on "Remembering and Judging," this dyad makes an early appearance with the primordial mother appearing in the form of the *Nebenmensch* ("fellow human-being" in Strachey's translation). This *Nebenmensch* is described as "the first satisfying object," and the child's ability "to cognize" is said to depend on its relationship to her. There is from the start it seems a structural disturbance of this relation, which is here theorized by Freud as a splitting of the *Nebenmensch*/mother into "two components, of which one makes an impression by its constant structure and stays together as a *thing* [als *Ding*], while the other can be *understood* by the activity of memory—that is, can be traced back to information from [the subject's] own body."[35] In his gloss of this text, Lacan designates the two components of the subject's experience of the *Nebenmensch* as (1) *das Ding,* that part which "remains together as a [*Fremde,* alien] thing" and thus, as Freud says, "evades being judged" (SE 1:334); and (2) *Vorstellungen,* ideas or representations through which the *Nebenmensch* can be cognized or remembered. The act of judgment falls then into two parts, as Freud will elaborate more extensively in his essay on "Negation," and the sense of reality is said to be constructed through the "specific action" of reexperiencing or refinding the first satisfaction with which the *Nebenmensch*/mother was synonymous. The various aspects of the mother, what she was like, will be captured by the *Vorstellungen,* the system of representations or signifiers that form the relatively stable and familiar world we share in common with our "fellow human-beings" or neighbors. But some aspects of the primordial mother cannot be translated into these representations, since they are, Freud says, "new and non-comparable" to any experience the child has of itself. A hole thus opens in the system of signifiers since those that would enable us to recall these new and noncomparable or singular aspects of the mother are simply unavailable, they simply do not exist. The *Ding*-component is this alien, untranslatable part of the *Nebenmensch,* which is thus forever lost to the subject and constitutes, as Lacan puts it, "a first outside" (S VII: 52).

Until this point it is possible to think simply that the maternal Thing is lost for want of a signifier, that is to say, that the fault lies with the signifiers. Representation fails, by its very nature, to capture the being of the Thing, which is thus inaccessible to the former. A Kantian analogy would thus suggest itself: the *Ding*-component of the *Nebenmensch* is to the *Vorstellungen*-component as the noumenal Thing-in-itself is to the idea we have of it, its phenomenal appearance. This would make the two components of the *Nebenmensch* a psychoanalytical endorsement of the philosophical separation of thinking and being: as we gain access to language and thus thought, we lose our access to that being which is the maternal Thing. Numerous passages from Freud's texts spring to mind in support of this thesis, including this famous one from *Three Essays on the Theory of Sexuality:* "At a time at which the first beginnings of sexual satisfaction are still linked with the taking of nourishment, the sexual instinct has a sexual object outside the infant's own body in the shape of the mother's breast. It is only later that the instinct loses that object, just at the time, perhaps, when the child is able to form a total idea of the person to whom the organ that is giving him satisfaction belongs."[36] The child is able to form an idea of the mother through thought, but it is precisely thought that forces the child to forfeit its link to the mother.

The radicalization of Freud by Lacan constitutes a refusal to be seduced by this analogy. At the core of this matter of the unforgettable but forever lost Thing, we find not just *an impossibility of thought,* but *a void of Being.* The problem is not simply that I cannot think the primordial mother, but that her loss opens up a hole in being. Or, it is not that the mother escapes representation or thought, but that the jouissance that attached me to her has been lost and this loss depletes the whole of my being. But why continue to insist on the unforgettableness of the Thing or lost jouissance? If we must not forget this jouissance that stays together as a whole, it must be because some trace of it remains behind even if the nature of that trace must be reconceived.

The point is this: Freud did not rest content with the division of the *Nebenmensch* into two parts. When there are only two components, as here, there is not yet any notion of drive. Drive emerges only with the introduction of another term that has far-reaching consequences for the way we perceive the *Nebenmensch* complex. The term is *Vorstellungrepräsentanz,* or "ideational representative" in Strachey's translation. Lacan, attuned to the nuances of Freud's thought, recognizes immediately the implications of this notion, which he defines in the following way: *"Vorstellungrepräsentanz . . .* is a matter of that which in the unconscious system represents, in the form of a sign, representation as a function of apprehending" (SVII: 71). Represents representation as a function of apprehending— what? Lacan answers this time, "the good that *das Ding* brings with it," even though a page earlier he insisted that the primordial loss of *das Ding* entails a loss of that Sovereign Good which had once been the goal of classical ethics. There is no longer any Sovereign Good any more than there is a Being that "stays together as a *thing,*" as a "constant structure," or as One. But, surprisingly, Lacan now informs us that representation, or thought, can "apprehend," can by itself grasp hold of some good. Not some of *das Ding*—this possibility is foreclosed as the subject finds itself perched over *the void of das Ding,* the void of its absence—but some good, something in place of *das Ding. Vorstellungrepräsentanz,* in other words, is not any ordinary representation (insofar as representation is thought to be what causes the loss of being as well as the loss of the jouissance of the incestuous relation), but a peculiar kind of representation that permits us to grasp hold of some nonbeing, some jouissance, or satisfaction.

Lucan will further flesh out the implications of the notion of *Vorstellungrepräsentanz* when he says, with explicit reference to the drive, "In my opinion, it is not in this dialectic between [the thing and the thing itself, the phenomenon and the noumenon] the surface and that which is beyond that things are suspended. . . . I set out from the fact that there is something that establishes a fracture, a bi-partition, a splitting of . . . being"(SXI: 106). The old dialectic between *das Ding* and *Vorstellungrepräsentanz,* or the noumenal and phenomenal mother, is disbanded with the development of the concept of drive, because the drive lets us conceive satisfaction not as always already lost, but as attainable by the subject. This is where we rejoin the argument we were following in *Beyond the Pleasure Principle,* where Freud opposes the object of the drive, *Vorstellungrepräsentanz,* to Kant's "necessary forms of thought." The ruin of the noumenal beyond and, Lacan adds, the fracture that is thus installed in the surface order of appearances emerge together and are somehow related to a new notion of jouissance that is inaccessible to the subject. This jouissance or satisfaction is represented as an object, such as a breast or a voice, that has been detached from the mother.

The development of the concept of *Vorstellungrepräsentanz* appears, then, to sever the *Ding*-component of the *Nebenmensch* complex into two parts, into *das Ding* and *Vorstellungrepräsentanz,* although *das Ding* is no longer conceivable as a noumenal object and is retained only by the description of *Vorstellungrepräsentanz* as *partial.* It is clear from the theory that when this partial object arrives on the scene, it blocks the path to the old conception of *das Ding,* which is now only a retrospective illusion. It is similarly clear that when he describes the *Vorstellungrepräsentanz,* or ideational representative, as a "delegate" of the body in the psyche—a delegate, specifically, that betrays its mandator—Freud is actually allowing this ideational representative to displace and forbid passage back to the naive notion of a body existing apart from its delegate, which sends the latter forth as its representative. The traitorous delegate and the partial object act not as evidence of a body or a Thing existing elsewhere, but as evidence of the fact that the body and satisfaction have lost the support of the organic body and the noumenal Thing. It is the loss of these supports that causes the fracturing of the surface order of appearances, a splitting within being and not between being and its beyond.

The introduction of the term *Vorstellungrepräsentanz,* in other words, coincides with a splitting that opens up in the phenomenal world *and* the attainment of some jouissance. What, more specifically, is the relation among these terms? This question provides an opportunity to clear up a lingering misconception. The moment one says that the aim of the drive is its own satisfaction, or that the drive has no purpose other than the repetition of its own trajectory, one is tempted to assert, as an obvious corollary, that the drive is indifferent to external objects. Virtually any object will serve as well as any other to satisfy the drive, which aims not at the object but at the satisfaction it can derive from it. Here the object remains, precisely, external or is incidental to the drive, a mere alibi or prop serving the end of satisfaction. Although the drive may be obliged to make use of such an object, this is only so it can get at its real aim, jouissance.

The first thing to note is that this idea of the drive's indifference to an external object is at odds with Lacan's definition of sublimation as "the elevation of an ordinary object to the dignity of the Thing." This formulation is admittedly confusing; it misleads Lacan himself at points to conflate sublimation and idealization. In these instances the ordinary object seems to become the representation of the Thing, of a noumenal beyond, and this has the effect of erecting a barrier to jouissance, which is now conceived as inaccessible. But there are also moments when elevation does not seem to entail this function of representation, but rather entails—in a reversal of the common understanding of sublimation— the substitution of an ordinary object for the Thing. One seeks satisfaction from an ordinary object instead of waiting vainly for the arrival of the Thing. This is the only way to comprehend the satisfaction Lacan experiences on seeing a series of matchboxes, found objects, that were collected by his friend, Jacques Prévert. What strikes Lacan is the extraordinary dignity of these little cardboard boxes, the dignity of their thingness.

It would be preposterous, of course, to speak of the dignity of the instinct's object, which is unceremoniously gobbled or used up once found. Instinct is satiated by the object, but also extinguished by this very satiety. The instinct and its object finish each other off, as it were, as the former quickly has enough of the latter. The drive, on the other hand, does not finish so easily with its object, but keeps turning around it, just as Prévert continues to collect and arrange his proliferating series of matchboxes. If the drive is not only satisfied, but continues to seek and derive satisfaction in the object, this has no doubt something to do with the splitting in the order of appearances of which Lacan speaks. The point is that the drive does not aim beyond the ordinary object at the satisfaction to be attained on the other or thither side of it. This is what happens in the case of the oral instinct, where the goal, food, is used to secure the satisfaction of one's hunger. The food is here merely the means by which the stomach gets filled. If the drive, on the contrary, is said to have no goal, but only an aim, this is because its object is no longer a means of attaining satisfaction, it is an end in itself; it is directly satisfying. It is not a means to something other than itself, but is itself other than itself. The bi-partition takes place within the object, not between the object and the satisfaction that lies beyond it. Lacan puts this another way in the *Ethics* seminar when he proposes that sublimation ought to be thought not as the substitution of a culturally valorized object for one that is immediately gratifying sexually, but as a *changing of the object itself.* The object of the drive is never identical to itself.[37]

Since an illustration of this point will no doubt be useful, I would like to consider the work of Jasper Johns. It is not only a particular work—*Target with Plaster Cast,* with its anatomical fragments, or partial objects: hand, heel, ear, foot, penis painted and primly placed in boxes atop a painted canvas target—that brings this artist to mind in this context, it is also his enlightening yet matter-of-fact answers to a series of questions put to him by the critic Leo Steinberg. Steinberg observes that the commonplace objects that are the subject of Johns's work are chosen precisely because "they are nobody's preference, not even his own."[38] For instance, the clothes hangers that appear in some of his pieces are not fine-crafted wooden ones such as might have been selected to connote, derisively or admiringly, values of elegance or wealth; nor are they the pastel-colored plastic ones one might find in the closet of a teenage girl. They are rather the plain, wire hangers one gets back from the cleaners and to which no one ever really pays much notice. "No attitude of anger, irony, or estheticism alters the shape" of the objects Johns paints, rather "it's the way things are that is the proper subject [of his] art" (31). The American flags for which he is perhaps most famous do not "stand for" any specific American values, they are not the flags of a chauvinist or a flag-burner. Yet Steinberg keeps pressing, trying to find some preference to explain Johns's choice of objects. Finally the critic asks for this minimal explanation, "Do you use these letter types [commercial stencils] because you like them or because that's how the stencils come?"—to which Johns replies, "But that's what I like about them, that they come that way" (32). Bull's-eye! This answer hits its mark and Steinberg, recognizing this, uses it to summarize Johns's relation to his objects: "He so wills what occurs that what comes from without becomes indistinguishable from what he chooses."

There could not be a better description of drive/sublimation: *it so wills what occurs that the object it finds is indistinguishable from the one it chooses.* Construction and discovery, thinking and being, as well as drive and object are soldered together. The drive's creation, ex nihilo, of an object, a thing in the very place where unified jouissance, *das Ding,* is absent, is evoked in this description but without calling up along with it the Romantic image of the artist-creator. On the contrary, Johns seems to disappear, leaving his objects to stand by themselves, "without any human attitude whatsoever surrounding [them]," Steinberg remarks. The objects stand alone; they do not stand for anything else, reflect anything else, not even Johns's attitude toward them. The will that chooses these objects is absolutely Johns's and yet absolutely impersonal. Lacan sheds some light on this paradox when he speaks of the "headless subject" of the drive. If the ordinary objects of Johns's work are somehow disturbing, it is not exactly correct to say with Steinberg that they are "relieved of man's shadow" or that they "insinuate our absence." What they insinuate is the absence of that egoistic self-consciousness which causes us to bow to external circumstances, to the wills and desires—the preferences—of others or to be moved to pity by their pains and sorrows. Johns's work is affectless only in the sense that it is not passively affected by the objects it paints. But this is not to say that there is no subject, no will or passion discernible in the work which, on the contrary, displays a remarkable passion for and satisfaction in the plain object. The affect of jouissance, satisfaction in the object, is not passive; it arouses itself through the active gift of love. If Johns keeps painting the same objects again and again, it is because their ability to fascinate him is inexhaustible—not because they stand for or represent something more than themselves, but because for him they are always more than themselves.

THE OBDURATE DESIRE TO ENDURE

Antigone exemplifies, we said, that which Freud designates under the term *Haftbarkeit*—or *perseverance*—with all the ethical connotations the word conjures up. She steadfastly persists in carrying out her implacable resolve to bury her brother, despite the remonstrations of the pliant and conservative Ismene and the wavering indecision of her community, that is, the Chorus, which is swayed by the merits of both sides to the conflict, just as Hegel will be. In fact, a significant difference between Hegel and Lacan is their respective relations to the Chorus. Whereas Hegel places himself roughly in their role as moderator, partially swayed by each side, Lacan regards the chorus more skeptically. Moreover, whereas Hegel focuses on the merits of Antigone's act of installing Polynices as "a member of the community . . . which sought to . . . destroy him," Lacan views the act of the loving sister as a definitive break with her community: "because the community refuses to [bury Polynices, she] is required . . . to maintain that essential being which is the family *Até*." In other words, the deed Antigone undertakes traces the path of the criminal drive, away from the possibilities the community prescribes and toward the impossible real. That she is "required" to do so testifies to the *Zwang* or compulsion of drive, which is indifferent to external criteria, such as the good opinion of others. It will not be for Lacan a matter of setting another place at the table, of making room for the one brother who was formerly excluded from the rites of the community, but of destroying that community in the name of what is impossible in it. This is not to say that the polis of Thebes is founded on the forbidding of certain ideas or actions, on declaring them off-limits. The impossible is impossible even to conceive under existing conditions—how then could it be forbidden? Ismene's primary role in the drama is to mirror what is currently possible and to mark the unthinkable nature of her sister's decisive deed; she goes so far as to express skepticism that Antigone will be able to carry off her outrageous plan. Informed by her headstrong sister that she *would* do so, Ismene replies, "*If* you can do it. But you are in love with the impossible" (ll. 104–105). And when Antigone persists, Ismene's skepticism switches to warning, "It is better not to hunt the impossible at all" (ll. 107–108).

Lacan rejects Anouilh's portrayal of Antigone as a "little fascist" hellbent on annihilating everything in her path. What he opposes is not the thesis that her deed destroys, but that it is conducted out of a pure will to destruction, for such a characterization overlooks the affirmation and the satisfaction from which her act derives its unstoppable force. That which Antigone affirms in no uncertain terms is her love for her brother, which, she insists, must be proclaimed, must be exposed to the light of day. Ismene is willing to go only this far in aiding her sister: she will remain silent and not tell anyone of Antigone's crime. It is this offer that provokes Antigone's greatest ire: "I will hate you still worse for silence—should you not proclaim it to everyone" (ll. 99–101). This small exchange goes to the heart of the matter: the singular truth of Antigone's love for her brother must have a universal destiny, must be openly declared. The proclamation of love occurs in a passage that has struck several critics as so strange as to provoke the wish that it would one day be found to be an interpolation: "If my husband had died, I could have had another, and a child by another man, if I had lost the first, but with my mother and father in Hades below, I could never have another brother" (ll. 908–912). This is the sentiment we express when we say of someone, "They broke the mold after they made him." Antigone lets us know that her brother is unique, irreplaceable. There will never be another like him. His value to her depends on nothing he has done nor on any of his qualities. She refuses to justify her love for him by giving reasons for it, she calls on no authority, no diety, none of the laws of the polis to sanction the deed she undertakes on his behalf. She says only, tautologically, "from my point of view, my brother is my brother." Lacan summarizes her stance this way: "Antigone invokes no other right than that one ['this brother is something unique'], a right that emerges in the language of the ineffaceable character of what is ['my brother is my brother']. . . . What is, is, and it is to this, to this surface, that the unshakeable, unyielding position of Antigone is fixed" (SVII: 279).

Some readers of Lacan may be tempted to turn Antigone's stance into a demand for a certain type of community, one in which the "otherness of the Other" would be respected, differences tolerated, a community of "singularities," where by "singularity" is meant that which cannot make itself public, that which is in retreat from publicity and thus inaccessible to others. But the argument Lacan advances does not support such an extrapolation. The point of his reading is not to insist on the radical, umplummable otherness of the Other, quite the contrary. The singularity of the brother is not in doubt; it is not his "otherness," his inaccessibility that is in question. That Antigone does not give reasons for her love does not imply that her brother is unfathomable to her but that she is, as even the Chorus perceives, autonomous. She gives herself her own law and does not seek validation from any other authority. In other words, it is not the otherness but the nonexistence of the Other on which Lacan's interpretation turns.

Antigone's affirmation of love is, I am arguing, similar to Jasper Johns's affirmative declaration, "But that's what I like about them, that they come that way." Like Antigone, Johns declines to offer reasons for his fascination with targets or American flags or a particular set of commercial stencils; he, too, attests, in Lacan's phrase, to the "ineffaceable character of what is." We are invited once more to taste the tautologism of love, and perhaps now we can say in what it consists, namely, the coincidence, or near coincidence, of the drive with its object. This is what Lacan sometimes called the "illusion of love": one believes the beloved is everything one could hope for without recognizing the role one's love for him or her plays in one's satisfaction. Though her love for her brother does not depend on any of his qualities, Antigone is not indifferent to them; she accepts them all, lovingly. For, love is that which renders what the other is loveable. This is not to say that Antigone overlooks part of what he is, that she fails to see that he is a traitor to Thebes or that he has any personal flaws. It means she loves him as he is, the way he comes. This is quite different from saying she loves something ineffable, unfathomable in him. To be sure, the Lacanian phrase "I love in you something more than you," taken alone, lends itself to either interpretation.

Everything depends on how one interprets the "something more." Advocates of absolute otherness will see it as an "inaccessible more"—I love your inaccessibility, what I cannot reach in you—whereas Lacan means to say that this "something more" is accessed through love. If one were to receive identical gifts or identical reports of an event one has unfortunately missed both from an acquaintance and from a beloved friend, one would get more, a surplus satisfaction, from the latter. A gift given by a beloved friend ceases to coincide with itself, it becomes itself plus the fact that it was given by the friend. The same is true of everything I get from the beloved, all the qualities, everything he or she is. That is, the "is" of the beloved is split, fractured. The beloved is always slightly different from or more than, herself. It is this more, this extra, that makes the beloved more than just an ordinary object of my attention.

I spoke above of a "near coincidence." The theory of the drive seems to issue forth in a series of such near coincidences: not only of the drive with its object, but also the drive with sublimation, and the external object with the object a. It is as if the very function of the drive were this continuous opening up of small fractures between things. Immediately after noting that Antigone's proclamation of love is expressed in the "ineffaceable character of what is," Lacan adds that what is is ineffaceable "in spite of the flood of . . . transformations." Here again the being, the "what is" that is the object of the drive is described as ever so slightly different from itself, as indistinguishable from a flood of transformations. The singularity of Polynices, what he is, is synonymous with these *surface* transformations, the ruptures in the order of his appearance. The drive continues to circle the object because the latter is never identical to itself, is split from itself.

Lacan's claim is not that Antigone immortalizes her brother, erecting a monument to his memory, but that she immortalizes the family Até, that point of madness where the family lineage is undone or overturns itself. "Immortalize" does not mean here to preserve in memory, but to continue not to forget that vitalizing fracture that permits one to "go mad," to dissolve oneself in a transforming act. One must not confuse the fact that Antigone is unyielding in carrying out her deed with a rigidity of being. If she is able to undertake such a fundamental break with the existing laws of her community, this is only because she has first been able to unloose herself from the fundamental law of her own being. It is not only the object of the drive that is split from itself; the subject, too, is fractured through the drive's repetitions. Because the play begins only after the critical events of her brother's death and Creon's cruel edict, some readers have been persuaded to see her as simply intransigent, unchanging in the very core of her being. But Antigone is portrayed on the contrary as a figure of radical metamorphosis, whose terrifying transformation we are not permitted to witness but are required to imagine. For the most part this metamorphosis must be supposed to have taken place just before the play begins, but some trace of it remains in the messenger's report of the screeching, birdlike cries that Antigone emits on learning that her brother's body has been re-exposed after the first burial. It is this wild tearing away from herself, this inhuman rather than heroic metamorphosis that is the subject of Lacan's analysis. For, the ethics of psychoanalysis is concerned not with the other, as is the case with so much of the contemporary work on ethics, but rather with the subject, who metamorphoses herself at the moment of encounter with the real of an unexpected event. Lacan's ethical imperative, "Do not give way on your desire," proposes itself as anything but an insistence that one stubbornly conform to one's own personal history. In short, the ethics of psychoanalysis filiates itself with Kant's argument that ethical progress has nothing to do with that form of progress promoted by modern industry, or the "service of good," but is rather a matter of personal conversion, of the subjective necessity of going beyond oneself.

A perennial accusation against psychoanalysis is that Freud's thesis that the subject is driven to reproduce an initial state, to recapture or find again its first satisfying object, is determinist. This accusation appears to be confirmed by the notion of the archetype invented by Freud's disciple, Jung. According to this notion, we can find in the psyche of each individual subject "some archaic relation, some primitive mode of access of thoughts, some world that is there like some shade of an ancient world surviving in ours" (SXI: 153). But Freud opposes Jung when he argues in *The Ego and the Id* that "[n]o external vicissitude can be experienced or undergone by the id [or: by the drive] except by way of the ego, which is the representative of the external world to the id. Nevertheless, it's not possible to speak of direct inheritance in the ego. *It is here that a gulf between an actual individual and the concept of a species becomes evident.*"[39] Freud here takes his distance not only from Jung, but from the description Aristotle offers of animal instinct's obedience to the species' dictates, and from Feuerbach's contention that the happiness drive inscribes the requirements of the individual subject in the researches carried out by the species. What is wrong with all three, in Freud's opinion, is that they attempt to eliminate the gap between individual and species in some way. Freud argues that this gap can never be reabsorbed; moreover, it is the very maintenance of this gap that permits the individual subject from being annihilated by the history she inherits. That which the individual inherits from her species, her family, her race cannot be located merely in a stateable law or dictate, but includes also the *Até* of the law, that excess in the law which cannot be articulated within it. Because the law contains this mad excess where it loses its head, as it were, the subject can carry out the law or carry on the family name without simply repeating in the present what has already been forseen and dictated by the past. Antigone is not fated by the crime of her incestuous parents to a similarly tragic crime. The criminal being she safeguards is that of the law itself, which contains its own transgression. If Antigone is fated by her family *Até,* it is in this paradoxical sense: she is *destined to overturn her fate through her act.*

Antigone's *Haftbarkeit,* her perseverance to the end or to the momentous conclusion of an act that will necessarily overturn her, is contrasted to the *Fixierarbeit* of Creon as conversion, or self-rupture, to modern progress. This contrast lets us observe the difference between "acting in conformity with the real of desire" and acting in a self-interested way, or acting to preserve one's own continuity with oneself. The principle of *Fixierarbeit* is articulated by Lacan as: "Carry on working. Work must go on. . . . As far as desires are concerned, come back later. Make them wait"(S VII: 315). *Work* here signifies something different, something opposed to the act insofar as work never concludes, it keeps going—or rather waiting. What is it that holds one back from satisfaction? On what is Creon fixated?

To answer, one must refer to the concept of inhibition. In *Inhibitions, Symptoms, and Anxiety* Freud offers as a memorable example of inhibition the hand of the obsessional, which is suddenly incapable of performing the simple act of writing. To release his hand and the flow of his thoughts, the obsessional, it is often said, must first de-eroticize the process of writing and thinking. This theory has no doubt contributed to some of the confusion surrounding sublimation, which is assumed to spring from a separation of thought from sex or jouissance. But our account of sublimation paints a different picture; sublimation does not separate thought from sex, but rather from the supposed subject of knowledge, that is, from the Other. For, the satisfaction of the drive by sublimation testifies to the autonomy of the subject, her independence from the Other, as we have argued. But if the *inhibition of the drive* by the achieved aim of its satisfaction bears witness to our independence, the *inhibition of the obsessional's hand,* and of Creon's fixation on the laws of the State, betray a dependence of jouissance on a supposed subject of knowledge. This does not mean that enjoyment becomes proscribed, that pleasure is forbidden by the Other, but that jouissance is now prescribed: "Henceforth you will find your enjoyment in the following way!"

This thesis garners support from something Freud says in *Beyond the Pleasure Principle*. Quoting a phrase from *Faust*'s Mephistopheles, he speaks of a "driving factor which will permit of no halting at any position attained, but, in the poet's words, '*ungebändigt immer vorwärts dringt* [presses ever forward unsubdued]'" (SE 18: 42). This phrase seems to apply to the intransigence of Creon and Antigone, both of whom appear to be, in the technical sense, driven. But Freud then *distinguishes* this particular "driving factor" from that which produces sublimations. To what does Faustian drivenness owe its unsubduable pressure? This is Freud's answer: "it is the difference in the amount between the pleasure of satisfaction which is *demanded* and that which is actually *achieved* that provides the driving factor which will permit of no halting." The phrasing recalls Feuerbach's damning critique of a certain modern notion of immortality.

While Antigone is driven by the satisfaction afforded by her love for her brother, which provides the pressure or tension necessary to act, Creon is driven by an idealization of the difference between the satisfaction demanded and that which can be achieved through work. In psychoanalytic terms we would say that Creon is driven by his superego, which is that psychic agency which fosters in the subject a distaste for mundane, compromised pleasures and maintains us in a state of dissatisfaction. Creon's fixation on the lost object causes him to be relatively indifferent to all others available to him. He remains glued to an ideal he will never attain, since it is dervied from his nostalgia for something he never possessed. One often hears it said that the superego is an internalization of the laws and ideals of the culture or community; this simplification misses the fact that the laws and ideals of the community are themselves fabricated only on the basis of an idealization of dissatisfaction. If the superego always demands more sacrifice, more work, this is because the ideal it sets in front of the subject is kept aloft by a loss that the subject is unable to put behind him. The superego attempts to mask the loss of the Other by posing as witness or reminder of that absolute satisfaction which can no longer be ours. The stubborn unity of purpose Creon displays is indistinguishable from the aggressivity he unleashes toward everything—even his own ego—that falls short of this ideal. This stubborness is thus not inconsistent with his failure of nerve toward the end of the play, his bending to public opinion. The fixation on dissatisfaction, in other words, does not always manifest itself as consistency of character, since it exposes the ego to the vicissitudes of public opinion in which it is always possible to find validation of the superego's harsh judgment.

The superego thus maintains a rigorous division between that satisfaction available to us and the one that lies beyond. It is possible to argue that there where Agamben has observed the notion of "bare" or "nude" life emerging out of the metaphysical positing of a realm of pure Being, "indeterminant and impenetrable" and located beyond an "unthinkable limit" that separates us from all it offers, there, too, one can recognize the handiwork of the superego. If, as Lacan argues, Creon represents a sovereign law that knows no limit, if he seeks "the good of all without limit," this is because his superegoic positing of a pure satisfaction or absolute goal is founded on the prior positing of an external limit to the world. This limit decompletes, empties out, all his endeavors, all his satisfactions, causing him to strive fruitlessly toward a goal he will never attain. Creon's hounding of Polynices beyond the limit of death prefigures modern science's hounding of the subject beyond death, apparently without limit, into infinitely extendable states (in principle, at least) of *coma passé*. When she covers the exposed body of her brother, Antigone raises herself out of the conditions of naked existence to which Creon remains bound.

Narcissism, Approached Obliquely

From the mouth of Timaeus of Locri (in the Platonic dialogue bearing his name), we learn that Earth was created as a globe that because it contained all things, had no need of sense organs or, indeed, of organs of any kind. As Timaeus explains, there would not have been any use for such organs "by the help of which [Earth] might receive his food or get rid of what he had already digested, since there was nothing that went from him or came into him, for there was nothing besides him."[1] This description of Earth as an immortal, self-sufficient "body without organs" has echoed through the ages into our own (as Deleuze and Guattari's famous phrase testifies). Novalis, for example, invokes the description at the beginning of the modern period: "If every organic part had the life-duration of eternity, it would need no nourishment in the stricter sense of the word, no renovation, no elimination."[2] But the status of this immortal body is for us moderns not in doubt, it would seem: it cannot and does not exist, except as a quaint and rather absurd notion. And for us the idea of an original plenum, of an All that would contain everything, has been destroyed; we speak now of the collapse of the universal, the end of Grand Ideas. Totality is an impossibility for speaking beings. As modern subjects, we are born into historical time with no promise of an eternal resting place outside time, no hope of everlastingness, and it is precisely our bodies that bring home to us this truth. Embodied, we are time-bound, condemned to finitude.

It is with this conviction that historians of the body have for several years now delighted in laying bare—through those literal and figurative transparencies that are one of the mainstays of biology textbooks—the organs of our *mortality*. The exposure by Foucault of the penetrating medical gaze, which opened up the nineteenth-century body to scientific scrutiny, is appropriated by these historians to sanction their numerous studies of the historical constructions of the body or, to put it differently, the peeling away of the historical and institutional layers of its construction. In this way the body has been shown to be neither a self-sufficient entity, nor eternally enduring, but finite and dependent on—to the point of being a product of—its immediate milieu. It is possible to think, then, of this historical work as that which has finally, definitively endowed the body with organs. One might even risk an analogy between this work and that performed by the famous eighteenth-century thought-experiment devised by Condillac. In this experiment the philosopher mentally chips away at the marble layer of a human statue in order to lay bare, one by one, the various organs of sense supposedly buried beneath. First the nose is exposed, allowing the statue to smell; next the exposure of the mouth allows taste, ears hearing, eyes sight, until finally the removal of all the marble from the entire body—or from the largest of the organs, the skin—pries open the dimension of touch. In other words, the statue, stripped of its marble, loses its status as classical, abstract ideal and becomes a living, mortal body dependent on and in touch with an external, temporal world. Time itself floods into the body, which now becomes vulnerable to the destructive powers of temporality. No longer frozen in time, the body will slowly decrepitate and eventually die.

THE PARTIAL OBJECT

Now, insofar as it claims that the Other does not exist and that the subject is constituted from an originary lack, psychoanalysis should, one would assume, be equally committed to the notion of the body's mortality. For psychoanalysis, too, one would expect the body to be the seat of death. But before rushing to this conclusion, it will be useful to examine the myth Lacan substitutes for the Timaean one found in Plato. Unlike the latter, this myth presents the image of a body that "gears into" the world, or comes into contact with an outside, through a "number of mouths at [its] surface." I am referring to Lacan's elevation to the status of myth Walt Whitman's lyric description of the body's "palpating expansiveness," which allows the subject to dream of "total, complete, epidermic contact between his or her body and a world that [is] itself open and quivering."[3] From Timaeus to Whitman something has changed in the description of the relation between the body and its outside; not only is the Whitmanean body endowed with organs, a myriad of mouths that form the skin and connect the body to a world outside it, but a kind of voluptuousness, absent from the Timaean body, infuses the poet's. The mouth is no longer simply that which ingests or spews out, but also and significantly that which kisses and sensuously sucks. Behind this change lies an even larger, systematic alteration: the classical, Platonic model, wherein the body is conceived as capable of *incorporating* that which is outside, has been replaced by the modern model, wherein the body is capable of *incarnating* what is other to it.[4] The psychoanalytic notion of the body aligns itself with the second model, with its way of privileging the voluptuary dimension of corporeality. Before we can begin to understand this change, however, we need to note that Lacan cites Whitman not simply in order to embrace his myth of "dilation," but also to register this dissent: we are *not* inserted into the world through total epidermic contact with it—Lacan says, contra the poet—but more narrowly and precisely at those limited and irreducible points that Freud designated as points of the drive. At these junctures we come into contact with "residues of archaic forms of the libido."

Let us contemplate what this implies: first, the body's "mouths" do not take in, incorporate objects from empirical reality, but rather they reincarnate, give body to, archaic or lost forms of libido in the form of small objects: gaze, voice, breast, phallus, and so on, the objects of the partial drives. One can recognize in this shift to the second notion of the mouth, or bodily opening, something of Freud's shift from the first to the second topic. The first, which consists of the perception-unconscious-consciousness system, assumes a reality that impinges on the psyche through perceptions, whereas the second, which consists of the intrapsychic agencies, ego, id, and superego, theorizes psychic life not as issuing from perceptions that impinge from without but from a longing for a pleasure remembered yet never experienced. As is often noted, the break between the first and second topic was precipitated by Freud's 1914 essay "On Narcissism." It is against this Freudian backdrop that we notice that the *organs of sense* so central to the Platonic myth of the body virtually disappear in the modified Whitmanean myth—which later becomes, in Seminar XI, the myth of the *lamella*—in favor of what Lacan calls the *"organ of the libido."* This formulation—"organ of the libido"—is striking and surely we are meant not to miss it: the myth of the lamella replaces the myth of the body without organs. Listen to what Lacan says: "This lamella, this organ, whose characteristic is not to exist, but which is nevertheless an organ . . . is the libido." And this libido "*qua* pure life instinct, that is to say, immortal life, or irrepressible life, life that has need of no organ, simplified, indestructible life," is, he admits—just as we would naively have expected him to—"precisely what is *subtracted* from the living being by virtue of the fact that it is subject to the cycle of sexed reproduction."[5] Lacan seems to be saying here that the human body is not a "body without organs," not an immortal body, for indestructible life has been drained, like the Zuider Zee, from it; the body therefore dies and can "live on" only by reproducing itself in another generation. The *individual* body is destructible, mortal; only the *species* survives the cycle of sexed reproduction. Our original, naive expectation is met, then; we even refind here in Lacan a truism of German idealism: sexed reproduction gives birth to death.

But this characterization of Lacan's argument turns out to be precipitous, for although immortal, indestructible life has been subtracted from us, there remain these *representatives* (not representations) of it in the form of little libidinalized objects. Let us unfold this logic in a slightly different way. That organ—the libido—which has no need of organs, since it is itself pure and total self-sufficiency, does not now and never did exist (or: there is no original plenum), yet something nevertheless remains of that never-existing, mythical time and self-sufficiency. Bits and pieces of that originary, purely mythical organ have remained behind in the form of partial objects. To these objects Lacan gives the names of bodily organs: gaze, voice, breast, phallus. But why? Explaining this conception of the libido as an organ, he says, laconically, only that he means *organ* in both senses: organ-part of the organism and organ-instrument.

It is odd to meet here the term *organ-instrument,* since it is already clear that the organ of the libido is meant to veer away from any instrumentalist or functional argument regarding the fitness of the body organs to predesignated tasks. Lacan is far from endorsing that claim of "purposiveness" which presumes eyes were designed for seeing, mouths for eating, and so on. And noses, were they designed for holding up our glasses, or hands for holding cell phones? The direction of Lacan's argument leads away from this supposed preprogramming of body organs toward an account of the way the organ of the libido *invents* our organs of sense, which owe their existence to our capacity to use them. We must approach the first answer, "organ-part of the organism," with an equal amount of wariness in order to avoid a spontaneous and thus spurious conclusion: *part* is no less tricky than *instrument* here.

What does it mean to say that the drives and the objects of the drive are partial? To help de-automate our response, I am going to leap to another field and a different vocabulary. The other field is film theory, and my suggestion is that the organ is a part of the organism in the same way as the close-up is a part of a visual field. Here is what Gilles Deleuze, following the early Hungarian film theorist, Béla Balázs, says about this cinematic device: "the close-up does *not* tear away its object from a set of which it would form part, . . . but on the contrary it *abstracts it from all spatio-temporal co-ordinates,* that is to say, it raises it to the state of Entity. The close-up is not an enlargement . . . it implies a change of dimension, this is an absolute change."[6]

Deleuze is claiming that the close-up is *not* a closer look at a part of a scene, that is, it does not disclose an object that can be listed as an element of that scene, a *detail* plucked from the whole and then blown up in order to focus our attention. The close-up discloses, rather, the *whole* of the scene itself, or as Deleuze says, its entire "expressed." This argument is strikingly similar to the one Roland Barthes makes in his essay, "The Reality Effect." Carefully reading a thick, realistic description from one of Balzac's novels, Barthes isolates a detail that turns out not to be one at all, inasmuch as it functions not, as the other details do, by adding to or thickening the description. What, then, is its function? It establishes the reality effect itself; without it, all the other details together would compose not a realistic scene, but a hallucinatory one. The barometer—which is the odd detail Barthes picks out—in Balzac and the close-up in film represent objects that though *included* in the scenes, do not properly *belong to* them; they are not subsumable as elements of the set of details composing the scene. The partial object of the drive, I will argue, exemplifies this same logic; it does not form part of the organism, but implies an absolute change.

It would seem on the face of it foolhardy to propose clarifying the distinction between a part that belongs to a whole and one that functions *as* a whole via a discussion of the partial drives, for it is just at this point that Freudian theory seems particularly resistant. Freud first conceived the partial drives—or, "component instincts"—as fragmentary and fragmenting. They produced a dispersed body and polymorphous and perverse pleasures that were later susceptible to the secondary operations of Oedipus and castration, which supposedly bundled the component instincts together and subordinated them to the primacy of the genital function. In the scenario proposed, then, there are two stages: the first concerns the child's libidinal attachment to its scattered body parts; the second involves the supercession of the first via the threat of castration, which severs the child from its autoerotic relations and directs the libido outward—"altruistically," Freud says here—toward another.[7]

The full extent of the revisions to this scenario demanded by the theory of narcissism is not often grasped, and so the scenario persists untouched in the popular imagination. This results in further misunderstandings down the road. For example, the primary claim of the essay, "On Narcissism"—in order to account for the emergence of the ego out of the *disjecta membra* of the child's original autoeroticism one must posit a "new psychical action"—is generally assumed to mean that the ego emerges *directly* from this psychical action. What Freud actually says, however, is quite different: "The development of the ego consists in a *departure* from primary narcissism."[8] Whereas the misinterpretation would retain the outlines of Freud's first theory (that is, autoerotic dispersal gives way to narcissistic wholeness), his actual statement alters that theory profoundly by insisting on *three* stages or structures (autoeroticism, primary narcissism, and "egoism," or "nostalgic" narcissism) and defining the relation between the second and third structures as antagonistic. The first and third structures alone may be still comprehensible in the terms provided by Freud's original theory, but the second, primary narcissism, and the "new psychical action" giving rise to it are opaque, not only to the terms of the first theory but to most commentators as well.

What then is the "new psychical action" to which Freud refers? Since he never explicitly offers an answer to this question, either in this or in subsequent essays, it is necessary to deduce one from what he does say. Leo Bersani argues, quite convincingly, in "Erotic Assumptions: Narcissism and Sublimation in Freud," that this new action is none other than sublimation. This seems to me exactly right and I will thus follow Bersani in this direction, but I first want to consider what happens in the process of these revisions to an old, familiar action—namely, castration—whose notion seems to be rejunevated along the way. In the year after the essay on narcissism is written, Freud spends his attention on reexaminations of the drives, repression, and the unconscious, all in order to emphasize less the split between the conscious and the unconscious than *a split within the unconscious itself,* between the objects of the drive and something that exceeds them. This shift in the location of the primary psychic division prompted Lacan to contest with regularity that the cut of castration does not separate the *child from its mother* (which is where it is ordinarily thought to fall and where it does appear to fall in Freud's first theory, considered above), but instead separates the *mother from the breast.* Rather than two objects, mother and child, we have now three: mother, child, and breast, with the last operating as a strange "delegate" or "representative" of the primordial mother. The mother falls into a void precisely at the moment when something—the breast, placenta, or some other object—is detached from her.

Moreover, castration takes on a different function in this new configuration. It appears now to participate in the *formation* of the partial drives rather than, as formerly, to intervene belatedly after they are formed, to bundle them.

It is, in fact, this later notion of castration that informs Lacan's myth of the birth of the body: castration banishes us from the paradise of immortal life by detaching from immortality these small representatives, or incarnations, of it. In place of the All, the original Plenum, we have these little objects, which are the source of our immortality, and partial incarnations of a lost maternal One.

In the period in which he is attempting to develop his new notions of narcissism and castration, Freud, by his own admission, keeps Kant's theory of the subject's relation to itself in mind. This much can be gathered from the opening of his 1915 essay, "The Unconscious," where he poses the following question: how is it that we are able to distinguish our own unconscious, which is after all alien to us, from another or second consciousness, which is also alien to us? That is, how is it that our unconscious appears to us as "inside," rather than as "outside," in the world? This is a variation on Kant's question regarding the difference between the perception of external objects and the apperception of the transcendental "I." The problem is that if thinking were able to catch the "I" in its nets or consciousness were able to catch hold of the unconscious, that which was caught would cease being what it is—spontaneous thought or unconsciousness—and become instead an object of consciousness. Yet clearly something has to appear to consciousness to cause us to suspect and therefore to posit the existence of the transcendental "I" or the unconscious in the first place. In attempting to think this peculiar object of thought—peculiar in that it cannot possess any objectivity, since this would make it indistinguishable from an external object— Freud is led to contemplate the unsituatable nature of the drive, which is neither inside nor outside. Let me quote from his argument:

> I am in fact of the opinion that the antithesis of conscious and unconscious is not applicable to instincts. An instinct can never become an object of consciousness—only the idea that represents the instinct can. Even in the unconscious, moreover, an instinct cannot be represented otherwise than by an idea. If the instinct did not attach itself to an idea or manifest itself as an affective state, we would know nothing of it. When we nevertheless speak of an unconscious instinctual impulse or of a repressed instinctual impulse, the looseness of phraseology is a harmless one. We can only mean an instinctual impulse the ideational representative of which is unconscious, for nothing else comes into consideration.[9]

In this passage Freud is plainly drawing *within the unconscious* the division of which we spoke earlier, between the ideational representative of the drive—the *Vorstellungrepräsentanz*—and what Lacan refers to as "the drive to come." "Drive to come" translates the idea that the object of the drive is partial; it does not promise a future free of this partialness. The problem raised by the passage from Freud is that of maintaining a distinction between inside and outside once the notion of drive is introduced, and this has the further consequence of making the "I" of the subject more elusive. Once the subject "gears into the world" through the drive, she begins—not to fuse with it, as per Whitman's description of "amatory adhesiveness"—to be unable to locate herself in an outside.

NARCISSISM AND SUBLIMATION

The central problem confronted by Freud in his groundbreaking but contorted and nearly unreadable essay on narcissism is connected to the complex of problems just cited. If self-consciousness does not allow us to turn around and grasp hold of ourselves, how do we know that we exist as subjects of consciousness? If the distinction between inside and outside begins to falter, how can I be sure there is an "I" separable from consciousness? On its face, this late focus on the partial objects and the partial drives seems to doom the project of finding a solution. Amid all this apparent fragmentation, would it not seem more difficult rather than less to speak of *a* subject of the unconscious? The question of why the subject does not simply dissolve or disperse herself amid her experiences does not seem answerable in terms that appear only to create dispersal. Castration, recall, is no longer available to bind either the drives or the subject; it intervenes instead between the *disjecta membra* of the morcelated organism and the partial drives of the subject. In what, then, does the subject's narcissism consist? How does the subject come to love herself as something separate from her experiences?

Since Bersani, in his previously mentioned essay, has already exhumed the central confusion in Freud's exposition, we will follow his reading, as a thread through a labyrinth. Although it names the self-love that detaches an "I" from the subject's experiences and perceptions, the concept of narcissism does not present a consistent theory of this "I." In the first part of the essay, Bersani argues, narcissism is synonymous with a "nonmoralistic masochism," or a "passionate suffering," in which the subject seeks to dismantle the infantile ego without destroying it. It is through this desire to shatter totality that the "first psychic totality," or primary narcissism, comes into being, as nothing but "a passionate inference necessitated by [the ego's] anticipated pleasure of its own dismantling" ("Erotic," 37). Or: the subject infers the something-to-be-shattered, the "I," on the basis of the shattering. Later, however, when Freud begins to speak about the adult subject's attempt to recover a former totality, a lost wholeness, he reconceives narcissism in *moralistic* terms, as the dutiful but inevitably masochistic effort of the ego "to find pleasure in loving an ideal to which it is guiltily inferior" ("Erotic," 40). The "I" is now a totality, a whole, that may be inferred from the guilt the subject experiences as a result of failing to attain some ideal rather than from the pleasure she experiences from dismantling the ego. In his theoretical confusion, Freud cannot see his way clear to distinguishing these two as separate operations, *narcissism proper,* on the one hand, and *nostalgic narcissism* or *egoism,* on the other. The question to be asked in differentiating the two is this: what does self-preservation, the preservation of the "I," mean in each case?

Bersani surmises that the theoretical back-pedaling in the second part of the essay is due to Freud's failure of resolve regarding his own conviction that the drive is intrinsically indifferent to external objects, that human sexuality is not basically "other-directed" or "altruistic," as he tended to believe in *Three Essays,* for example, but is on the contrary "autistic," or narcissistic, has no goal other than its own satisfaction. Fearful, perhaps, of the actual consequences of his notion of an autistic or solitary pleasure on his theory in general, or of the way it might appear to others, Freud reacted by rethinking narcissism as a derivation of object relations. That is, he reconceived narcissism as *loving oneself as an object.* The notion, then, of an *objectless* enjoyment or, in Bersani's words, "the pleasure of self-shattering," which briefly makes an appearance in Freud's essay, is quickly whisked offstage; it becomes, precisely, an obscene notion.

But although the fears, hesitations, and confusions are as visible as Bersani alleges, it is nevertheless true that Freud persists in subsequent essays, as I have been arguing, in his radical theorization of that unconscious division which alone makes the first theory of narcissism comprehensible. So that, though one would have to agree that Freud stumbled in those moments when he seemed to recast narcissism as a kind of object-love in which the ego played the role of the loved/despised object, one is also convinced that there is more to be learned from the curious twists and turns of his argument, particularly as it concerns the intrications of ego-libido, which accounts for the erotic passion for the "I," and object-libido, which is directed at external objects. Moreover, while one can agree with Bersani that narcissism cannot mean loving oneself *as an object,* that *narcissism* is objectless (at least in this sense), it is impossible to accept the proposal that *sublimation* has no object. Bersani's decision to make sublimation objectless, to define it as "the first deflection of the sexual instinct [drive] from an object-fixated activity to another, "higher aim" . . . [namely] to repeat the activity of an eroticized consciousness" ("Erotic," 37) or to repeat the self-shattering of consciousness, is all the more striking given the fact that Jean Laplanche, whose work on this subject was influential to Bersani's own thinking, noted that sublimation is associated in Freud with "the *genesis* of objects."[10] Now, the vulgar misinterpretation of sublimation, to which Freud himself is not always immune, is that it substitutes a culturally valorized object or goal for a nonvalorized, sexual one: the pleasure of drawing up orderly budgets and accounts, for example, for the anal eroticism of feces retention. Bersani persuasively attacks this widespread misunderstanding and returns to sublimation the sexual enjoyment that accompanies it. This is a significant achievement, but it overshoots the mark by denying sublimation not only a culturally valorized object but any object at all.

The question of the object must be approached from two directions, as it pertains to narcissism and as it pertains to sublimation. Bersani's conceptualization of the relation between narcissism and sublimation is not sufficiently effusive, however, to allow us to distinguish them. Both seem in his account to consist in the pleasure of a shattering of self. It is left to us then to try to pry the two apart. Bersani borrows the notion of self-shattering from Laplanche, who derives it from the Freudian definition of sex as that which overwhelms every psychic attempt at self-binding. Sex is traumatic by its very nature, in precisely this sense: it shatters the ego's boundaries. But the relation Bersani establishes between sublimation and narcissism may also have its roots in Foucault. In "What Is an Author?" one finds a definition of writing that is very close to Bersani's definition of sublimation; writing, Foucault says, is "a voluntary obliteration of the self."[11] He continues, "Where a [premodern] work had the duty of creating immortality, it now attains the right to kill, to become the murderer of its author." A psychoanalytic thinker, Bersani knows not to conclude from statements such as this, as historicists have, that shattering annihilates the subject. For him the point is not that the subject is obliterated but that this obliteration constitutes the subject's experience of itself as a separate existence, an "I." These obliterations locate themselves in the element of the same, in the subject's passionate regard for itself as subject of these shatterings. They become proof of the subject's existence, not of the "deconstruction" of the subject. Freud's intent is not, however, to reintroduce through this route a substantial subject "behind" or "beneath" the experience of shattering, an essence of the subject that withstands the destructive force of jouissance. The subject or "I" slips into the argument, rather, as a mere logical inference: "primary narcissism . . . is less easy to grasp by direct observation than to confirm by inference from elsewhere"(*SE,* 14:90). It is then Freud's solution that Bersani adopts when he defines the "first psychic totality," or the subject itself, as nothing but a "passionate inference" derived from self-shattering jouissance. If we are able to perceive very little difference between naricissism and sublimation in Bersani's argument, one surmises that this is partially because the notion of narcissism adds nothing, no positive beyond, to the self-obliterating sublimations; narcissism seems to be little more than a retroactive positing of an *X* as—as what? It is no longer possible to say, with Kant, "as the condition of the possibility of sublimation," for the addition of the qualifier *passionate* removes narcissism from the logic of transcendent conditions.

Despite the shadowy existence ascribed to narcissism, we must not allow it to disappear into the notion of sublimation and must interrogate Bersani's near conflation of the two terms further. The conclusion that narcissism has no object is arrived at by discrediting the almost universal assumption that the ego is the object of narcissistic love. The conclusion that sublimation has no object is partially supported, we said, by discrediting the assumption that this process strives to obtain a socially valorized object, but it is also supported by the view that the drive in general is indifferent to external objects. As Lacan put it, "Even when you stuff the mouth—the mouth that opens in the register of the drive—it is not the food that satisfies it, it is, as one says, the pleasure of the mouth" (*SXI,* 167). The mouth of the drive opens, as Whitman might have said, "electrically," in an erotic stirring, not "electively," to take in this particular object. Bersani ratifies this view by defining sublimation as "the project of distilling sexual excitement from all its contingent occasions," as a "burning away of the occasion, or: *the dream of purely burning*" ("Erotic," 37). The pleasure of the mouth depends on its being stuffed with it-matters-not-what; it is the erotic stimulation, the shattering excitement, that stuffing occasions which counts, not the particular object with which it is stuffed. Any object will do as well as an other.

But this is not true. Since the last chapter contained a refutation of this position, I can be brief here. It is insufficient to say that the mouth that opens in the register of the drive is not satisfied by the milk without immediately adding that the drive *is* satisfied nevertheless—by the breast. That is, there is an object of the drive, and this object does not require any social acceptance. What sort of object is this—this breast that is capable of satiating the oral drive, or this gaze that satiates the scopic drive, this voice . . . ? Lacan calls these "objects of lack." This, then, is the crucial difference: where Bersani discovers a *lack of object,* hence only shattering, Lacan discovers an *object of lack,* which lodges itself in the opening of the drive and fills it.

This term, "object of lack," cannot be understood outside the Timaean/ *lamellian* myth from which it derives. The partial object or object of lack is the one that emerges *out of the lack,* the void, opened by the loss of the original Plenum or *das Ding.* In place of the mythical satisfaction derived from being at one with the maternal Thing, the subject now experiences satisfaction in this partial object. But to say that it is this object, the breast, that satisfies, rather than the milk (or some other actual object), is not to say the milk is irrelevant or incidental to the satisfaction. The breast is not something other than the milk, something the milk represents or "stands for," it is the milk's otherness to itself. One can approach this point from another direction: it is not that the breast satisfies rather than the milk, but that the milk fills more than the stomach, it fills the gullet of the drive. The object a, the breast in this case, is that something more in the external object, the milk, which adds nothing to this object, predicates nothing more about it— except that it satisfies the drive. Bersani proceeds as if there were two objects or, rather, as if the external object were merely the contingent occasion of the non-object, the self-shattering jouissance. But there is only one object of the drive in Lacan; the object a and the external object are not two different objects but, as objects of the drive, a single object that has the peculiar "feature" of not coinciding with itself. The elevation of the external object of the drive—let us stay with the example of milk—to the status of breast (that is, to the status of an object capable of satisfying something more than the mouth and stomach), does not depend on its cultural or social value in relation to other objects. Its surplus "breast value," let us say, depends solely on the drive's election of it as an object of satisfaction. Thus, the self-shattering jouissance on which Bersani focuses is dependent on a "shattered" object that exceeds itself and renders jouissance accessible.

Bersani's brilliant argument sorts out a major confusion in Freud's narcissism essay, but it fails to rescue one of the major discoveries Freud was attempting valiantly, amid all this confusion, to expound: that of the intricate relation between ego- and object-libido. Bersani forces us to question the appropriateness of the term "ego-libido," since narcissism concerns libido that is proper not to the ego but to the subject or "I." Yet with this point in mind we must now redirect our attention to this key moment in Freud's argument:

> We form the idea of there being an original libidinal cathexis of the ego, from which some is later given off to objects, but which fundamentally persists and is related to the object-cathexes much as the body of an amoeba is related to the pseudopodia which it puts out. . . . [T]his part of the allocation of libido necessarily remained hidden from us at the outset. All that we noticed were the emanations of this libido—the object-cathexes, which can be sent out and drawn back again. We see also, broadly speaking, an antithesis between ego-libido and object-libido. The more the one is employed, the more the other becomes depleted. The highest phase of the development of which object-libido is capable is seen in the state of being in love, when the subject seems to give up his own personality in favour of an object-cathexis. (SE, 14:75–76)

In this important passage, Freud states that all libido is narcissistic because all libido belongs to the ego. His later work allows us to reassign (narcissistic) libido to the drive, to the "headless," or egoless subject of the drive. It would be impossible, however, to detect the presence of libido—or narcissism, for that matter—*were it not for the libidinal cathexis of objects.* Narcissistic libido is never directly evident; we infer it only on the basis of object-libido or object cathexes. A moment later Freud reiterates this point: "during the state of narcissism, [ego-libido and object-libido] exist together [but] our analysis is too coarse to distinguish them; not until there is object-cathexis is it possible to discriminate a sexual energy—the libido—from an energy of the ego-instincts" (SE, 14: 76). This spells out a clear difference between Freud, who infers narcissism from object-cathexes, and Bersani, who infers narcissism from an objectless self-shattering.

What are the stakes of this difference; what follows from it? Conceiving sublimation as well as narcissism as independent of any object-cathexis, Bersani is left with a kind of autistic notion of erotic passion. But having sacrificed relationality or sociality in this way at this stage in his work, he later finds himself in the position of having to reintroduce a notion of "connectedness" (in *Caravaggio's Secret* and essays written since) by going beyond psychoanalysis. Certainly he can be seen to have been moving slightly away from psychoanalysis for some time if one considers that his long-time theoretical interest in sublimation had at least in part to do with the fact that it was, as he saw it, a borderline concept, the point where psychoanalysis took stock of its own limits and began writing itself out of business (insofar as this business could be defined as that of interpretation). But Bersani's recent work takes this decision to explore the limits of psychoanalysis much further.

In one recent essay Bersani confesses to being quite nonplussed by the enthusiastic reception his earlier work had received from the French *Ecole lacanienne,* which was delighted to see in it confirmation of Lacan's aphorism, "There is no sexual relation." This only goes to show that being French does not automatically entitle one to understand Lacan. For, Lacan did not maintain, as the *Ecole lacanienne* put it, that "the sexual [is] an *absence of relations, a failure to connect.*"[12] Lacan says only that there is no sexual ratio or formula, no predefined aim of the sexual drive; he fully acknowledges that sexual encounters happen, that the drive, working blind, without guide or goal, does occasionally stumble on a satisfying object. And though jouissance may be a solitary business in the sense that one only ever experiences one's own jouissance, this does not mean that this experience is not made available through the subject's relation to another. Erotic love does exist. Lacan agrees with Freud, who celebrates this achievement in an already-cited passage from "On Narcissism": "The highest phase of development of which object-libido is capable is seen in the state of being in love." One's comprehension of this simple declaration begins to unravel, however, at either end, threatening to undo this midsection. First, the object-libido whose "highest development" is found in the state of being in love turns out in fact to be one of the "pseudo-podia" of ego-libido, that is, it turns out to be fundamentally narcissistic. Second, in this state of being in love the subject's personality is said to be surrendered. In its distilled form, then, Freud's observation seems to see-saw back and forth from the object to the subject back to the object once again: the highest form of object-cathexis, love, is fundamentally narcissistic and entails the surrender of the subject's personality.

Mikkel Borch-Jacobsen, though he reads Freud's argument carefully and intelligently, finds it fruitless and absurd, something akin one imagines to "holding a sieve under a he-goat while some one else milks it."[13] If this analogy was the first to spring to my mind, this is no doubt due to the fact that what so disturbs Borch-Jacobsen about Freud's theory of narcissism is not just that it seems to him to collapse the distinction between object- and ego-libido, but that this collapse takes the distinction between male and female libido down with it:

When Freud persists in placing woman in the role of Narcissus, we may be sure that he himself, in this "dialectics" of mistress and slave, occupies the servile position. This entire theory of love is written from the clouded vantage point of the slave who believes in the narcissism of the other, does not want to see that he has yielded her "his own," and thus avoids acknowledging that there is no narcissism that has not already been "yielded," . . . no mastery that does not depend on servitude.[14]

There is an excess of affect here which registers the exasperation Borch-Jacobsen feels, for when he looks carefully into Freud's essay, all he sees is confusion. The problem is that although he, unlike Bersani, correctly keeps in sight the complex relation Freud tries to establish between self-love and object-love, Borch-Jacobsen makes the mistake, which Bersani's reading corrects, of confusing primary narcissism with the subject's imaginary capture by the ego. Thus is he led to condemn Freud for enclosing narcissism in "the topology of the imaginary" ("Ecco," 125). That is, he finds in Freud's essay only an unresolved oscillation between an impoverishment of the subject's identity and an impoverishment of the object's alterity. The essay on narcissism offers, he believes, two unacceptable alternatives: either "the ego is a 'model' reflecting itself in objects and narcissistically enjoying itself in that reflection," or "the ego 'models itself' on objects or 'forms itself in the image' of the other" ("Ecco," 118).

By identifying sublimation as the "new psychical action" that allows narcissism to replace autoeroticism, Bersani removes narcissism from the problematic of the imaginary and inserts it within the problematic of the drive, whose circular trajectory has nothing to do with imaginary specularity. The drive's movement out toward the object and back toward the subject is not one of reflection or identification, but of the attainment of satisfaction. This is an important point because it tears narcissistic love from the grip of phenomenological speculation. Moreover, if the subject in the narcissistic state of being in love seems to surrender her own personality, it is not because she fuses with or effaces herself before the object of love. Once the problematic of specularity, or of self-reflection, has been set aside as inadequate to account for love—which we have now determined is a matter of the drive—one can no longer expect to find the subject among the sedimentations of imaginary identifications, that is to say, in the evidence of personality. The evidence of narcissism is decidedly *impersonal*. To paraphrase the insight of Leo Steinberg with regard to the striking absence of personality—or "human attitude"—surrounding the objects painted by Jasper Johns: the subject in the state of being in love so wills the object of his or her love that what comes from without, from the beloved, is indistinguishable from what the subject chooses. That is narcissism: neither the fusion or melding of the subject with a hypnotic, mermerizing object nor the subject's discovery of its own reflection everywhere outside himself in the objects he sees, but an encounter between the impersonal drive and the object as is.

A further observation. The situation is precisely opposite to what Borch-Jacobsen fears. The sexes do not become undifferentiated in Freud's theory of narcissistic love; on the contrary, it is through love that their radical disjunction is exposed. This is one of the conclusions Lacan draws from the concept of narcissistic love, where, he says, "old father Freud breaks new ground."[15] While the idea of love starts out from a "relationship with the One," as Lacan puts it, that is, from the idea that "we are one," Freud did not approach this One of love in a fusional way; lover and beloved do not disappear into each other to form a single entity, the couple, say, which was the goal of Hollywood film or the myth of Aristophanes in Plato's *Symposium*. The lover does not take leave of herself, does not abandon herself while loving another. We have noted that this is the point Freud makes in "On Narcissism," and we now witness as Lacan pushes this point to a new level of awareness by insisting on the fundamental disunion or disharmony of the sexes ("there is no sexual relation") at the very moment he is engaged in highlighting the paradoxical nature of the One of love (the "relationship with the One"). What is Lacan up to? Is he attempting to dispel the One of love as illusion, as "false consciousness" of the actual failure of every love relation? No, it would be a mistake to think so. He is trying to preserve the One, to hold onto the Freudian discovery: the One of love does not fuse the two in love—subject and object; or lover and beloved, of whatever sex; or *man and woman*—into one, but exposes their disjunction.

But why should this be so? Why insist on a disunion or disjunction where others have discerned only a dissolve—either of the *enamored subject* in the beloved object or of the *alterity of the object* in the self-enamored subject's regard? The theory of narcissism inaugurates Freud's mature speculation on the drive, which—the theory will show—secures for the subject a jouissance on the very spot where the original Plenum or fusional One has collapsed. The jouissance of the drive, of the organ of the libido, replaces the jouissance attributed to the primordial union, the blissful state of the body without organs. But if the original

Plenum no longer exists, what remains is only our condition of immanence. This means that there is no point of transcendence from which the two in love would be able to be *counted as two*. One must be careful, then, to distinguish

> love and the couple. The couple is that which, in love, is visible for a third party. This two is thus *calculated* on the basis of a situation where there are at least three. . . . The two that the third party counts are thus . . . a two completely *exterior* to the Two of the disjunction [or: the two in love]. The phenomenal appearance of the couple, submitted to an exterior law of calculation says nothing about love. The couple does not name love, but the state (even the State) of love: not the amorous presentation but its representation. It is not *for love's sake* that this two are calculated from the point of the three. For love, *there are not three,* and its Two remains subtracted from all calculation.[16]

That is, the two in love are not distinguishable or separable as two distinct ones, but as "One and the Other . . . and the Other cannot in any way be taken as a One" (SXX, 49). What we have instead is One plus a ($1 + a$), a being plus an object without any "objectivity," or which cannot be objectified as a free-standing entity. The dissymmetry of the two in love, or between the One and the Other, comes to figure in *Encore* as the dissymmetry of the sexes, in which the woman is defined as "the Other sex" or as that sex "which is not One."

But what to make of this dissymmetry? We know that the psychoanalytic theory of sexual difference does not constitute the sexes as complementary, as two separate terms external to each other but capable of coming together to form a couple, in Badiou's derogatory sense. But if the man is the One (1) in Lacan's little algebra while woman is the a, what does this imply about the woman? That she is a blot or stain, an anamorphosis, in the humdrum land of men? And if we would say she were, would we know what this means? Alain Badiou, whose extraordinary essay "What is Love?" was just cited, worries that in the final analysis the formulas of sexuation Lacan constructs to describe the paradox of the amorous disjunction (rather than separation) of the sexes may assign woman too "classical" a role. For, by attributing the universal quantifier to the male position and defining woman as the not-all, Lacan does not go beyond Hegel's famous description of woman as the "eternal irony of the community," that is, as the "existential border" that "breaches the all that men strive to consolidate."[17] If Badiou's fears were justified, Lacan's notion of the stain or anamorphosis would have to be equivalent to Hegel's notion of irony, which it is not.

If one examines the formulas of sexuation against the background of Freud's concept of narcissistic love, the position of the woman in them emerges as far less "classical" than Badiou supposes. Like Freud, Lacan seems to credit woman with a stronger inclination toward narcissism than men. Freud damns this observation from the start, of course, by introducing it through the clumsy—not to say calumnous—analogy that equates the "charming inaccessibility" of women with that of small children, cats, and large beasts of prey. Yet the psychoanalytic position, however retrograde it may appear, needs to be reexamined from the vantage of all we have just said about narcissism. Leaving aside the defamatory lining of the analogy, let us attend a bit more closely to the nature of the inaccessibility it ascribes to the narcissistic woman. For a moment Freud forgets himself and allows this inaccessibility to denote a kind of inwardness or unreachability, the haughty unlovingness of these women, about whom he also says, "Nor does their need lie in the direction of loving, but of being loved" (SE: 14:89). But to take what he says here at face value would be to ignore what Freud is in the process of discovering about narcissism: it is not so much inaccessible as *accessible only indirectly*—through object cathexes. So far this may look like additional support for the anamorphosis as irony thesis of Badiou, but this support falters in the next step. For, despite the implications of Freud's characterization of narcissistic women, his concept of narcissism says that their wanting to be loved, their narcissism, is not opposed to loving, but is expressible only through loving. To love is to want to be loved; love is always narcissistic. One must remember that these statements do not issue from a phenomenological approach to the question of love; therefore, they do not mean either "I love you so that you may be induced to love me back" or "I love you because you remind me of myself." One cannot—even if one is a narcissistic woman—love onself directly because one cannot take oneself as an object. The "I" of the subject is a hole in being. How then can one love onseself; whence comes the experience of "oneself" on which narcissism depends? From the shattering jouissance one experiences in loving another. The "I" is a "passionate inference," as Bersani correctly says, an experience of the body, that comes from the libidinal cathexis of objects. What looks like an impatiently passive stance at first—wanting to be loved—is in fact the return curve of the drive to love.

The year following the publication of "On Narcissism," Freud plainly delineates the active nature of narcissism in a passage added to a new edition of

Three Essays: "ego-libido is . . . only conveniently accessible to analytic study when it has been put to use cathecting sexual objects, that is, when it has become object-libido. We can then perceive it concentrating upon objects, becoming fixed upon them or abandoning them, moving from one to another and . . . directing the subject's sexual activity" (SE, 7:217). What strikes us immediately about this passage is its resemblance to Freud's description of Leonardo da Vinci, who took up and abandoned paintings and motifs restlessly, interrupting one to go onto another. This resemblance further confirms Bersani's thesis that narcissism is approached only via sublimation, but does so while making obvious the role of object cathexes in this relation. At the same time, this reconfirmation of the essential link between narcissism and sublimation rotates our perception of the dissymmetrical relation between the sexes. Although Badiou's observation is consistent with the way this dissymmetry is normally read—it leaves the woman, the "Other sex," in the default position of being only the eternal irony or bane of community (the destroyer of civilization, in Freud's vocabulary)—it is now possible to see that the woman, as anamorphosis or stain in Lacan's sense, *is the subject par excellence.* For it is the subject, the "I," the "forger of new passions" that appears only indirectly among the objects of the world.

CINDY SHERMAN'S *UNTITLED FILM STILLS*

According to one of the most popular forms of criticism practiced today, a text of whatever sort must be examined as a product of its historical context, which forms the framework of what is thinkable at a particular moment. Not only texts but historically located subjects, too, conceive themselves, we are told, in terms permitted by this framework. This belief informs much of cultural theory and nearly the entire reception of Cindy Sherman's name-making series, *Untitled Film Stills,* produced between 1977 and 1980. In these photographs, Sherman masquerades in a wardrobe to match the various background settings she has designed to evoke some Hollywood period, genre, or directorial style. In an early article, Judith Williamson put her finger on what would become in subsequent criticism the central issue of the photographs: "What comes out of the imagined narratives is, specifically, femininity. It is not just a range of feminine expressions that are shown but the *process* of the 'feminine' as an effect, something acted upon."[18] The passivity of the feminine refers to the fact that in the culture evoked by the photographs woman is not allowed to become the "bearer of the look," but is condemned to be its object. She is forced to see herself—more so than men—in

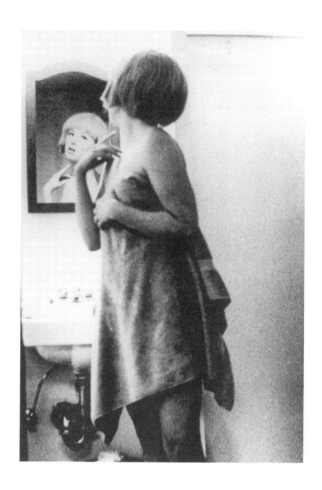

Figure 2.1 Cindy Sherman, *Untitled Film Still,* #2 (1977). Courtesy Metro Pictures.

Figure 2.2 Sherman, *Untitled Film Still,* #56 (1980). Courtesy Metro Pictures.

Figure 2.3 Sherman, *Untitled Film Still,* #35 (1979). Courtesy Metro Pictures.

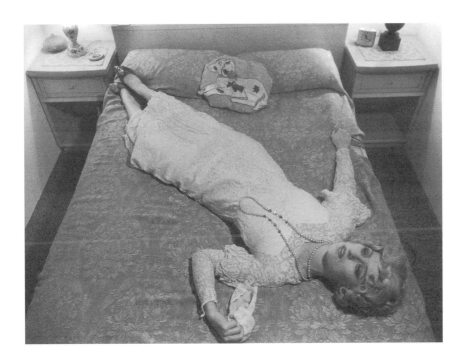

Figure 2.4 Sherman, *Untitled Film Still,* #11 (1978). Courtesy Metro Pictures.

Figure 2.5 Sherman, *Untitled Film Still,* #46 (1979). Courtesy Metro Pictures.

the images culture produces of her. She must compose herself in their terms, compose herself for the gaze they presuppose.

Accordingly, Sherman's photographs are almost always read as images of women attempting to see themselves in a number of culturally approved forms, as women attempting to adapt themselves to stereotypes. These are women who want to be loved. Sometimes a critical effort is made to pull these women away from the image that informs her self-presentation by drawing attention to the photograph's exposure of its own "constructedness." Ideology may construct the woman but the photograph or critic can deconstruct the ideology. Another strategy points out that the aspirations of these women are tripped up by the bodies that strive after them. The photographs open a gap between the ideal images the women emulate and the noncompliant fact of what they corporeally are, their real bodily circumstances: this one's arms are a bit heavy, her ankles too thick, that one's tawdry dress ill-fits the romantic scenario she is fanticizing. The body of the woman is always in these readings "finite" in the cultural theory sense of that term, in the first case because it, like the photograph, is simply constructed, a simple realization of conditions existing elsewhere. In the second, the body is doubly finite, a mere object exposed to the look of the spectator or any diegetically conceivable passerby *and* a simple opacity resisting the woman's hopeful look, an inert unyielding to her idealizing demand.

I argue, however, that one can locate in the *Untitled Film Stills* a gap between the women and their immediate surroundings without giving in to the preemptive narrativization of that gap that generally follows. The rush to narrativize, to compose the background story that landed these women in the places where they now find themselves, is problematic on a number of counts. First, linking woman to her concrete milieu, this reading strategy proceeds as if each photograph contained a *different* woman; that is, it fully diegeticizes each woman. It asks us to focus on the relations that bind the particular situation to the particular woman contained in it, without recognizing that the very process of constructing this narrative produces the particularity it finds, or to say it better, reduces what it finds to particularity. No, there are not several different women in these photographs, there is only one, the *same* woman, Cindy Sherman, who appears over and over again, and one of the profound question posed by the photographs—"How can someone be the same if all her appearances are different?"—is slighted if we do not privilege in our analysis the fact that it is she who reappears again and again in her photographs. This is the question raised by feminine being as such, by femininity, which is, to reinvoke Badiou's term, "multiple being" or multiple *appearings/masqueradings.* The implication here is not that the masquerade of femininity is only a semblance that hides a being which is beneath, but that semblance or appearance is what feminine being is. On the other hand, however, the fact that Sherman is the subject of all her images, that she has consistently chosen to place herself on display in them, has hardly gone unnoticed. In fact, her supposed narcissism is a constant of the critical literature. The problem is that the notion of narcissism sustaining this evaluation is so thin that it seems to require repeating just to create an echo: Sherman so loves being looked at that she herself takes pleasure in looking only at herself. Moreover, the issue of Sherman's narcissism is never integrated into the analysis of the relation of the women (who remain pluralized) to their surroundings in the photographs, except to suggest that "they," too, nourish themselves on the meager diet of their own self-regard.

The second major difficulty with the narrative—and (it must be said) *psychologizing*—reading of the photographs is a corollary of the first: it drains from the woman's face all expression but that which is able to feed the narrative. It is not that a certain determinate ambiguity of expression, a hovering between fear and defiance, for example, or longing and resignation, has escaped these readings. But it is always assumed that *the situation imprints itself,* however ambiguously, *on the woman's face.* She is stamped by her setting. What is thus overlooked is the Kuleshovian nature of Sherman's photographic experiment.

Lev Kuleshov, one of the first of the Soviet montage theorists, devised experiments that became the basis for much of the later thinking about montage. In one of these (of which there is no clear evidence that it was ever carried out), it was planned that a single close-up of a famous actor's face (the Soviet actor, Mozhukhin) would be juxtaposed to three different cinematic scenes in order to create an imaginary geography of their linkage. In the first scene, Mozhukhin would seem to sit in a jail and watch the sun rise over the landscape outside his window; in the next, he would seem to stare at a half-naked woman; in the third, he would appear to stare at a child's coffin. When the film was projected, it was anticipated that Mozhukhin would be perceived to express a range of emotions according to the scene beside which the shot of his face was placed: joy and longing for freedom; lasciviousness; sorrow. While this proposed experiment is usually taken to illustrate the way the association with an object anchors or determines the meaning of the facial expression, Gilles Deleuze makes the point that the opposite seems rather to be the case. It is the very ambiguity of the facial expression that allows it to "receive" or be appropriately juxtaposed to so many different scenes, scenes that do not exhaust its meaning.

Deleuze takes his cue from the pioneering study of the close-up by the Hungarian film theorist, Béla Balázs. Writing, for example, about close-ups inserted into sequences of high drama—one imagines, say, the opening of *Vertigo*, where in the midst of a police chase over San Francisco rooftops, we are shown a close-up of Scotty's (Jimmy Stewart's) face—Balázs remarked: "However much the precipice may be the *cause* of vertigo, it does not explain the expression it produces on a face. Or, the precipice over which someone leans may perhaps explain his expression of fright, but it does not create it. For the expression exists even without justification, it does not become expression because a situation is associated with it."[19] The point Deleuze draws from Balázs's observations is that the facial close-up is *not a part of the scene,* an enlarged detail, whose continuity or discontinuity with the "rest" of the scene (expressive of fear/expressive of defiance) can be established in a narrative account. The close-up cannot be fitted into the spatiotemporal coordinates of the scene, because it opens onto a different dimension, a dimension that is not of the spatiotemporal order.

Although Deleuze—who, unlike Balász, sees *all* close-ups as *faces,* as "*faceified*"— attempts on this ground to *distinguish* the close-up from the psychoanalytic notion of the partial object—"the close-up, the close-up of the face, has nothing to do with the partial object"[20]—it should be obvious from our discussion that he has misunderstood the psychoanalytic notion, which does not pretend to be a part of some whole, but is instead a part that replaces a whole. In this sense, the partial object is quite similar, mutatis mutandis, to Deleuze's notion of the *face.* In fact, one can detect a broader resemblance between this argument about the status of the *face* and Lacan's argument concerning the status of the *gaze,* which also appears *in* the field of painting or film without being a part of that field. The face of the woman in the *Untitled Film Stills* functions more like the gaze than the close-up, in that in them the woman's face appears within the scenes rather than alongside them, though this difference is fairly trivial, having to do with the difference between a still and a moving image, not with any real theoretical discrepancy between the two concepts. Basically I am arguing that the images of Cindy Sherman's face function as close-ups in the *Untitled Film Stills* even before they actually become close-ups, in the purely technical sense, in Sherman's later work. Included, then, in the various diegetic spaces of this photographic series, the face of Sherman does not belong to them.

The face of Sherman, in short, does not play the ordinary role of the face, which is, as Deleuze describes it: "individuating (it distinguishes or characterises each person); . . . socialising (it manifests a social role); . . . relational or communicating (it ensures not only communication between two people, but also, in a single person, the internal agreement between his character and his role)." Individuating, socializing, relational or communicating. In other words, the face displays the features of the individual's *particularity* as it is defined differentially, through one's relations to other people and objects, or to a situation; the face relates the person to its milieu. In the close-up, however, the normal role of the face is suspended; it no longer individuates the person, but serves, on the contrary, to de-individuate or impersonalize her. The close-up discloses a de-predication of the subject, an emptying out of personality. The face, then, withdraws from the represented space, retreats into an "other dimension," as Deleuze says. This withdrawal is thematized in many of the films that rely significantly on close-ups. Deleuze mentions specifically Ingmar Bergman's *Persona* (in which a woman abandons her former life, renounces her profession as well as her role as wife and mother, and retreats into almost total muteness, or, in sum, uncompromisingly separates herself from all that individuates her) and Carl Dreyer's *The Passion of Joan of Arc* (in which Joan is filmed almost exclusively in close-up and seems to have detached herself from the historical state of things to which her accusers attempt unsuccessfully to make her answer).

This antinomic relation between the space of the close-up and the diegetic space of the film is echoed in Lacan's account of the antinomic relation between the gaze and the represented space. The antinomy defines the difference between two levels of representation: the level of enunciation, marked by the appearance of the gaze, and the level of the statement or represented space. That is, a surplus object appears in the field while announcing itself as *not* part of the represented, as being of a different order than the one in which it shows itself. Lacan links the manner of identifying this split between enunciation and statement, gaze and representation, to Descartes's procedure of radical doubt, in which the entire content of the represented is effectively negated by being thrown into question. At the end of this procedure, however, something is left standing, something resists the erosion by doubt: the cogito or the instance of enunciation. The fact that it escapes the annihilating gesture that demolishes all else is proof that the cogito is not identical to the represented or thought.

The theory of this split sets a trap, however, which the *Untitled Film Stills* will help us evade. Running the various positions (from Descartes to Deleuze via Lacan) together (for the sake of some average argument), let us consider a reading of the photographs obviously suggested by this argument. One can detect in the face of Sherman a certain distractedness, as though she were lost in reverie and thus not actually present to her current situation, in some way untouched by it. The sole figure in all the photographs, the lonely one in each, she interacts with no one and is absorbed in no activity but that of her silent musings. The uncompromising withdrawal of the film women Deleuze discusses, the much remarked solitude of women who want nothing more than a room of their own, even the already mentioned role as "ironists of community," all leap to mind in support of this reading, giving it resonance and credibility. The only difficulty is that the photographs themselves do not yield to it. They resist, we might say, the analogical impulse to attribute to woman the same charming inaccessibility one finds in small children, cats, and large beasts of prey. For, the look of reverie on the face of the woman in these photographs—a familiar topos of painting and film alike (think of the countless images you have seen of women peering dreamily out of windows or simply out of frame)—does not lift her from the space that surrounds her. Why? Because she happens to be represented in the very sort of imagined elsewhere, the cinematic or screen space, we imagine her to be fantasizing, the melodramatic spaces of "female fantasy." It is as if these photographs were endorsing the thesis of film theorists regarding the closeness of the woman to the screen image. Inseparable from the image, from appearance, woman is theorized as incapable of distancing herself from it, of occupying a position beyond. She remains instead immersed in the world of appearances. But where film theorists condemned this theoretical and cinematic conflation of the woman with the image, the *Untitled Film Stills* does not. It accepts that there is "no exit" for woman from the level of appearance, that "womanliness" *is* always but masquerade.

This is how the photographs avoid the trap I mentioned a moment ago. But what is the trap to be avoided? It is believing in a world that is elsewhere, in a place to which one can withdraw in solitude to safeguard the precious core of one's being. One could argue that Freud himself succumbed, in a curious way, to the false lure of this belief in his study of Schreber's psychosis. For, what Freud finds after examining Schreber's wholescale destruction of his world, the psychotic phenomenon of "the end of the world," through the withdrawal of all object-cathexis, is that something, one thing, remained intact: the narcissism of Schreber. This theory of psychosis reads as a kind of parody of Descartes's procedure of radical doubt in which everything is destroyed in order to produce the precious core of the cogito, only here, instead of the unshakable cornerstone of rational thought, the process precipitates a delusional megalomania. Almost immediately Freud recognized that his account of psychosis was proof of nothing so much as the pressing need for a theory of narcissism, and indeed the case study of Schreber became one of the major impetuses for writing "On Narcissism." What Freud learns from Schreber, in short, is that primary narcissism, the subject's libidinal sense of his own integrity, his separability from the world, cannot come from anything so simple as a negation or decathexis of the world, which leaves nothing in its wake but destruction—not only of the world but of the self as well, which is then imaginarily reconstituted in the pathological form of delusional megalomania. Primary narcissism must be theorized by a different route.

The boldness of the theoretical act through which Freud succeeded in carving out this theory of narcissism is best understood as what Lacan, in his seminar on transference, calls an act of *Versagung*. Lacan writes about the heroine Syngne de Coûfontaine (from Paul Claudel's dramatic Coûfontaine trilogy), who sacrifices the ethical principle most dear to her, the principle with which she herself identifies and for which she formerly stood ready to sacrifice all else.[21] The sacrifice of the only thing that could not be sacrificed, the exception to the list of sacrificable things, is described by Lacan as the ethical gesture par excellence, for what it surrenders, finally, is the *pedestal* that allows one to raise oneself above the battleground of decision and action. If "On Narcissism" is such an act, it is because Freud there strikes a fatal blow to that notion of the cogito which excepts it from the entire order of the world. Or: if Freud's gesture in this essay is as groundbreaking as Lacan claims, it is because it severs psychoanalysis from the idea that the self can find safe harbor outside thought or action. The proposition it puts forward, "I love therefore I am," can impress us as riskier and bolder than "I think therefore I am," because it appears to put in jeopardy something more precious to us than the world, namely, the "I." More than doubt, it is object-cathexis that threatens to unseat the subject, and yet it is precisely through object-cathexis that Freud proposed to arrive at a confirmation of the "I" of the subject.

The question is often asked why Freud came to recognize the need to theorize the female subject so late in his career. One possible answer (though one of course is not enough) is that he had to await the development of his theory of narcissism. For, prior to this point, when ego- or self-preservation instincts and sexual instincts were held too strictly apart and the subject was posed too rigidly against the libido, this same subject could seem to occupy a place apart from the rest of the world. With the development of the theory of narcissism, the problematic of the female subject, or feminine being, opened up, since now the subject would no longer be sought in a point beyond its libidinal investments. At this moment the woman began to be, I will not say accessible, but accessible indirectly to psychoanalytic theory.

The point of course is not to forget everything "On Narcissism" teaches us about the ontological paradox of love and thus confuse love with its phenomenological representations. The association of woman and love has a long and nauseating history that drags both down to the sentimental level of nurturing and care. In combination with a rereading of Freud's essay, perhaps another look at the *Untitled Film Stills* will help if not eradicate at least slow down this dissolution of the paradox of love. The close-up or face of the woman does not transport her, we noted, out of the space in which she finds herself, despite the dreaminess of her expression. Her blank or objectless look of longing, directed out of frame, is, filled by the scenes that surround her. Blocking or filling the blankness of the woman's look, the photographs shift attention away from an imagined elsewhere onto the object they actually represent. What is that object? Film, cinema, represented in a series of scenes that reproduce a variety of periods and styles. The *Untitled Film Stills* represent film as an object of amorous fascination.

What prevents the love of cinema from being a banal subject for a series of photographs is the series' brilliant demonstration of the truth of Freud's thesis that love, any love, is always and fundamentally narcissistic. Again: when one loves something, one loves something in it that is more than itself, its nonidentity to itself. But a new point can now be made, one that was only inadequately expressed before. To say that what we love in the object is something more than that object is not to say only that we love that real point in the object from where it can cease being what it was to become something different from itself, but also that *what we love in the object is ourselves*. One must refrain from the temptation to turn this observation back into a banality by making it a matter of resemblance; one does not find in the loved object a reflection of one's own image, as we pointed out earlier, one finds rather in the jouissance loving it affords a corporeal experience of the self. It is equally important that one distinguish the object of love from the "pathological" object, in Kant's sense of the term. The difference bears not only on the distinction between passivity and activity (we are not passively affected by the object of love, we actively affect ourselves by loving it), but also on the nature of the object, since the pathological object—unlike the object of love—does not affect us from the point of its difference from itself.

When Lacan makes the claim that in love there are not two ones, but a One and an Other, or One plus a, we must understand the One to be not the lover, but the beloved object. This is at least the way Freud's theory of narcissism demands we understand Lacan's statement. The lover, on the contrary, is locatable only in the object a, the partial object or indivisible remainder of the act of love. Indivisible (because irreducible to spatiotemporal coordinates) and the product of no division, part of no whole. We should not be surprised, then, to find the face of Cindy Sherman returning consistently as close-up (in Deleuze's sense) or as object a in all her photographs, the perennial residue of her love for the cinematic-photographic image. We should rather take to heart the lesson her photographs teach us: genuine love is never selfless—nor, for that matter, is sublimation. This lesson is the very opposite of a cynicism.

Moses the Egyptian and the Big Black Mammy of the Antebellum South: Freud (with Kara Walker) on Race and History

Nearly all the work of Kara Walker produced thus far—including *Gone: An Historical Romance Of A Civil War As It Occurred Between the Dusky Thighs of One Young Negress And Her Heart* (1994); *The End of Uncle Tom and the Grand Allegorical Tableau of Eva in Heaven* (1995); *The Battle of Atlanta: Being the Narrative of a Negress in the Flames of Desire—A Reconstruction* (1995); *Presenting Negro Scenes Drawn Upon My Passage Through the South and Reconfigured for the Benefit of Enlightened Audiences Wherever Such May Be Found, By Myself, K. E. B. Walker, Colored* (1997)—I cite a few titles to give you some flavor of the work—nearly all the work employs the same technique: the adhesion of black paper cut-outs to white gallery walls. These cut-outs depict larger-than-life-sized human figures, amid occasional tufts of landscape, set within snippets of narrative of the antebellum South. Composed of black paper, all the human figures are, technically, black, though we are able to distinguish the diegetically white "folk" from the diegetically black on the basis of their stereotypical profiles, postures, and clothing. Glued to the walls, the figures become part of their flat surface rather than standing out in front of them as they would had they been mounted on canvas. Depth is subtracted also from the relations between the figures, who do not so much stand in front of or behind each other as they mingle and separate, protrude from and merge with each another.

These flat, black figures recall a number of proto-photographic techniques: the shadow projection theaters of the nineteenth century, with their curiously weightless, atopic images; the cycloramas (enormously popular at the end of the nineteenth century, before cinema permanently displaced them) that dwarfed their spectators by enveloping them in exaggerated-scale reconstructions of historical events; and, not least of all, those black-paper silhouettes that preceded and partially overlapped the advent of photography and served as a quick, inexpensive means of preserving the likeness of one's loved ones. Walker's cut-outs, then, recall the antebellum South in the sorts of images available to people living at the time. Yet it would be wrong to conclude that the work attempts to efface the distance that separates Walker from her figures. Signing her work "Miss K. Walker, a Free Negress of Noteworthy Talent,"[1] that is, in the style of the historical romances she recreates, and writing of herself as if she were one of the "nigger wenches" she portrays, Walker, while donning period costume, is nonetheless not trying to locate herself outside herself, in these figures from the old South. She is not, in short, immediately or naively identifying herself with them. When, for example, she relates the question that motivates her technique, "Could I possibly make the art work that should have been made by a woman like me before the turn of the *last* century? Using just the methods available to her coupled with a lofty ambition and a checkered past?"[2] we do not fail to hear in her phrasing—just as we see in the silhouettes themselves—the humorous distance that separates the "lofty ambition" and "checkered past" that belong to her from the turn-of-the-century figures to whom she anachronistically lends them. That is, Walker acknowledges the gulf that separates her from the antebellum past even as she ponders and avows her relation to it. Young, middle-class, RISD-educated, mostly urban-dwelling, Kara Walker is a black artist, who has been abundantly honored by established art institutions. The life experiences of the figures she draws are notably alien to her, and the inquiry in which her work is engaged is that of figuring out how this largely foreign past could still be said to form part of her own. This aesthetic inquiry thus approaches the problem of identity in a way contrary to the standard one. Ordinarily the question is asked how one group— blacks, say—differ from others; Walker asks how, given the differences among them, its members can be counted as belonging to the same group.

The "plantation family romances,"[3] as Walker calls her vignettes, have not been warmly received by everyone. In the black community, particularly, they remain controversial, with many blacks fiercely agitating against the work and even mounting letter-writing campaigns to protest her exhibitions. The problem for these protesters is that rather than narratives confirming the dignity of the race or reflecting the actual achievements and steady integrity of a downtrodden but spirited people, rather than positive and uplifting images of defiant or self-sacrificing and virtuous black slaves, Walker's nursery-rhyme raunchy vignettes offer a fulguration of uncouth "sex pickaninnies."[4] Hottentot harlots, sambos, mandigos, Uncle Toms, churls and scallywags of every sort engage nonchalantly in violent and licentious acts of parturition, sodomy, cannibalism, and coprophany, as well as in other acts we have no idea how to name. The charge made against Walker is both that her representations are sexually and racially derogatory

Figure 3.1 Kara Walker, *Presenting Negro Scenes Drawn Upon My Passage Through the South and Reconfigured for the Benefit of Enlightened Audiences Wherever Such May Be Found, By Myself, Missus K. E. B. Walker, Colored* (1997). Courtesy Brent Sikkema, New York City.

Figure 3.2 Walker, *Slavery! Slavery!* (1997). Courtesy Brent Sikkema, New York City.

Figure 3.3 Walker, *Camptown Ladies* (1998). Courtesy Brent Sikkema, New York City.

Figure 3.4 Walker, *African't* (1996). Courtesy Brent Sikkema, New York City.

Figure 3.5 Walker, *A Work in Progress* (1998). Courtesy Brent Sikkema, New York City.

Figure 3.6 Walker, *The End of Uncle Tom and the Grand Allegorical Tableau of Eva in Heaven* (1995). Courtesy Brent Sikkema, New York City.

and that they have no basis in fact, but simply recycle stereotypes found in that racist memorabilia or Americana that Walker, like many other blacks, admits to collecting. What she calls her "inner plantation," this criticism implies, has been implanted in her by white racists; she owes it to herself, and her race, not to recreate these fictions, but to exorcise them through a recovery of her actual, truthful, and, by the way, glorious origins.

The first thing to note is that Freud, the inventor of the family romance whose plantation variation Walker wittily fabricates, made an equally scandalous gesture in the eyes of others of his race as well as in the eyes of historians who thought he had not shown sufficient respect for history, or for the standard notion of history to which they subscribed. In *Moses and Monotheism,* Freud laid out a theory of Jewish racial identity that, rather than celebrating Moses, the most cherished ancestor of the Jews, deprived them of him, in effect, by repositioning Jewish origins in a prior and unprovable source: an earlier, Egyptian Moses, who was a fanatic follower of the "Pharaonic" monotheism of Aten. Eventually murdered by the Semite tribe he had attempted to indoctrinate into his religion, this first Moses returned centuries later to inspire the teachings of the Jewish prophets. Ernest Jones, aghast, stupidly mused that Freud seemed not to have been enlightened by the theories of Darwin. This uncomprehending remark simply underscores the fact that Freud's poorly named notion of "phylogenetic inheritance" (which means something like "an unconscious rather than ego transmission of the past") would never become the stuff of positivist historians, who could easily admit the existence of orangutans, the big gorillas in a group of apes, because these could be observed, but not the Egyptian Moses, who had no coordinates in actual experience.[5] Freud is not, of course, the idiot Jones takes him for; his theory of the origins of Jewish identity and of the survival of the Jews despite the harshest of circumstances was erected on different historical tenets than those that hampered his empirically minded biographer. For Jones and company, history must contain no unfillable gaps and must be materially documentable. Yet Freud insisted on the "historical truth" of his admittedly improbable and undocumentable story of the martyred and resurrected Egyptian Moses and contrasted it explicitly with the "material truth" of "objective" historians.[6]

Walker and Freud are alike, then, in eschewing identification with the traits of empirical (and, one hopes, noble) ancestors as the basis of racial identity, and both begin their inquiry by wondering how the differences separating them from others of their race fail to disqualify them automatically from membership in it. In the Hebrew translation of *Totem and Taboo,* for example (this book being a theoretical forerunner of *Moses and Monotheism*), Freud pointedly asks himself, "What is there left to you that is Jewish?" after admitting his ignorance of Hebrew, his lack of religious conviction, and his detachment from Jewish nationalist ideals, that is, after admitting the absence from himself of what are traditionally considered the salient characteristics of Jewish identity.[7] It is not difficult to recognize in Freud's opening sally a quintessentially modern move. Peeling away or erasing all positive traits of Jewishness, he then wonders what, if anything, survives their removal. The surprise is that he does not come up with the quintessentially modern answer, which would have been: a tabula rasa; a nobody who could be anybody; a flat, blank canvas, or screen, or page. From politics to aesthetics, the negative gesture that helped define modernism—erasure—was able to wipe the slate clean, all the way down to the material support itself, pure, pristine, and generalizable: humanity itself; Being as such; a neutral, Cartesian grid; the white walls of modern museums on which paintings of all historical periods could be equally well displayed; and so on. But when Freud tries it, he discovers that something resists his efforts at erasure, something refuses to be wiped away. Casting off the features that ought to have been the tell-tale source of his Jewishness, he does indeed arrive at a certain featureless "impersonality," but this is not to say that he finds buried within himself that neutral, uninflected, untinctured, dispassionate humanity that modernists often claimed to have discovered or encouraged us to expect. Freud surprises us, and most likely himself, by discovering that he is Jewish after all, that is, after all the positive traits of Jewishness have been rubbed away. And let us not forget that this discovery is made even as Freud continues to maintain that psychoanalysis is a science per se, not a Jewish science, and that one of the greatest contributions of the Jewish religion is monotheism, the belief in one God for all. So that while he remains convinced that science and religion have to address themselves to everyone, he does not end up believing that this necessity depended on or stemmed from the existence of a universal humanity in which everyone shares.

What happened in this case to interrupt the usual modern procedure? What resisted the negation, the erasure, by which Freud might have been expected to arrive at the clean slate of a neutral identity? Moses, the Egyptian; a fulginous stain that not only Freud but history and death itself proved incapable of rubbing out. This Egyptian appears to have been endowed with a kind of "immortal, irrepressible life" to which only the undead can in modern times lay claim.[8] The art-work of Walker thwarts the modern gesture in a similar fashion, for it stains the white walls of the exhibition spaces in which she shows with antic and obscene ghosts who, long dead, refuse to die, with silhouettes that have long ago lost the bodies to which we might have expected them to be attached. The empty white halls of the gallery spaces are thereby converted into a series of "barracks filled with stubborn back-looking ghosts still recovering . . . from the fever"[9] of their ante-bellum past.

One must be careful not to mistake this indivisible and invincible re-mainder of the process of erasure—this "hard kernel" that Lacan would come to call the real—for some essence or quasi-transcendental a priori that manages to escape the contingent processes of history. Judith Butler, in her continuing ar-gument with the real, seems not to want to let go of this misunderstanding, but I see no reason for this. The fact is that the real is what guarantees that nothing es-capes history. What is it that motivates erasure as a privileged modern practice? What does it wish to accomplish? Erasure is intended precisely to foreground his-torical contingency, to demonstrate that the accretion of particular features by this or that subject, that the cumulate deposits of ego identifications, are the result of historical circumstances that could have been otherwise and that these particular features are therefore inessential. They could easily be stripped away, effaced, by subsequent or alternative circumstances. And yet this process of erad-ication, as practiced by modernists, culminates in the production of its own limit or exception. Despite its self-presentation, erasure encounters its *limit* when it reaches the empty page or blank slate, not evidence that the process has been fully accomplished. As long as this empty support—an uninflected, neutral humanity; Being as One, as uniform—remains behind, we can be sure that something has survived untouched by the processes of historical contingency. The notion of a universal humanity stands outside and domesticates history, making the latter the agent of merely minor variations on its already decided script.

I suggested earlier that the Egyptian Moses uncovered by Freud's feature-effacing efforts represented a limit or exception to the process of erasure in the form of an ineradicable stain. This characterization is at once accurate and totally misleading. Although it remains true that neither Freud nor history nor death it-self is capable of putting an end to the eternal return of the first Moses, of re-pressing him finally, this is not because he resides outside the reaches of history or limits the reign of radical contingency. On the contrary, that this Egyptian remainder insists in the history Freud devises of the Jewish race testifies to the fact that the father of psychoanalysis bore down more heavily than other modernists on his historical eraser, that he allowed nothing, no exception to escape eradication, that is, that he allowed nothing to escape being caught up in history. Freud encounters the ghostly double of the Jewish Moses by eradicating the exception to erasure; everything, he effectively says, belongs to the domain of history, since history has no outside. For, if history has no outside—and on this point, at least, Freud seems to have been aided by his Jewish education, which taught him to disbelieve in a life after death or beyond the one that is historically lived—if history is without limit, then it must accommodate or be invaded by the infinite, the never-ending, by undying repetition, or the undead. This reasoning proposes something other than the simple truism that history is an ongoing process stretching indefinitely into the future; it proposes that history consists of something more than just the long "cortège of a 'One dies,'" that is to say, something more than the mere finitude of existence, of a coming into being and fading away.

Deleuze speculates that Foucault realized he had backed himself into a corner with the writing of *The History of Sexuality,* that he knew his thesis that relations of power have no outside had led to a dead end since the thesis made it impossible "to conceive a 'power of truth' which would no longer be the 'truth of power,' a truth that would release transversal lines of resistance and not integral lines of power."[10] In Deleuze's reading, Foucault broke through this impasse in *The Use of Pleasure* by reconceiving sexuality not simply as something that could be constructed by power but as an interiorization of power's outside, or a folding back of the outside of power into its inside. You will note that the thesis, which is capital, that power has no outside is not damaged by this revision; it remains intact. There is still no outside on the other side of power, though there is now an outside within power. Because Deleuze links this revision of the theory of sexuality to what he perceives as Foucault's continuing fascination with the double, we are encouraged to suspect that Foucault in some respect reinforces the view of Freud, who also associates the uncanny double—the Egyptian Moses, in the case we are considering—with an eradication of the outside conceived as a beyond.

What are the steps of this reasoning? Foucault launches his argument in *The History of Sexuality* by opposing immediately the "repressive hypothesis" on the grounds that, contrary to what that hypothesis claims, power does not say "no," does not wield a negation that produces a beyond. That on which power frowns is not denied and does not thereby fall outside the law or outside power but is rather part of power's own territory, what it positively makes. In Foucault's account, sex does not fall outside the law and does not have the power, then, to counter power. The problem, of course, is that power loses its meaning if there is nothing that is not power, if nothing opposes it. It seems that Foucault had given negation too slight a role to play, and its relative default leaves power bereft of meaning and endowed with a counterfeit force. But how to revamp the role of negation without at the same time reinstating an outside?

What is the answer Deleuze gives to this question? Or rather, what, according to Deleuze, does Foucault do to resolve his dilemma? He shows us how the Greeks folded force, bent it back on itself. This description refers to Foucault's argument that the Greek practice of sexual austerity was not motivated by a morality of renunciation or sacrifice, but instead constituted an act of self-formation, an exercise of self-mastery aimed at transforming the self. The Greeks engaged in a self-limitation or inhibition of their sexual drive in order to free themselves from sexual passivity, to escape enslavement to their passions. In Deleuze's reading this self-inhibition emerges less as an ascetic curtailment of sexuality than as a definition of sexuality as such, seen now as a relation primarily to oneself—rather than to others—that resists external determination. In Deleuze's essay one hears echoes of the psychoanalytic notion of the sexual drive, which is theorized as a force that turns back on itself to encircle not an external object, but an internal one. It is striking that Deleuze similarly describes the trajectory of folded back force as an encircling of an immanent outside.

What is it that allows force to become suddenly bendable, self-limiting? One could argue that it is the intrusion of the real. If power is to have no outside, if there is to be, as Foucault insists, no place beyond power from which someone or some state agency might seize hold and remotely control it, while remaining unentangled in its networks, then there must be something in power itself that negates the possibility of escaping it. And that which negates this possibility would itself have to be unnegatable, since its removal or negation would trigger the collapse of power itself, as Foucault is endeavoring to define it. Lacan's definition of the real is precisely this: that which, in language or the symbolic, negates the possibility of any metadimension, any metalanguage. It is this undislodgeable negation, this rigid kernel in the heart of the symbolic, that forces the signifier to split off from and turn around on itself. For, in the absence of any metalanguage, the signifier can only signify by referring to another signifier. The point is that if one wants to prevent the formation of an outside, one must not, as was said, avoid any negation for fear that it would cause a domain to emerge that would limit power from the outside—as the domain of immortals limits that of mortals, say, or feathered bipeds that of the featherless—but must rather inscribe in the interior a negation that says "no" precisely to the possibility of an outside. This type of negation would look like the one that is inscribed in language: a certain self-imposed impotence of the signifier itself, a kind of active retardation of its own power. Far from positing the existence of an elsewhere, the real as internal limit of the symbolic—that is, the very impotence of the signifier—is the obstacle that scotches the possibility of rising out of or above the symbolic. It is as if the symbolic increased its power by checking itself, by actively holding back from positing an outside. It is only when power, like the signifier, is conceived as limitable only by itself, by a self-imposed impotence, that the subject, while unable to extricate himself from its network, is nevertheless able to be thought as capable of subjectivation rather than as passively subjected to power. For, it is only insofar as he is held within the internal limit of power, the minimal gap that divides power from itself, that the subject is able to free himself from submission to the forceful pull of his own determined and determinate identity. To summarize: to say there is no outside of power and therefore nothing that opposes it is incorrect. It is more accurate to say that power, and it alone, operates on power. Power has the power to curb itself.

This late Foucauldian/Deleuzian thesis on power is strictly analogous to the Freudian thesis on history. There is no history without an internal limit within history itself, without an irreducible element, a negation that forbids the emergence of an outside of history. Again, this negation is able to be designated by its Lacanian name: the real. There is no arguing with the real, no negating it, since history itself depends on it. It is precisely because it cannot be negated that we say it eternally returns or repeats. This is to say that the real produces temporal anamorphoses within historical time that take the form of uncanny repetitions or anachronisms. These uncanny phenomena represent not the persistence of essences indifferent to historical contingency, but emerge rather from the adamant insistence of a refusal of the ahistorical, of essences. Referring to the real as empty, Lacan underscores this fact that what returns is nothing but the negation that prohibits any exception to history.

One must not, however, make the mistake of imagining the real as an inert void, a stark limit. Lacan pictures the real as *teeming with emptiness,* as a *swarming void.* What is implied in this characterization? How is it that something that has the

function of an internal limit, the negative function of ensuring that nothing escapes the finite processes of history, can so enchantingly be described as teeming
or swarming, that is as endowed with a kind of wiggling vitality or indestructible
life rather than as standing firmly on the side of an inescapable death? (This is
true as well, by the way, in the rendition given by Deleuze, who designates the in-
carnation as the Christian origin of the fold.) Recall the way the real divides the
symbolic, installs a rupture in it such that the signifier is unable to signify without deferring to another signifier. The intrusion of the real makes it impossible
for language to function literally. One way of recognizing this is to say that the real
marks the failure of the signifier. Language fails to designate literally what it wants
to say. But it is precisely this failure that allows the symbolic to grasp hold of some
excess, some surplus existence over sense, over what it signifies. This excess, which
is *produced* by language, is not to be confused with a true beyond, since the actual
existence of this excess is not posited. It is simply an opening, or tension, or possible line of flight that Deleuze tries to capture with the term *the virtual* and Lacan
hints at through his references to a teeming. The virtual and the real are both
atopic; they have no place of their own either outside history, in some eternal
realm or waiting room, or within history itself. Placeless, homeless, they are able
to be imagined only as "parasitic" on historical phenomena, as a certain disturbance or dislocation in the order of historical being.[11]

    In short, this excess is uncanny in the precise sense. Freud was careful to
explain that the uncanny is not the opposite of the canny, the inverse of the familiar or homely. That is, the uncanny or unhomely negates the homely not from
outside, not by returning from an elsewhere, but limits the homely from within.
It leeches familiarity from the familiar. The uncanny ghosts or undead of history
are not refugees from another place but are homeless in a more profound sense.
Not simply displaced from their real homes, which exist or once existed elsewhere, they give body rather to a certain displacement or out-of-jointness in the
homely place where they appear. They thus hold open or maintain a gap or limit
within history, which gap ensures the very contingency of history, that it will proceed unpredictably and cannot be manipulated from some other place apart.

    Freud, as was noted, scandalized historians and Jews alike by uncovering
an Egyptian Moses to whom he attributed "historical truth." It is now possible
to observe the compatibility between this concept of "historical truth" and
Foucault's "power of truth." Each is defined not in opposition to history but as
the very guarantee of history's unsmooth or contingent functioning. It is the

ineradicable "historical truth" of the Egyptian Moses that allowed Freud to con-template the eradication of the historically contingent features of Jewishness without eradicating Jewishness as such. That is, Freud located the source of Jew-ish survival in the fact of contingency itself, in the capacity of Jews to be otherwise, as I will argue later. For the moment I want to go back to the artwork of Walker, who defines the indestructibility of her figures not only through the shadowy ap-pearance she gives them, but through their cartoonish survival of the most ex-treme acts of violence and an aggressive sexuality that derides the very principle of self-preservation.

BLACK BAROQUE

It has been commented that Freud left the woman, specifically the mother, out of the Jewish family romance; she is nowhere to be found in the uncanny narrative he constructs in *Moses and Monotheism*. Walker offers a useful vantage from which to view this complaint, for her plantation family romance positions the "Big Black Mammy of the Antebellum South" in the very place where Freud located the Egyptian Moses, as the "anonymous root" of racial identity.[12] Asked in an inter-view to explain a particularly striking vignette from *The End of Uncle Tom and the Allegorical Tableau of Eva in Heaven*—"In the left side of one of the panels, there's this incredible image of four women—girls and women—suckling each other. What was this meant as a metaphor for?"—Walker responded: "History. My constant need or, in general, a constant need to suckle from history, as though history could be seen as a seemingly endless supply of mother's milk represented by the big black mammy of old. For myself, I have this constant battle—this fear of wean-ing. It's really a battle that I apply to the black community as well, because all of our progress is predicated on having a very tactile link to a brutal past."[13] We can agree that this is not a very satisfying answer insofar as it appears merely to restate a popular cliché in which the mother is viewed as a superabundant source from which future generations draw and to which all lines of filiation lead back. What captures our attention, however, is the discrepancy between the cliché and the image it purports to explain. What makes Walker's reply most unsatisfying is its failure to respond to the question posed to her: why are there *four* girls and women in this vignette rather than just the *one* superabundant mammy her answer im-plies? Why this duplication, this replication of women, suckling not their young (the descendants of the race whose source they are supposed by the cliché to be), but each other? One small silhouette is clearly that of a child, but the other three

Figure 3.7 Walker, *The End of Uncle Tom and the Grand Allegorical Tableau of Eva in Heaven* (detail, 1995). Courtesy
Brent Sikkema, New York City.

cannot be distinguished by age, and none can be isolated as *the* big black mammy. In this case, how can she be said to be represented in this vignette?

The discrepancy between image and reply shows Walker backing away in her artwork from the commonplace of the superabundant mother that prevails in psychoanalytic theory and in the vulgar imagination. Lacan, too, breaks from the stereotypical image and conceptualizes the mother, on the contrary, as a void, a hollow. The point of Lacan's conceptual intervention seems to be that whenever she is figured as a fully supplied container, the mother is made to represent a beyond or elsewhere, a paradise of pleasure, from which the subject has been banished and to which he or she then endeavors to return. It is in order to eliminate every trace of an outside, or a metadimension, that Lacan eliminates this mother-dimension. The absence of the mother from the historical romance he constructs is not the result of an oversight, the failure of Freud or Lacan to pay the same attention to the mother as was paid to the father; it is the result rather of the radical erasure of the dimension of the outside of history.

This flat statement first appears, however, to fly in the face of or to level a distinction psychoanalysis wants to maintain between the girl's and the boy's relation to the mother. On more than one occasion Freud made the point that the boy differs from the girl in that he is more able, because of the threat of castration, to separate himself from his mother or, in Freud's bombastic phrase (could it have been mocking?), the boy is more successful in accomplishing "the great cultural achievement" of turning away from his mother.

A whole feminist literature arose from this point. Because the girl cannot be threatened with castration, the deed having already been done, she has no incentive to abandon her mother and thus remains throughout her life doubled or haunted by her. The literary and cinematic phenomenon of the "female uncanny" or "female Gothic," in which young, often orphaned and/or unlovely women return to unnaturally ancient ancestral homes where they come under the spell of the undead presence of their mothers or some maternal substitute from whom they are incapable of breaking free (the former mistress of Manderley, Mrs. DeWinter, in *Rebecca,* for example, or the maternal aunt in *Gaslight*), was explored as confirmation of the girl's characteristic nonseparation from the mother. Lacan's theory was even enlisted to support this thesis. As is known, Freud maintained that anxiety was not occasioned, as some thought, by separation, by lack. In the situation of anxiety the subject is not overwhelmed by loss or the threat of loss. Lacan restated Freud's position by declaring that anxiety is occasioned by the "lack of lack," by a surplus rather than a lack. The step from this restatement of the Freudian position to the contention that the prevalence of anxiety in women stems from the suffocating presence of the unabandoned mother was, however false, an easy one to make. Those who took it were even prepared to accept what it inferred: that woman never properly, or only with the greatest difficulty, accedes to the status of subject. Her subjectivity is jeopardized by her inability to sever the connection to her mother and thus to establish an autonomous identity.

The problem is that this picture of uncanny doubling does not jibe with the one of uncanny repetition in the discussion of Moses. There it became clear that the phenomenon of the uncanny did not mark an unabandoned attachment to but the refusal of transcendence, of a domain outside history. The formation of the subject depends on this refusal. One is reminded in this context of a wry comment by Freud that has long seemed irksome. While repudiating the idea that woman had any significant access to either the morbid pain of moral accusation or the joy of moral exaltation, in short, to moral transcendence, he went so far as to bemoan the stubborn materialism of one type of woman who, he said, was susceptible to nothing but "the logic of soup with dumplings for argument."[14] The phrase was no doubt meant to be unflattering, but it would be wrong to dismiss the characterization totally as insult. Lacan, for one, showed he took it seriously when he translated it into his formulas of sexuation; the woman, he argues there, has no external limit and thus no outside. She is constituted by the negation of any transcendent beyond and thus lives in a "soup and dumplings" world of immanence. This distinction between her and the man, who is on the contrary defined by an external limit, allows us to reinterpret the distinction between the boy's and the girl's relation to the mother. The difference turns not on the fact that the boy separates himself more easily from the mother, but on the fact that this separation is more easily figurable in his case, since for him separation is simultaneous with an installation of the mother on the other side of a limit, in a paradisiacal beyond. Or: separation is achieved through an idealization that puts the mother out of reach, on a pedestal. A barrier separates the boy and his mother, and the ideal space she thus comes to occupy is the very one in which the superego will form.

The difference then is not that the girl does not sever the relation to the mother—she plainly does—but that separation is not accompanied by an idealization. This explanation raises a question. If the mother is indeed given up by the girl, by what is the orphaned and/or unlovely young woman in all that Gothic fiction haunted? Why is the woman more likely than the man to experience an uncanny doubling? Recall once again the earlier discussion of uncanny repetitions. They appear, I said, where one stumbles against the real or internal limit that refuses to admit a metadimension and thus splits historical phenomena from within. The uncanny that gives body to this split is not the unabandoned mother, but a part object that detaches itself from her. Woman is haunted by such a surplus, empty object—a breast, say—that forms as a result of her definitive, her radical giving up of the mother. The being of the woman is multiple not because she is doubled by another one, the mother, but because she is decompleted by the addition of a surplus object that interrupts or blocks the formation of a whole, the One, of her being. The being of the woman is multiple because she is split from herself.

Consider the description Deleuze offers of the double in his essay on Foucault. It is, he says, "not a doubling of the One, but a redoubling of the Other. It is not a reproduction of the Same, but a repetition of the Different. It is not the emanation of an 'I,' but something that places in immanence an always other or a Non-self. It is never the other who is a double in the doubling process, it is a self that lives me as the double of the other: I do not encounter myself on the outside, I find the other in me."[15] And now compare this description both to the vignette by Walker of the four suckling women and the following account by the Lacanian feminist, Michelle Montrelay, of feminine sexuality: "The woman's relation to her body [is] . . . simultaneously narcissistic and erotic. For the woman enjoys her body as she would the body of another. Every occurrence of a sexual kind . . . happens to her as if it came from another (woman). . . . In the self-love she bears herself, the woman cannot differentiate her own body from that which was 'the first object.'"[16]

The passage from Deleuze reinforces the one from Montrelay, while avoiding the suggestion that the "first object" is the mother. There are not two ones in the uncanny of feminine sexuality, the woman herself and the mother whom she could not abandon. The woman is not doubled by another just like her, by another one: the mother. Or simply: the mother is not the double of the woman, as we have already noted. Rather, the woman lives herself—enjoys her body—as if it were not her own but another's, as if she were the double of another. The woman does not encounter her mother in the uncanny experience of her own sexuality any more than Freud encounters a stranger on the train in the little vignette he offers in his essay on the uncanny of his own experience with seeing his double. This double turns out to be his own reflection in a mirror, although on this occasion that sense of familiarity which usually adheres to the sight of his own image seems to have been leeched from it. He glowers at himself as if he were a stranger who had wandered into his compartment.

Anxiety accompanies these uncanny experiences, not fear, which has an object and whose arousal would have meant that the woman or Freud, in his robe and slippers, had indeed encountered some other person, someone outside her-or himself, the mother or a disoriented fellow traveler. Anxiety signals that the threat cannot be exteriorized, objectified, that it is instead internal, brought on by an encounter with that limit which prevents one's coincidence with oneself. To theorists of the female Gothic who argue that the inability to separate from her mother prevents the young woman from becoming a subject, I would counter not only that it is not the mother who is the obstacle inhibiting the formation of a whole or complete being, but also that this very inhibition is what constitutes the woman as a subject. To be a woman is to be not-all, to be parasitized by an object that continuously unglues her from her own body, not by defining her as some-thing other than her body, but by making her jouissance a disruption of self-identity.

The image from *The End of Uncle Tom* . . . of the suckling women makes sense only against this background. It does not represent the big black mammy of the antebellum South as the external source of history. Only the internal void left by the definitive loss of the mammy can account for the replication of the woman, or the splitting of the image from itself, and the depiction of this uncanny form of sexuality in which "the" woman is shown to enjoy her own body as the body of another. If this is not an image of one superabundant mammy, neither can we de-scribe it as an image of four separate women. To count immediately four women is to commit an error of substantialization, for the vignette raises, rather, the question of how we are able to count as one a woman parasitized by a surplus that fractures her, splits her from herself. The repetition of suckling women registers, I would argue, the woman's reencountering of her difference from herself. Here we have the portrait, in other words, of what Deleuze referred to as an "aesthetic existence," the doubling or relation with oneself that is the rule of freedom. Yet this is not the portrait of any woman, but of a black American woman suckling not from her mother's breast simply but from history, and so we might say that the portrait also raises the question of how we are able to count as one, or as the same, a race that is always different from itself or not always the same as itself. Can we speak of a sameness that is distinct from the opposition between the sameness and difference of positive characteristics, a sameness that would be the return of self-difference rather than the elimination of it?

We must not lose sight of what is most extraordinary about the portrait; its analogization of history and the maternal breast. For if we insist on distinguishing the mother from the breast, as I have argued we must, then the analogy becomes both more profound and a more enlightening clue to Walker's artistic project. What does it mean to think of history not as a mother, that is, not as a container that holds subjects as part of its contents, but as an internal object that lives the subject as the double of another? How can history be thought not as objective, but as this internal object that lends the world its objectivity? From these questions one is led to the idea of a traumatic event, an event that cannot be an object of positivist historical study because it never takes place in the way historical situations do, but rather defines the place in which these situations come to inscribe themselves, a rupture that constitutes the never present origins of a race. Why "never present"? Because it is a structural impossibility to be present at one's own origin—except in the experience of the uncanny. This is as good a definition of the uncanny as one will find: the experience of encountering one's own origins. Freud theorized that such an encounter was felt by the ego as a threat that initiated a preparedness for action or flight. The flight that ensues need not, however, be considered as merely reactive; the act for which the encounter prepares us can also be one of invention or resubjectification.

THE ANONYMOUS ROOT OF RACIAL IDENTITY

In his catalog essay for the exhibition, *Voici: 100 ans d'art contemporain,* Thierry de Duve ushers in the art of the last century through the portal not of Manet's *Olympia,* which would have been the standard gesture, but through Manet's *Christ aux anges* (1864), a painting "never destined for any church" and thus a nonreligious painting, in which Christ is painted in a way that leaves him suspended, as if in a snapshot, between the status of an already dead, and thus no longer God, and a not yet resurrected, merely mortal man.[17] De Duve's critical argument, the one that secures for this painting its inaugural position, is that it is not as God but as man that Christ will resurrect himself in the next moment. If this painting can signal the beginning of modern art it is because this art understood the event of Christ's death to have bequeathed to it the task of resurrecting life, creating new life from the nothing it inherited from its break with the past.

Freud, the theorist of modern life, seems to have agreed with the premise of Manet's painting: some resurrection of man is possible. Like Manet, Freud disbelieved in the finitude of man, arguing in his essay on the uncanny that "although the statement 'all men are mortal' is paraded in text-books of logic as an example of a general proposition, . . . no human being really grasps it and our unconscious has as little use now as it ever had for the idea of its own mortality."[18] This essay on the uncanny, one of his rare forays into the field of aesthetics, argues that we moderns energetically deny the power of death by inventing a double as insurance against our own extinction. The feeling of the uncanny, he speculates, results from the fact that once formed as assurance of immortality, this double later "reverses its aspect" and returns as a harbinger of death, as a spirit or ghost of the dead.

It is as if in writing *Moses and Monotheism* Freud were returning to and expanding this argument, which is too truncated here in the earlier essay to make much sense. First, it is not as a "harbinger of death" or as a "spirit of the dead" but as *the undead* that this double reverses its aspect and returns. *Moses and Monotheism* clarifies this, as we saw, along with another confusion. There are, it would appear, two different ways of doubling oneself as insurance against extinction, but the only hint we receive of this in the uncanny essay is Freud's admonition that moral anxiety is not the same as the anxiety aroused by the feeling of the uncanny. Freud never explicitly elaborates a distinction between two forms of doubling, but by offering his theory of racial identity as an implicit critique of the racism fomented by Nazi ideology, he does most powerfully suggest a distinction.

Here is what we can gather from Freud's theory in general and from the specific arguments he makes about racial identity in the Moses book. Modern man, refusing to accept the finitude that modern thought thrusts upon him, doubles himself through a notion of race that allows him to survive his own death. Henceforth he is not only an individual subject, but also a member of a racial group. The phenomenon of race (and of racism) that results is unlike anything that preceded it and not only because race has now to assume the role of heaven, of eternity, in safeguarding the subject's immortality. Focused on the finite, modern man can no longer reliably sustain the old idea of eternity, but he does manage to reconstitute an alternative from a scrap left behind by the old idea. This leftover or remainder is the superego, the libidinally cathected belief that there is—if not a heaven—at least something that escapes the ravages of historical contingency. This idea is a negative one, nothing more than the conviction that between our expectations and their realization there is always a shortfall, some compromise. Yet it is what survives of eternity in the modern world, and it lends to a certain notion of race an element of ideality that is the source of its profound violence and its disdain for every historical obstacle, every contingency that opposes it.

While evidence of this idealized and thus unparalleled violence was mounting, Freud pressed forward with the composition of his Moses book. One has the sense that he would have effaced the notion of race altogether, but his theory would not let him. As we saw, his efforts at erasure, at driving out every exception where violence might take root, produced the uncanny form of doubling we have described—and another notion of race.

Since Nazi racial ideology was founded on an idealization—of the difference between what history had so far accorded them and what they could expect in the future—it was bound to a problematic of identification, the ideal being something with which one identifies. This had consequences, as we know, for the conception of the Aryan body. The ideality at the core of this notion of racial identity could not have resulted at this point in a naive forgetting or leaving behind of the body in favor of the disembodied contemplation of the ideal tomorrow for which the subject, as member of the Aryan race, would be saved. It resulted rather in an idealization of the body itself, in the construction of the notion of a "machine body," fit for use and even for useful pleasures, whose frailties could be disciplined by exercise. National Socialism thus encouraged identification with an ideal body.

Freud removed his notion of race from this problematic of identification; he stripped it of ideality. In the process he uncovered an anonymous root of racial identity, in a useless, exorbitant pleasure. This exorbitant pleasure, for which the subject is always unprepared, overtakes him as anxiety at the moment he encounters the double that, far from acting as prosthesis, as the protective armor that will allow him to survive the vicissitudes of history unharmed, tears him away from himself, undermines his very integrity. Freud identified himself as a Jew not because he shared any of their identifying traits or time-defying traditions, but because he believed that his own survival, like theirs, depended on his being able to overturn these stultifying traditions and modes of thought. What survives now, however, is no longer biological life but jouissance.

Kara Walker's silhouettes are filled with figures violently merging with and protruding from each other. They swallow and secrete, tear at and torture each other. It is as if they represented not just a number of different figures battling among themselves, but a parasitized body joyously trying to free itself from its slavery to itself. For this reason it is precisely wrong to criticize them as a recycling of stereotypes. They are on the contrary an erotic disassembling of them, a mad and vital tussle to break away from their stale scent and heavy burden. Allowing her work to be haunted by the traumatic event of the antebellum past, that is, by an event that neither she nor any other black American ever lived but that is repeatedly encountered in the uncanny moment, she opens the possibility of conceiving racial identity as repeated self-difference. What she shares with all the other members of her race is not simply a number of common experiences but this impossible-to-experience event that keeps tearing them from themselves, a historical rupture that cannot be "metabolized," but keeps depositing itself in those little piles of shit that turn up everywhere in the Walker's silhouettes. History flows through these figures but it does not contain them.

The Invention
of Crying and
the Antitheatrics
of the Act

HYSTERIA VERSUS ABSORPTION

My initial premise is this: crying was an invention of the late eighteenth century. I offer as proof of this thesis the fact that at this precise historical moment there emerged a brand new literary form—melodrama—which was specifically designed to give people something to cry about. Now, I realize that some of you are saying to yourselves, "I think she's got her dates wrong. I seem to remember something about people crying before then. Weren't there even professional mourners in some former societies?" I will grant you this: tears were shed from time to time before the eighteenth century, and even as a public duty, but never before was there such a universal incitement to cry. I suggest, then, that we pay closer attention to this social imperative in order to distinguish crying in the modern sense—the sense that accounts, for example, for Jean-Jacques Rousseau's dwelling, in *The Essay on the Origins of Language*, *The Confessions*, and *Emile*, on the importance and necessity of pity; for Denis Diderot's theatrical dictate, "First touch me, astonish me, tear me apart, startle me, make me cry . . . you will please my eye afterward if you can";[1] and for the wholly new emphasis in art and art criticism on the sentimental, empathetic relation between spectator and character—to distinguish this *modern* crying from all the lacrimation of earlier times.

I am, of course, not the first to view melodrama—the genre whose overt purpose was to facilitate this new outpouring of tears—as evidence of a social revolution. In *The Melodramatic Imagination* Peter Brooks also defines melodrama as an "enduring mode of the *modern* imagination" (my emphasis) and similarly links it to Rousseau, specifically to the opening passage of *The Confessions* in which Rousseau addresses himself to "my kind" even as he emphatically asserts his basic difference from them. Rousseau paradoxically insists not only on his uniqueness among men, but on the necessity of relating this uniqueness in its entirety, of "saying it all."[2] Brooks connects this modern compulsion to say all immediately to melodrama, arguing that the felt inadequacy of language to make everything absolutely clear is compensated for, in melodrama, by the grandiose gesture, the schematic tableau, the expressive mise-en-scène, music, the inarticulate cry, all those mute signs that we commonly take as characteristics of the genre and that make visible what is otherwise absent and ineffable in the narrative by words alone.

Although Brooks's basic argument is convincing, even inspired, several objections to it must nevertheless be raised. In preparation for doing so, I offer the following account—somewhat different in its terms from Brooks's version—of the source of the compulsion to speak the whole truth, which so suddenly erupted as the eighteenth century drew to a close. At this time, we know, a new entity—the citizen—was at once constructed and inserted into a similarly novel sort of space: a public space populated by the citizen's fellows, his kind. For just recently, the freshly minted notion of universal humanity had opened the door not only for the individual citizen, but for countless others just like him, all of whom entered through the same door. If the notion of universal humanity gave modern man the right to see himself as beyond compare, the only one quite like him, it also determined that he would not be alone in doing so; in this he was exactly like the others. In order, then, for the citizen to become countable among his fellows— to become comparable or equal to them in his right to claim his own uniqueness— something had to be *discounted*.

Michael Fried has analyzed the decisive shift that took place in painting during this period as a fundamental shift in representation itself, which abandoned its former "theatricality" to embrace a new strategy of "absorption." He argues that in mid-century painting began to obey Diderot's imperative, "Act as if the curtain never rose!"[3] That is, it began to carry on as if the beholder who stood in front of the painting were not there, even to obliterate his existence, by depicting characters who were totally preoccupied with their own autonomous world, intensely engaged in matters at hand. Curiously, however, this self-absorption of the represented space, this refusal to acknowledge the existence of any space outside its own, aimed not at an absolute denial of the beholder so much as at his "absorption" in the depicted scene. That is, the paintings' very pretense to ignorance of the beholder's presence worked to arrest the beholder's attention, to capture him in their thrall. By sealing the space of the representation off from that of the audience, at which the scenes were in fact directed, these paintings did not completely sever their relation to their beholder but, on the contrary, emphasized that relation, gave it new weight and significance. If the empathic critical literature of the time is to be credited, the obliviousness of the painting to the beholder caused him to become transfixed by it, to stand motionless and silent before it for long periods of time and to be deeply moved by it.

Anyone who has studied film will recognize in Fried's description of the techniques of absorption the strategies of classical cinema, which is also assiduous in its disregard of the spectator and maintains a rigorous taboo against any character's looking directly at the camera, that is to say, at the spectator, who comes to occupy the place of the camera during the film's projection. In cinema as in the late eighteenth-century paintings Fried analyzes, the apparently autonomous world of the representation depends on the outlawing of any exchange of looks between its characters and its spectators. And in cinema, too, this taboo functions to help hold these same alienated spectators spellbound, to move them profoundly.

Lacan, I argue, gives an account of this same antitheatrical logic of absorption when he draws an analogy between the world, which he designates as "all-seeing," and "the satisfaction of a woman who knows that she is being looked at, on condition that one does not show her that one knows that she knows."[4] This analogy is particularly felicitous as a description of the cinematic form of absorption, since it recalls several memorable scenes in which the look of a woman is cast almost directly at the camera/spectator, but misses it, significantly by only a few degrees. In these instances the woman turns out to be looking not at the camera, but at her own image either in a mirror supposedly placed in the camera's location or in her mind's eye. Think in the first case of Hitchcock's *Marnie,* where Marnie throws back her just-dyed hair and gazes with satisfaction at her image in the (unseen) mirror over the bathroom sink; and think, in the second case, of the famous scene at the end of Billy Wilder's *Sunset Boulevard,* in which Norma Desmond looks into the diegetic, off-screen camera, placed just slightly off-center from the one that is actually filming the scene, and announces her readiness for a close-up. It is as if this threatened transgression were periodically necessary to reimprint the taboo: do not permit this woman, this figure in the field of the represented, to see that we know that she knows we are looking at her. To distract her as she looks at herself by permitting her to direct her look at the spectator standing so tantalizingly close to the point where her own image is located would, of course, violate that taboo. But what does this strange rule signify? And what makes it possible for me to say that Lacan's "all-seeing" world is the "self-absorbed" world of representation Fried describes?

Lacan draws his analogy between woman and world as part of a historical argument he makes concerning a fundamental mutation of the relation between the seeing subject and the visible world. My point is that this mutation occurs in the very moment that both Fried and Brooks investigate. In Brooks's terms, this moment marks the point when the "post-sacred world" is installed, that is, the point at which moral and religious certainties are at once erased and melodrama springs into existence. The hermetic, self-sufficient, closed system of pictorial representation that is produced by techniques of absorption cuts itself off, in other words, not only from the space of the beholder, as Fried insists, but from the realm of the (now defunct) sacred as well. This new autonomous world, which relates to nothing but itself, is a world that has cut its ties to any transcendent divinity. Like Fried, Lacan discerns as one of the basic coordinates of this mutation the taboo against any exchange of looks between the world and its beholder. But here Lacan's distinction between look and gaze becomes absolutely necessary. For of course, it is not the case that the beholder cannot or must not look at the (represented) world; he can and does do so, even fixedly, as was noted. What is prohibited, however, is the arousal of the beholder's gaze. The world, Lacan says, "does not provoke our gaze."[5]

From this we can conclude that the difference between the antinomic Lacanian terms *look* and *gaze* will be at least partially clarified by understanding the representational taboo on which Fried's study focuses. This study, we have said, emphasizes throughout the dilegence with which the figures in the painting avoid acknowledging the presence of the beholder and purposefully busy themselves instead with the tasks at hand or their own states of mental distraction. Approaching the taboo from a different angle than Fried does, Lacan distinguishes not absorption from theatricality, but an all-seeing world from an exhibitionist one: "The world is all-seeing but it is not exhibitionistic—it does not provoke our gaze."[6] The avoidance by personages in the painting of any direct look at the beholder should, I propose, be considered in this way, as one of the means by which painting resists exhibiting itself.

The close parallels between the arguments of Lacan and Fried serve in the end to expose a major difference between them or, to state my observation more pointedly, to expose a significant absence in the analysis of Fried: there is in his work no indication of the fact that at the historical moment under scrutiny the world suddenly became "all-seeing." That is, at the precise point when the field of representation begins to announce its self-sufficiency, the beholders become "beings who are looked at in the spectacle of the world."[7] What is missing from Fried, in short, is a theory of the gaze. This observation does not fault Fried for not being Lacanian, but for not developing the implications of his own discerning argument to the end. For, though he attempts heroically to explain the paradox that permitted late eighteenth-century painting to draw its beholder empathically into its represented space even as it sustained the illusion of his nonexistence, one is not convinced finally that Fried sufficiently accounts for the paradox. While the thesis of its operation is often reiterated in the analyses of the paintings, the mechanism of their simultaneous binding and disregard of the beholder remains obscure. My point is this: the theory of the gaze, which is to say, the theory that *the world gazes back at the beholder, sees the viewing subject from all sides, even as it taboos the location of its gaze at any particular point or in any of the figures of the painting*, is necessary to explain the beholder's affective absorption in the world, his immersion in this new, realistic space.

Remarkably, the argument of Fried does come very close at one point to the one Lacan makes; it will be instructive to consider it. Following Diderot's comments in *Pensées detachées*, Fried explains the special problems the painting *Susannah and the Elders* presented to the taboo sustaining the turn toward "absorption": insofar as Susannah exposes her naked body to the eye of the beholder (rather than to the elders from whom she shields her nakedness by means of veils), she risks implicating the beholder in her exposure, or risks exposing the beholder as witness of her nakedness. Diderot's account of how the painting successfully sidesteps the taboo consists entirely in asserting a distinction between "a woman who is seen and a woman who exhibits herself."[8] According to this distinction, Susannah does not exhibit herself to the beholder who just happens to see her nakedness. Through this explanatory move Diderot—and Fried, who adopts his account—effectively blinds the visual world we behold: Susannah simply does not *know* that we are looking at her, does not see the beholder who sees her. The option Lacan offers—that she knows but does not want us to show her we know—is not considered. Fried quotes Diderot's various insistences that the scene must always be presented as a unified aspect, as a point of view, specifically that of the beholder. The tableau composition of these new paintings makes the scene visible only from the beholder's eyes. What would it take to move from this observation to the conclusion that the world composes itself for the beholder's eye or in some sense "knows" that it is being looked at?

Let us first consider why one would not make this move. Earlier we said that the development of techniques of absorption coincided with our entry into the postsacred world and the beginning of realism. This moment has sometimes been described as that of the disenchantment of the world. A disenchanted or re-alistic world could hardly be said to be all-seeing, to gaze back at us, or so some would say. But this is precisely what the Lacanian theory of the gaze does say: it is when the realistic world emerges from the collapse of a sacred beyond that the sub-ject comes to be submitted to the scrutiny of an unlocatable gaze and becomes vis-ible from within the world it sees. Visible not from outside the world, as formerly, but from within it. The beholder becomes visible in an all-seeing world when the place of an all-seeing agent is vacated. The subject encounters an elusive gaze in the world, not a seer beyond it, at the moment he is no longer submitted to the absolute condition of transcendence. Not a metonym of God, his remainder in the finite, realistic world, the gaze is, rather, a reminder of His absence.

But if this world is all-seeing, like Susannah it does not solicit our gaze by exhibiting itself. What does this mean? Exhibitionism, a perversion, seeks to avoid anxiety by inducing it in the other. The exhibitionist induces anxiety by try-ing to force the other's vision to coincide directly with his jouissance. He disre-gards the other's desire and aims at allowing the other to gaze on a vision that is immediately satisfying. The exhibitionist, who offers *himself* as the object of satis-faction, is able to dispense with all the ruses of seduction because he does not need to tease out what the other wants. He knows with certainty what it is. Were Susan-nah to look directly at the beholder or Marnie at the film spectator, their images would be perverse. The beholder would no longer be absorbed in the scene, lured there by desire, but would be made to experience anxiety.

The logic of the gaze and the all-seeing world will be treated more fully in the final chapter. For now only those aspects relevant to our discussion of melodrama need to be emphasized. The fundamental point here is that melo-drama employs methods not of theatricality, but of absorption to involve us in its world. Melodrama is in this sense solidary with the emergence of realism, with its new emphasis on the affective relation between visual representation and its be-holder, solidary with realism's invention of crying.

The point has been made that the representation of the world in visual *tableux*, in unified points of view, betrays a kind of "intention" or "purpose" on the part of the world or a kind of knowledge of the fact that it is being looked at by the beholder. Fried tells us that the primary function of the *tableau* in Diderot's esti-mation was "not to address or exploit the visuality of the theatrical audience so much as to neutralize that visuality . . . [in order to maintain] the illusion that the audience did not exist." It is true that a *tableau* was visible "only from the beholder's point of view. But precisely because that was so, it helped persuade the beholder that the actors themselves were unconscious of his presence."[9] There's not enough reasoning here. We get the idea: point of view pretends to represent a "found" reality, a reality on which the beholder has the impression that he simply happened. But the construction of this "found reality effect" is more complicated than either Diderot or Fried allow. It is necessary to state the obvious: a point of view gives only a partial view. How is it that this fragment, this limited view, does not appear solipsistic? How is the illusion created that this view presents part of the whole? Or: how is the solipsistic effect avoided and replaced by the reality effect? Something in the view must signal, without showing us anything more, without breaking out of the perspectival scene, that something is unseen. At this moment the beholder no longer simply sees but experiences himself as visible in the visual space; the painting, the *tableau* gazes back at him. The effect of reality is not, then, merely a matter of how the scene appears to us, it also depends on the sense that we are potentially visible in it. Kant, I would argue, attempts to make a parallel point when at the conclusion of the third *Critique* he elaborates a concept of "natural purpose." Nature gazes back at us, takes us into account, and it is by this that Kant assures himself and us that our subjective perspective is, in fact, objective. Our sense of objectivity depends on our conviction that nature constitutes an all-seeing world.

All-seeing, but not all-seen: this in brief is how the world that presents itself to our point of view appears. What Brooks refers to as melodrama's "moral occult," or quest for a hidden moral legibility, takes flight from the palpableness of this unseen. Problems emerged because one of the things missing from this new world was an objective moral code. My argument is that these problems were various; the difficulty does not present itself always in the same way. The question then becomes, "How is it presented in melodrama?" Since I intend to take seriously the common assumption that melodrama is somehow "female" specific, I will turn briefly to the psychoanalytical theory of sexual difference where we find, it turns out, two approaches to the problem of the all. Since I have detailed the logic of Lacan's formulas of sexuation elsewhere, I will be brief in stating how these formulas derive from Freud.[10]

Freud makes this fundamental distinction: while the boy's scenario of castration begins with the Oedipus complex and ends with the threat of castration, the girl's scenario begins with castration and ends with Oedipal love. What is the distinction Freud is attempting to draw? It is this: for the boy castration involves prohibition, whereas for the girl it does not. Her castration takes place without the father's intervention, without interdiction. The reluctance of some feminists to accord Freud's distinction the full value it deserves is due to the fact that it seems to depend on an immediacy of sight in the girl's case. The priority of castration in her scenario has been interpreted to mean that it is located in a visibility that precedes symbolic structuration. But it is possible to interpret the priority of castration in another way, as bearing witness to a certain inescapability or impossibility that contrasts with the prohibition that is crucial for the boy. Let me explain. The father's interdiction forbids the boy's access to something. To enter the world as a man, it cautions, you must give up one thing. The social order into which the boy makes his way is thus one that is always incomplete. Not everything can be included in it. The social world into which the girl enters similarly fails to form an easy or untroubled all, but not because it is incomplete or lacks anything. The fact that prohibition does not figure in her castration means not that everything can be included in it, but that nothing can be excluded from it. Yet the imperative to include, or to not say "no," does not give the woman any more opportunity to say everything than the imperative to exclude something, the paternal interdiction, gives the man, since no all can form where inclusion knows no limit. This impossibility of constructing an all does not mean, as is usually assumed, that some of her is lodged elsewhere, outside the symbolic, for this is rather the logic of the boy's scenario. We must conclude then that there simply is no all of feminine being. The impossibility of an all of being to which feminine being testifies is denied or refigured in masculinity through a prohibition that pretends to install being elsewhere, in a beyond.

If melodrama bears witness to an inability to say everything and a consequent compulsion to try to do so, we must ask ourselves which inability is at stake. In *The Melodramatic Imagination,* Brooks proposes that there is in melodrama a certain striving for more, a "striving beyond," or an "attempt to go beyond the surface of the real to a true hidden reality, to open the world of spirit."[11] Everything depends on how this striving, this quest for more, is thought. Melodrama displays a clear recognition and dissatisfaction with the way things actually are and a longing for something else, for some "should be" that remains inchoate. But generally speaking, there is a world of difference between that dissatisfaction which expresses itself in a feeling that the world does not measure up to some ideal, however vaguely this ideal may be conceived, and that dissatisfaction which expresses itself in a feeling that the world lacks any legitimate ground. In the first case, the world appears as a pale and degraded form of what it ought to be, in the second it appears as inauthentic. The melodramatic world is one in which masks proliferate as masks, as disguises that flaunt their thinness. The many copies or simulacra circulating through it refer not to an ideal lodged elsewhere that one strives to attain while feeling powerless to do so, but rather float the complaint that no such ideal exists. Everywhere one looks one finds instead façades without any real support. This sense of inauthenticity—which is a primary characteristic of the genre, one that makes sense of nearly all the others—is what determines melodrama as a "feminine" complaint. It is based not on the assumption that just beyond our reach there hovers an ideal we have failed to attain, but on the conviction that the world is not based on any ideal support. One thinks immediately of Douglas Sirk's famous claim that he would have made *Imitation of Life,* the film that culminated his career as a director of melodrama, for its title alone. From the costume jewelry of the opening credits to its garish colors and emotional pretenses, this film wears its inauthenticity on its sleeve. One would miss the point if one assumed that the imitations or simulacra that fascinated Sirk caused him to represent his characters as secondhand or sorry versions of something more true, for this would reduce the film to the narrative clichés it mocks. What determines the film's—and melodrama's—inauthenticity is not the fact that the characters all judge their own successes and failures in someone else's terms, but that none of the characters can provide the measure of any other. A critical perception exists that the characters in melodrama are defined through conflict with other characters. This is not exactly true; the conflict between characters is never exhaustive, it does not take place without leaving a residue of questions or opening other narrative avenues than the ones it purportedly concerns. It is because the characters are not reducible to their relations with each other that a seriality infects the genre from within. The "infinitely expandible middle," or seriality, of melodrama stems from the inexhaustive nature of character conflicts. Think again of Sirk's *Imitation of Life.* In this film the narrative of the black family (Annie and Sarah Jane) is ultimately revealed to extend beyond the supportive and subservient relations mother and daughter have with the white family (Lora and Susie). Annie's funeral, which takes place in a black church, introduces us to characters, music, and events that are completely new to us, though they have been part of Annie's life all along. Because we have been viewing her until now from Lora and Susie's point of view, we have seen nothing of this part of her. The shift of focus, the disjunction, is felt to be radical because we have been unprepared for it. What we took for a diegetic world commonly shared by two families suddenly collapses. Sirk's strategy here is not to be viewed as an attempt to produce a "Roshomon effect," wherein different points of view collide and vie with each other regarding the truth of their representations of the same event. In *Imitation of Life* the dominant point of view is hollowed out not because it is directly challenged by that implied by the funeral sequence, but because the relations we took to be the subject of the film are abruptly exposed as nonnecessary ones. It is, it turns out, mere chance and contiguity that bound the narratives of the two families together, and in a much more external way than we were ever led to suspect before the final scenes. Before the ending we had believed that the chance encounter of the two families had forged a more intimate relation; now we can see that this is not so. Living alongside Lora and Susie, Annie and Sarah Jane have lived substantially alone.

It is often noted that melodrama's focus is on innocent and powerless victims whose suffering is extolled as virtuous. The argument given for this is similar to one Roland Barthes makes about wrestling: in a world from which objective, commonly held standards of the good have disappeared, justice is specularized not by fixing it so virtue always wins out in the end, but by amplifying the gestures of suffering.[12] In this way moral law is installed *a contrario*, by making transgressions and transgressor as legible as possible. Consistent with my conviction that the genre condemns the world it presents as inauthentic, I argue that melodrama dwells on figures of innocence not to provide testimony for the need to install a law, but rather to indict existing laws and standards as unfounded. Thus, although recognition of the real but elusive—or unrecognized—virtues of the innocent are demanded, the genre seems most intent on finding ways of prolonging its complaint against any public or any authority who might be able to provide the desired recognition. This is, I argue, the effect of the generic emphasis on the belatedness of public recognition; the sought-for prize is always marred by the painful proof of its ineffectuality at the moment it is finally won. Recognition often arrives too late, but even when it does not, its arrival is treated more as a coincidence than a testament of the well-foundedness of the standard of judgment.

VARIETIES OF SPECTATORSHIP IN *STELLA DALLAS*

One of the problems of defining melodrama comes from its sheer pervasiveness, particularly in American culture. From the early films of D. W. Griffith to television soap operas, melodrama seems to be a dominant mode of the modern (and especially American) imagination. Thus, descriptions one plausibly advances for some instances do not seem to work for others. For example, the rigid moral polarizations—featuring pre-Raphaelite virgins and fiendish rakes who try to take advantage of them—that are the ubiquitous signature of early instances of the genre disappear in later, more realistic melodrama. Suffering is still rawly exposed in the later films, but it is not immediately evident what else links them to their generic predecessors. In order to answer these definitional concerns I will turn my attention from a general consideration of the historical emergence of the genre to a specific film, chosen primarily for the heated debates its final scene managed to ignite about the fundamental characteristics of the genre. One can only imagine the paroxysms of emotion this tearjerker, *Stella Dallas,* would have released in Diderot.

Here, for those who still have not seen it, is a summary of the plot: Stella, an energetic, ambitious, working-class woman, marries the rather dull, upper-class Steven Dallas. Soon after, they have a child, a girl, and Stella begins to devote all her attention to her, attending less and less to Steven. The couple become alienated from each other and start to live apart. Eventually Steven reencounters his former fiancé, a woman more suited to him, temperamentally and socially. Believing her daughter will be better off with her father and this woman whom he plans to marry, Stella pretends that she has decided to pursue interests other than motherhood and absents herself from her daughter's life. In the final scene, the daughter's wedding day, Stella shows up in the street outside the apartment where the ceremony is taking place and, unobserved by anyone inside, gazes through the window as the vows are pronounced.

The question on which most analyses of the film hinge is this: how are we to account for the rhapsodic look on Stella's face and her jaunty gait as she turns away from the scene of the wedding and walks toward the camera? Two quite different accounts mark the extreme poles of the debate. According to one, what lights her face and lightens her step is passive, spectatorial pleasure: she is suffused with a reflected glow from the happy image she sees through the window. This glow, however, comes at a cost; Stella has had to make herself a blank screen to receive it. She has, through her self-sacrifice—that is, by surrendering her daughter by disappearing from her life—made herself an anonymous outcast.[13] A second interpretation focuses not on this sacrifice, but on the fact that the look of triumphant pleasure adorns a face turned away from the window; it argues that this look indicates Stella's jubilant detachment from the world. She has finally said good-bye even to her spectatorial attachment to it.[14]

These two readings, seemingly at odds, are united on certain points. Both view Stella as exterior to the epithalamial world on view through the window, whether her exteriority is read as an exclusion she is tricked by society into accepting or as a detachment she freely elects. That is, whether she is thought to surrender her daughter and her own pleasure in order to experience the world from a distance, vicariously, or to leave the world completely behind in order not to surrender anything, Stella and the world are presented as mutually exclusive. My own view impeaches both claims. I will argue instead that the final scene presents us with a world in which Stella finally includes herself.

Let us focus a while longer on Stella's position as spectator. Most critics have noticed a parallel between the final scene and an earlier one in which Stella, on a movie date with her future husband, Steven, watches spellbound as a love scene unfolds on the screen. The equation of these two scenes has led critics to associate Stella's pleasure not with her own involvement with a romantic love, but with her viewing of it. This would make the scene a prologue to the final one in which Stella watches passively and enjoys only vicariously the scene of her daughter's wedding. But is her spectatorship necessarily passive? Isn't it more accurate to say of Stella, as Lacan does of Dora, that she has a certain "passion for identifying herself with all the sentimental dramas . . . , of sustaining behind the scenes everything that can pass for passion, but which is not her affair"?[15] Here again the pleasure Stella takes from the scene is associated with her position outside, not in it. The difference, however, is that she is now recognized to be pulling the strings behind the scene, controlling the image.

Stella's passion is, in psychoanalytic terms, hysterical. To the hysteric, the fact that the father is a "man without means," that he is impotent or incapable of rising to the level of his function, is never disguised. She is acutely aware of it, as all her constant complaints, stormy refusals, and bitter objections testify. She is alert to the fraudulence rampant in her world. Yet she is not content simply to complain; like the beautiful soul she is, she always takes an active—and ingenious—role in securing her own dissatisfaction. If she cannot find in the whole wide world a man who can measure up to her expectations, well, then, she will make one up. The hysteric, Lacan says, "makes the man." Knowing that her father is impotent with Frau K., Dora shrewdly arranges it so there is at least an appearance of his amatory potency. Yet in order to stage this little theater of satisfaction, she has to keep herself unsatisfied, disgusted with the whole mess. She thus withdraws herself not only from the immediate tawdry quadrille in which everyone wants to embroil her, but from the whole pathetic bourgeois milieu in which she is condemned to live. Distancing herself from her world, the hysteric eroticizes her solitude while acting as puppeteer of an erotic coupling elsewhere.

I am suggesting that the hidden or misunderstood virtue so dear to melodrama is not best approached as that of a passive victim of forces the characters cannot control but of an active manipulation designed to sustain the illusion that there can be an existence that evades inclusion in social space. I take Stella, whose parlousness is underlined by regular camera shots of her scheming look, as a figure of this structure of manipulation in melodrama as a whole. Indeed, the narrative of *Stella Dallas* needs to be reconsidered in this light. Let me explain: early in the film we are presented with an image of Stella reading a newspaper that reports the breakup of Steven and his fiancé, Helen, after the suicide of Steven's father. The images of the severed couple are seen over the spectatorial shoulder of a passionately interested Stella. A surface reading of this shot would see it as the moment when the scheming Stella hatches her plot to snare Steven, to escape her working-class existence by seeking security in the arms of an upper-class man. But the framing of the shot and the fact that it is not only Steven's image but Helen's as well that is pictured in the paper demands that we place this scene alongside the other two in which Stella is seen gazing at romantic couples. What information does the newspaper impart to the sentimental Stella? It tells the story of a ruined father (also pictured in the newspaper) who had, he thought, no other option than suicide and of a son so broken that he could not sustain his relation with the woman he loves; in short, it gives further evidence that her social reality—upper as well as lower classes—is littered with weakened and disappointed men. Nothing prevents us, then—in fact the entire working out of the narrative encourages our suspicions—from reading Stella's response as part of a scheme much more complex than the one the surface reading allows. From the beginning, I am arguing, what Stella's actions ultimately aim at is not her union with Steven, but the salvaging of his relation to Helen—in other words, to the forming of a couple from which Stella will be excluded.

It is only by recognizing this structure that we can make sense of otherwise incomprehensible details. We see, for example, almost nothing of Stella's marriage to Steven. At almost the first possible (screen) moment, that is, after the birth of their daughter, Stella turns away from Steven to embrace her child. If Stella were simply the fun-loving, adventurous spirit critics have taken her to be, this would be intelligible only as a terrible miscalculation. As she herself says later and in various ways, "I don't get any fun out of a good time anymore. All the time I'm out, I'm thinking of her . . . and I just want to get back to her," or: "Lollie uses up all the feelings I've got and I don't have any left for anyone else." In turning toward Laurel, Stella turns to embrace not life but isolation; she retreats from the world into a fantasy of self-sufficiency.

As the regrets come in one by one while mother and daughter await the arrival of birthday party invitees, the shrinking of their world becomes painfully palpable. It is as if we were witnessing the progressive vanishing of any outside, while the two women are abandoned to their solitude. One might object that this is a condition that Stella endures rather than courts, but the film offers contrary evidence. The train ride that precipitates the onslaught of civilized refusals is undertaken immediately after Laurel's teacher asks Stella to allow her daughter to go on a trip to Boston. At the moment she is threatened with the loss of her daughter, Stella uncharacteristically leaves her to enjoy a rare moment of pleasure outside her home. On the train she and her déclassé friend, Ed Munn, engage is some harmless fun by putting itching powder on their fellow passengers. This provokes the censorious look of the passengers, primary among them the teacher who proposed taking Laurel to Boston.

Two points should be noted. First, her railway antics end up protecting Stella against the threatened loss of her daughter. Second, the censorious look Stella solicits is marked as blind. Since the film's audience is first made privy to the innocence of these antics—the platonic nature of Stella's feelings for Ed is made explicit in this scene—the passengers' subsequent misreading of them as vulgar erotic display is clearly undercut. We know what this playful behavior looks like to the passengers and we know that they are wrong. In other words, the film contains a denunciation of the snooty upper-class look and does not offer it, as other critics have wrongly insisted, as a privileged point of view. Our position as audience is parallel to the hysterical one, distanced from and critical of the social milieu that cannot afford Stella a place in it.

This is a good point to return to the more general discussion of melodrama and my promise to try to elucidate the relation between its early and late forms. First, it is necessary to reconsider the avowed relation of melodrama to the modern problematic of ethics, wherein an objective standard of the good can no longer be employed. As I have argued, since the girl's castration takes place without the father's intervention, the (moral) world into which the woman enters appears to her flawed in a different way than it does to the man. For her the fault establishes itself in the absence of a limit, hence a beyond, which absence robs the world of its base or ontological prop. If she is obliged to assume a skeptical attitude to this world, this is because it appears to her to be unfounded, a mere semblance. The ethical imperative calls on the woman to respond to this ungroundedness of the world. And melodrama, for its part, not only exposes us to the fraudulence, the inauthenticity of the world, but also presents a particular kind of response to it. It attempts to redress the particular failure it perceives by making up for what appears to cause it. In brief, it responds to the absence of any limit by imposing imaginary limits on it.[16] I am not proposing that this response is characteristic of woman as such, but only of a particular kind of woman, the hysteric, and of melodrama.

Hysteria attempts to "cure" the inauthenticity it finds in the world by imaginary means. Freud's dictum, "hysteria condenses," is a more pithy way of saying that the hysteric is especially prone to the sort of synthesizing or schematizing we connect with the philosophical imagination.[17] Confronted with the very real inadequacies of phallic jouissance, the insufficiency of ardors that stumble and cool before obstacles, that go endlessly astray, confronted with the monotony of a passionless succession of events, the hysteric takes the reins of the world by constructing imaginary resolutions, that is, by imposing limits via a comprehensive, imaginative seizure of events. The static *tableaux*, the schematic and stereotypical polarization of characters, the *voix du sang* plot twists by which improbable discoveries of previously unknown blood relations bring disparate events to a sudden and climactic halt, all these well-known elements of early melodrama, I claim, result from the violent imposition of imaginary boundaries on a world that presents itself as pure succession and that will not allow itself to be otherwise grasped. The imaginary brings into being a passionate world, but it does so by spatializing time, freezing it in rigid constructions. Like Dora, who stood for two hours before the Sistine Madonna, the hysteric attempts through her picturing imagination to hold back the relentless and lackluster progression of time.

What we see in early melodramas are the effects of the limits imposed by the imaginary: the spatialization of time. These effects have largely disappeared from later, more realistic melodramas and are replaced by narrative accounts of how such effects are achieved. Limits are imposed, the world is comprehensively seized only because the hysteric purchases this comprehension with her person. That is to say, the condition of the world the hysteric thus constructs is that she never set foot in it. As I indicated earlier in speaking of Stella, the hysteric *makes herself the limit* of the world she brings into being—and she does so precisely by withdrawing from it. What we find in later melodramas are "narratives of retreat," in which the heroine (or hero) removes herself from her milieu in order to give birth to a consistent social order, to narrative resolution and clarity. *Stella Dallas*, as I have so far described it—as a narrative of Stella's refusal to join the world—fits into this category.

But these attempts at an imaginary resolution create flimsy structures, as anyone familiar with melodrama knows—and they are marked as such. The schematizations of early forms are rigid and scarcely credible and the narratives of self-sacrifice common to the later forms index the deep inadequacies of the social world they depict. Melodramatic tales of innocence misrecognized, virtue unrewarded, secrets taken to the grave relate over and over again that something continues not to be written or made visible in a world too inadequate to do so. In making up and flaunting her romantic, imaginary scenarios and her various flashy images—including images of her own body—the hysteric also flaunts their stagey, cardboard character, the fact that behind this excess of visibility she remains invisible. Stella's "excess visibility" is to be understood in these terms. Whether or not she knows how to dress is not the point of *Stella Dallas* (which gives contradictory evidence on this question); the point is rather that she always dresses or makes up her body image so as to deceive the Other. Traipsing across the manicured lawns of the country club where she is staying with her daughter, Stella—dressed improbably not only in too many frills but in a fur stole that is entirely inappropriate for the warm weather that allows everyone else to go without wraps—does not expose her true, carefree and whimsical being, as the commonplace reading would have it, but, rather, calculatedly cloaks her being, guards its mystery, behind this ludicrous display.

But now that I have outlined ways in which *Stella Dallas* conforms to the definition of melodrama I propose, I want to reverse myself to say: it does not. That is, *Stella Dallas* is not a typical melodrama in that at the end Stella is shown to succeed where the hysteric, in celebrating failure, fails. Typically, I have been saying, the melodramatic heroine exiles herself from society; standing (literally or metaphorically) alone in the rain and cold, she insists on making her own body give mute testimony to all of society's failures. From the first melodramas to *The*

Bridges of Madison County—in which Francesca Johnson's dying wish is that her body not be buried, not be submitted to family and social rituals of mourning, but that it instead be allowed, as ashes, to pursue beyond death the very icon of a lost ideal, a lost love—it is the (usually female) body that resists society's clutches and submits itself as the very proof of that society's fraudulence. In the face of the uncertainties, ambiguities, and disappointments the world offers her, the hysterical/melodramatic heroine chooses the certainties of a body in retreat from and thus untarnished by social encroachments and constraints or, in the words of Dora: "adorable" and "white." For this belligerent refusal to sacrifice her unsanctioned enjoyment, she sacrifices everything—all her claims within society—which in turn justifies her complaints that she gets nothing out of it, that it constantly fails to take account of her, to write her into its scenarios.

There are several reasons why this description cannot be made to fit the final sequence of *Stella Dallas.* The comparison between the ending and the earlier scenes of Stella's gazing at couples breaks down because in the final scene, we are presented not with Stella's withdrawal from the world, but her presence within it. In the end the film ceases to represent the impossibility of representing a world in which Stella, too, would have a place; it ceases to represent the contingent events—Steven's arrivals home just when Ed Munn happens to be there, Laurel's teacher's chance witnessing of Stella's antics, and so on—that function as the fulcra on which the hysteric balances her lack of faith. And rather than viewing the final scene of passion, Laurel's wedding, across the neurotic barrier that Stella has always until now erected between herself and the world she viewed, this time we spectators enter the scene before her, from the other side. Helen orders the curtains to be drawn open so that the ceremony will be visibly accessible to Stella, the beholder she knows will be looking in. Thus, as we come to take a position beside Stella and watch from her point of view the ceremony that unfolds "as if the curtain never rose," that is, a scene that pretends to be ignorant of Stella's presence, we know that she is in fact visible within the scene, that she has finally herself become a spectacle in the world from which she has for so long alienated herself. In other words, Stella has ceased placing herself in the hysterical position.

If the hysteric's response to the world's unfoundedness is a comprehensible solution, it is not the best one. While exposing this unfoundedness, it makes itself impotent, for it leads only to skepticism regarding what we can expect from a flawed society or to a naive voluntarism about our possibilities of escaping from it, and often to both at once. Kant, a fierce enemy of skepticism, has then something to teach the hysteric. While maintaining that it was impossible to determine whether any particular act was free, or ethical, he was certain we were free and sought to find positive evidence of our ethical nature. In his theory of the sublime he proposed that certain ideas of reason allowed us to triumph over impasses and thus to think and act freely. In the dynamically sublime the triumphant idea is that of might, or of an absolute force, which is able to make rugged overhanging cliffs, thunderclouds, volcanoes, the boundless ocean, and all the most terrifying forces of nature sink into puny insignificance in comparison to it. In the mathematically sublime, the idea is that of magnitude, or of an absolute all, of a measure beyond measure, a grandeur that exceeds every conceivable greatness and gives greatness itself its size. These ideas of reason are manifest in the world, however, only in the positive feeling of the sublime, in "the *frisson* that . . . flashes through the body everywhere there is life in it," in the feeling of an exalting satisfaction.[18]

It is tempting to read the jubilant look on Stella's face and the lightness of her step as evidence of this sublime voluptuosity of spirit. The problem is that although psychoanalysis concurs with Kant's conviction that proof of our ability to act and think freely is to be found in an experience of jouissance, of corporeal pleasure, it also instructs us that jouissance comes in various forms. We cannot therefore immediately distinguish that jouissance which evidences our ethical nature from that which is secreted by acts of sacrifice and which are not ethical. Insofar as the sublime ideas of reason posit a superior force or a superior measure from whose heights the subject can look down and find herself inferior, insufficiently strong or great, they cannot be associated with that jouissance which disposes us to ethical action. These ideas, rather, enslave the subject to a force or a measure to which she can never quite measure up and to which she is compelled to sacrifice her efforts and pleasure in an attempt to do so.

It is at this point that Lacan's concept of the feminine not-all and of another, non-phallic jouissance intervenes. For what is this not-all—or as we can now say, this absolute not-all—if not the extraction of Kant's absolute all or absolute measure from the all? That is, the absolute not-all is formed by removing the exceptional magnitude, or unmeasurable measure against which all others are measured, from the all. It is for this reason that feminine being is, in Lacan's phrase, "not one," but multiple. Whereas in the logic of the sublime, the subject is able to surpass or exceed herself by finding herself lacking in relation to an exceptional force or measure that, by tracking the various self-surpassing appearances of the subject, constitute them as appearances of one being, feminine being on the contrary goes beyond itself without relating itself to any such measure; its various appearances, then, are not appearances of one being that acts as their ground.

In proposing this concept of the feminine not-all, Lacan appears to have elevated Freud's many declarations of the absence of a superego among women to the status of an ontology. The lack of a superegoic structure becomes the key to understanding feminine being. This is not to say, of course, that this lack of a ground or of a One of being now (in a reversal of expectations regarding the relation between ethics and the superego) guarantees that the acts of all women will be ethical. Individual women respond to the absence of a ground or of a One of being in different ways. As we have seen, the "sublime" hysteric responds by complaining about the "inauthenticity" she observes, not in herself, in her own being, but in the world. Accordingly, she is not filled with the self-accusations by which those who fall under the influence of the superego are burdened, but on the contrary, becomes, as it were, superego to the world. Her self-exile from society is a withdrawal to the heights of moral disdain from which she feels justified in proclaiming the inferiority of all she surveys. Such a retreat, which abandons the pleasures of society, can hardly be mistaken for free, ethical action, for the hysteric remains enslaved if not to an idea of reason, then to an idea of the idea of reason. She still wants a master, keeps going (and complaining) in hopes of finding a master—whom she can master. This is to say that she will be the judge or the measure of the man, she will determine whether or not—and it is always "not"—any of the pretenders is master enough in her estimation.

The jubilant Stella is no longer in the position of the hysteric, no longer places herself in the position of outside observer of the world. If she had remained until the end satisfied with that external position we can be sure that the final image of the film would not be the one we are given, but one of her gazing up at the window. Only in this way could the joy on her face have been read as the joy of sacrifice. Instead a surfeit of space unfolds as she walks toward the camera. Because this space unfurls before our eyes as yet unclaimed by narrative action, it has a presence that strikes us as more immediate than the other spaces of the film. It is as if space itself had not been exhausted by the narrative which has just played itself out to some conclusion, but some surplus remained ready to support another, as if Stella could no longer be reduced to her role as mother, but were "something else besides." What I claim is that the end of the film is no longer about giving something up, about maternal sacrifice, but about giving, or maternal love, about the creative act in which one gives precisely nothing.

As mentioned, the critical tendency is to view the scene of Stella looking up into the window at her daughter's wedding as parallel to the earlier scene of her looking up at a movie screen, on the grounds that Stella in both cases remains outside the scene, its passive witness. Yet in the final scene it is her own daughter rather than a fictional character who is on view; this daughter whom she has previously kept by her side, in the audience, now appears on life's stage. The final scene calls up not only the scene at the movies but another in which the relation between Stella and Laurel takes a decisive turn. The scene to which I refer is the one at the resort in which Laurel, having just been pinned by her boyfriend and future husband, is seated with him at a soda fountain. Facing the counter at which she sits there is a long wall mirror. Glacing up at one point she chances to see a reflection of her mother, who has just strolled in, outrageously dressed and behaving like a vulgar floozy. In order to avoid detection as daughter of this mother, Laurel flees.

One's first impulse is to interpret this scene as the moment at which Laurel suddenly sees her mother from the perspective of the social class into which she has now formally been inducted. But to assume that it is the intervention of another determinate point of view (that of her boyfriend's social class) that arouses Laurel's intense feeling is to misjudge the nature of the feeling aroused. This is a scene not of simple embarrassment but of shame. Shame is awakened not when one looks at oneself, or those whom one cherishes, through another's eyes, but when one suddenly perceives a lack in the Other.[19] At this moment the subject no longer experiences herself as the fulfillment of the Other's desire, as the center of the world, which now shifts away from her slightly, causing a distance to open within the subject herself. This distance is not that "superegoic" one which produces a feeling of guilt and burdens one with an uncancelable debt to the Other, but is, on the contrary, that which wipes out the debt. In shame, unlike guilt, one experiences one's visibility, but there is no external Other who sees, since shame is proof that the Other does not exist. Glimpsing the outlandish image of her mother in the mirror, Laurel for the first time notices a lack in her mother, the veneer of maternal self-sufficiency is stripped from her. Shame does not attempt to redeem this lack by substituting for her mother a different Other; Laurel does not simply switch loyalties, to put it perhaps too crudely. As we watch the penetrating sense of exposure, the brilliant flush of shame rise in her, we understand—or should—that it is the door of the social as such that has blown open in this scene. The presence of the long mirror helps to suggest that Laurel now feels herself to be visible not merely from some specific point, that of her upper-class friends, but from all sides.

From now on Laurel ceases to be fused with her mother; she takes the part of an independent, social being. The question of the film becomes how Stella will respond to this social being, her daughter, who no longer sits with her on the sidelines but joins the world. The final scene gives the answer: she responds with an act of love. Lacan has said that suicide is the only successful act; what he should have said, and perhaps meant, is that love alone is successful, for only in love do we encounter the Other. The implication of a link between suicide and love is not intended to rehearse the usual humanist claptrap about love's being an immolation of the self on the threshold of the Other's otherness. Some such sentiment does, however, inform readings of *Stella Dallas*'s conclusion, where the plain-clothes anonymity of Stella is perceived as a sign of her self-abasement before the radical otherness of her idealized—that is, now unreachable—daughter. This notion of love really is melodramatic because it depends on one of those heart-breaking missed encounters for which the genre is properly known. The point is not that in melodrama love is always misrecognized or too tardily recognized. It is rather that melodrama conceives love as necessarily entailing these bungled encounters, or to constitute the very stuff of amorous relations, precisely because the latter are assumed to bring with them the annihilation of one or the other of the lovers. One cries in melodrama because the love it celebrates always and only consists of a suffering through a series of failed rendezvous.

If the ending of *Stella Dallas* is not generic, as I have been arguing, this is because it represents love as a successful encounter. Within the framework of Lacanian theory it may sound strange to speak of an encounter that comes off successfully, since Lacan himself unfailingly characterized the encounter as missed. This suggests that we need to distinguish two senses in which an encounter can be said to be missed. In the first or melodramatic sense—which echoes Freud's famous diagnosis that a man and woman are always a phase apart psychologically, or is epitomized by Sarah Jane's arriving too late, at the end of *Imitation of Life,* at her mother's funeral to tell her that she loves her—the intractable differences between the sexes and the generations, their "out-of-synchness," is emblematized by their not showing up at the same place (psychologically or physically) at the same time. One arrives at a point, awaits the other, despairs and leaves or goes about life without him, who later arrives and finds no one there waiting for him. We see one, then the other, but not both at the same time, or: we see two but not a meeting of two.

Lacan's concept of the missed encounter is different. It declares not that there is no encounter, but that there are not two in the encounter. Love takes place not between two ones but, as Lacan said, between one and *a*. What does this mean? An encounter is not an ordinary circumstance; it is rare. Among the possible scenarios for tomorrow's lunch, my having lunch at Babbo with a famous Hollywood director might not seem to you one of them—until I told you that the director was a friend of my friend, Nevin, who worked as a script doctor on his last film and that I had sent him my screenplay about the Lafayette Escadrille just at the moment he had the idea to do a film about this off-beat group of World War I fighters. Then, however doubtful you might be about my ability to write a credible screenplay about war, you would at least admit that such a meeting was a possibility. After all, I had shown you that promising novella I wrote awhile ago, and the director could just be doing Nevin a favor. It would be possible, barely, to imagine my sitting with the director at one of the tables in the front of the restaurant. But were such a meeting to take place between the director and me, it would not be an encounter. Too much preparation has gone into it; I have had to string together a chain of reasons for it, the director and I had already to be bound together by our mutual friend and our mutual interest in the Lafayette Escadrille, to make it appear as a possibility.

An encounter is not constructed out of such narrative possibilities. This is to say no reasons can be given for the encounter. In the encounter of love, for example, the lover gives nothing, no reasons for loving the other nor for being loved by him. One does not offer one's interest in the Lafayette Escadrille, one's talents as a writer, or a list of one's well-placed friends, nor, on the other side, one's Hollywood ambitions or desire for fame. No reasons pave the way to the encounter, which remains, for this very reason, impossible. What one encounters then is not another fully realized thing (trailing behind it an array of reasons for its being in this place at this time), but the real, insofar as the real is that which is impossible (preceded by no reasons that would insert it already, half-expected in my path). Again, this is not to imply that an encounter does not take place, that it fails to happen, but that what one happens upon, what one encounters, is experienced *as real, as impossible—or as unrealized.* This is why the encounter cannot be represented as a meeting of two, but only as a rift, a disjunction.

Stella Dallas ends with a missed encounter not in the melodramatic but in the Lacanian sense, for the point of the final scene is not that Stella does not get a chance to be present at her daughter's wedding, but the rift that interrupts the narrative and opens up a surplus of nonnarrativized space. Yet the disjunction in which the encounter is registered accounts not only for this excess of space, but also for Stella's jouissance, manifested in her joyous tears and radiant appearance. Lacan is only one in a long line of thinkers who have stressed that the modern subject is out of joint with her world, such that where world is, subject is not. Only love accomplishes the impossible by allowing the subject to encounter its world directly, that is, to experience the elusive "I" that always seems to disappear in any experience of the world, into the very content of one's thoughts or perceptions. This is not to say that the "I" shows up at this point as a fully realized thing that can be added to the world as $1 + 1$. No, the "I" is there, is present, rather, in a corporeal marking, in the experience of jouissance that suffuses the subject's body.

It is only through love, through the encounter with her worldly daughter in the window, that Stella is finally able to experience herself as a transcendental "I," not just herself as mother. The joy that love makes available to her shatters the casing of her self-sacrificing maternal role. In this way, I would suggest, the film's finale operates like the realist paintings Fried studies. The tabooed exchange of looks between pictorial figures and the beholder prevents not their encounter, but the appearance of two at the encounter. What we get, rather, is the seemingly self-sufficient, realistic, and moving world of the painting plus—plus what? Not the obliteration of the beholder, but his (impossible) presence—in the form of the jouissance that flashes through his body and which Diderot describes as the cry of the beholder. By reconfiguring this encounter as something that could not take place, as an impossibility that does not happen, melodrama hystericizes this structure and produces an unhappier flood of tears.[20]

EVIL AND THE EYE OF THE BEHOLDER

Evil in the

Time of the

(In)Finite

World

5

When we contemplate the international situation, we cannot fail to be struck by the utter barbarity with which civilized nations cling fast to fundamental principles they refuse under any circumstances to abandon:

> Each separate state, so long as it has a neighboring state which it dares hope to conquer, strives to aggrandize itself through . . . conquest, and thus to attain a world-monarchy, a polity wherein all freedom, . . . virtue, taste, and learning, would necessarily expire. Yet this monster (in which laws gradually lose their force), after it has swallowed all its neighbors, finally dissolves of itself, and through rebellion and disunion breaks up into many smaller states. . . . The result is that the *philosophical millennium* which hopes for a state of perpetual peace based on a league of peoples . . . which tarries for the completed improvement of the entire human race, is universally ridiculed as a wild fantasy.

And if we were then to refocus our attention on a more intimate scale of human relations, we would find numerous examples of this same perfidious egoity, of "a secret falsity even in the closest friendships, . . . a propensity to hate him to whom one is indebted, . . . a hearty well-wishing which yet allows the remark that 'in the misfortunes of our best friends, there is something which is not altogether displeasing to us.'"[1] Such sentiments, common enough today, could be attributed to countless sources, who might be speaking of the breakup of the former Yugoslavia or the Soviet Union, the rash of "tell-all" books that betray the trust of intimates, the petty perfidies of talk-show guests. But these words belong to Immanuel Kant, who employs them in a late text, *Religion within the Limits of Reason Alone,* to acknowledge the "insurmountable wickedness," the *radical evil* that inhabits the heart of man and that he can "by no means wipe out" (66).

This acknowledgment will seem scandalous to those of us who see Kant as the apostle of reason and progress. It is as if in evil progress had hit a bump that threatened to expose it as mere anthropomorphic illusion, or reason had suddenly been shown to be corruptible at its core. That is, in admitting the innateness or radicality of evil, Kant could seem either to have discarded his belief in the powers of reason and the perfectibility of man and reverted instead to a belief in original sin, or to have found in these Enlightenment notions a new source of evil. It was easier for his contemporaries to take the former position, to think that Kant had in his old age returned to one of the traditional religious views against which they were then battling. To us, the latter position comes more easily; we almost spontaneously assume that Kant must have begun, in his old age, to renounce his former optimism and to fear that the Enlightenment principles he had so long preached might themselves become the doctrine of a modern-day religion, more dangerous than the kind it superseded. The difference in these reactions stems from the fact that between Kant's contemporaries and us there have intervened numerous colonialist battles and two all-out wars that have been borne by a kind of implacable fury and devastation that could not possibly have existed during the centuries before Kant wrote and of which even he could only have had abstract glimmerings.

Let us not forget that the "international situation [*den aüszern Völkerzustand*]" Kant contemplates was just barely formulatable as a notion at the end of the eighteenth century. The contemporary ring of his complaint is slightly off; it sounds a bit prematurely. For, nations in the modern sense, republics rather than monarchies, whose very destiny depended on the will of their people, were at this time in the earliest stages of conception and formation. And thus the conflicts, the colonial and world wars, that would break out between these nations—and would give rise to the very notion of the "international situation"—were merely an emerging possibility when Kant expressed his bleak sentiments. When these wars did in fact take place, they would be unlike any that had been fought before, more barbarous, more cruel. What would make them so different from earlier wars is that they would be waged by nations who were able to enlist the will of the people, who were for the first time free to dispose of it as they chose. It was only when war had will on its side that the former acquired its limitless capacity for destruction.

The question that must immediately be asked is this: how base is will, that is, is it *fundamentally* base; what, finally, does Kant mean by the term *radical evil*? He most certainly means that evil is *rooted* in human will, has no existence apart from will and cannot be eradicated from it, but critics have been less sure how far down he supposes evil to go, how far a "secret falsity" and a "propensity to hate" permeates human will. The question is: does evil consume will entirely or does it leave behind something that might positively strive toward good?

An earlier version of this chapter was first written as an essay commemorating the 200th anniversary of the publication of *Religion within the Limits of Reason Alone.*[2] I wanted at the time to try to sort out some of the questions raised by what was re-garded by many as the thoroughly baffling concept of evil proposed in a book that, until recently, was considered relatively minor and was therefore critically ne-glected. Since the appearance of my original essay and the volume of essays it introduced, however, a new translation of Kant's book has appeared and the con-cept of radical evil has become more familiar, especially to those interested in his-torical phenomena such as the Holocaust. Yet the horrible evidence of what Kant variously called the *wickedness, corruption,* and *perversity* of the human heart is, un-fortunately, not only encountered in memories of past events, but also met with among our current experiences. We are daily obliged to witness fresh atrocities as ethnic and racial hatreds seek to express themselves in the annihilation of their proponents' enemies—all of them—and as nations decimate themselves, breaking up into ever smaller and more fractious units; as terrorists of every stripe blow up people and buildings in an effort to protect their own and the rights of their "un-born"; as multinational interests devise more advanced forms of exploiting labor and crushing resistance; and on and on. If Enlightenment philosophy's "wild fantasy" of "moral improvement" and universal humanity, of the fostering and protection of human rights, progress, universality is everywhere ridiculed, if the whole aureola of concepts surrounding that of will is tarnished, this is because— some would say—these concepts are responsible for bringing about the very di-sasters they pretended to ward off. In the last two centuries will has revealed itself to be free to will its own enslavement to fascist heroes and to "just" causes (such as freedom, humanity, human rights) that have demanded the torture and execu-tion of those who opposed them. And things keep going from bad to worse.

It would seem to be necessary, then, to take another look at the notions of will, progress, freedom, and universal rights that emerged in tandem with the notion of radical evil. By way of doing this, the first thing to be considered is the often forwarded proposal that Kant could not face squarely his own discovery of the radicality of evil; he could not admit that it ultimately extends beyond the corruption of all our moral maxims (the imperatives that command us to act disinterestedly, for the good)—which is what he conceded—to a corruption of the will itself. That is, some critics have claimed that if we pursue Kant's thinking where it refuses to go, we will find that radical evil is worse than he was prepared to admit, that it is, in fact, *diabolical* or *absolute*.[3] By this they mean that will is capable not simply of opposing the moral law, but of making this opposition the very motive of our actions. If this were so, we would be capable of doing evil simply for the sake of doing evil, not merely for the sake of some profit to ourselves. Kant firmly and expressly denied to man this decidedly *Romantic* capability. One such denial is expressed in the following way: "Man (even the most wicked) does not, under any maxim whatsoever, repudiate the moral law in the manner of a rebel (renouncing obedience to it)" (31). Some assume, however, that the horror Kant felt at such a possibility caused him to retreat into simple and questionable reassertions of the "fact" of will; they treat his insistence on the essential *goodness* of will as merely a defensive gesture designed to protect him from the shuddering thought of a diabolical will or a malign reason that aimed at pure destruction. This implies, of course, that after his confrontation with evil, Kant's belief in human perfectibility and the goodness of will was maintained in blatant contradiction with his own arguments.

I will propose, however, that the best way to understand the status of Kant's belief in the essential goodness of will is not to begin by looking askance at the seeming contumaciousness of his claim regarding its self-evidence, but by pausing to reflect on the obstinacy of his assertions regarding the self-evidence of evil. As I have been suggesting, this is what is really odd and not merely because it seems to be out of step with the newfound optimism of the philosophical age whose figurehead he was and out of line with the cherished convictions he held in common with educators that the world forges in a *positive* direction, from bad to better. When Kant immediately concedes that moral goodness cannot be deduced from experience, which only provides proof of the *badness* of man, we have to wonder at the readiness with which he accepts the fact of our wickedness.

We go only partway to understanding what he is up to when we note that in *Religion within* . . . , Kant's purpose is to contest previous accounts of evil, which could grasp it only it as a negative phenomenon. In his earlier writings, even Kant held to the long-standing religious or metaphysical view that considered evil to be nothing in itself, but merely the *lack* or deficit of something.[4] In this view, disease, disaster, political and social injustice, suffering of every sort were treated either as illusions fomented by the limitations of our merely mortal understanding, or as actual but temporary conditions attributable to the limitations of human will by earthly passions or by human freedom through original sin. By imputing evil to mortal defect or privation, as that which interfered with the full appearance of the Good, the various solutions to the problem of evil were designed to leave both the Good and God unscathed, and thus, ultimately, justified.

But in *Religion within . . .* , evil no longer has only this shadowy, insubstantial existence; it no longer has less reality than good does. Instead evil appears as a positive fact, firmly rooted in reality. At this point it ceases to be a religious or metaphysical problem and becomes, for the first time, a political, moral, and pedagogical problem. This conceptual "revolution" is brought about by detaching evil from human *finitude* (conceived as simply the limitations imposed by our mortal nature) and attaching it to human *freedom* (or: to our "immortal" aspirations). Kant's underlying question is historically posed. He does not ask himself how evil is possible; he asks, rather, how evil is possible given the fact of freedom. He wants to understand how it happened that men who had just recently won their freedom, who no longer needed to bow to external pressures, chose to calculate in terms of these pressures, that is, chose to act immorally. That is to say, Kant sees evil as uniquely the product of a free humanity, and it is this that is new in his thought.

But once having made the point that Kant's innovation was to link evil to human freedom, we are forced to acknowledge that the evidence of evil is not as simple as the constant consensual complaints against it would imply. For if evil is defined as a positive act freely carried out, then empirical evidence alone is no longer sufficient to identify it. We can only conclude that an act is evil on the basis of an *unobservable* condition: that it was governed by the free adoption of a bad maxim. Before Kant, it was possible to conceive the battle between good and evil as taking place between will and sensuous motives. It was thought that our mortal nature made us susceptible to worldly temptations that promised us pleasure and flattered our pride, and that our will, or moral nature, provided us with the only power we had to combat these temptations. One acted for ill out of a weakness or deficiency of will whose default allowed external, sensible incentives to control one's actions. Kant argued, however, that no external incentive, no pure animal interest, could in and of itself—that is, could in the absence of will—govern the actions of men. Will does not combat sensuous motives; it determines the rules of our actions. The battle between good and evil is thus redefined as taking place between the adoption of two possible types of rules: good or bad; disinterested (that is, based only on moral law) or self-interested (based on self-regard). If we act badly, out of self-interest, this is because we have *chosen* to be influenced by external concerns, we have incorporated a particular pathological desire into a maxim, we have allowed this desire rather than the moral law to become the motive of our action. In Lacanian terms, we must always desire to be lured by a particular desire. In the absence of this second-level desire to desire, we would be completely indifferent to even the most highly prized object.

One of the consequences of this redefinition of evil is that it burdens us with full responsibility for our actions; we are no longer able to exonerate ourselves by claiming to be victims of our passions and thus of external circumstances. Lately, we have been taught to refuse this position as politically naive, since it seems to isolate and elevate us above the entire set of our social circumstances, to disregard our embeddedness in historical time. Yet this dismissive reading of the Kantian position has not only sacrificed the astuteness of its historical insights, it has also stoked the fires of our modern misanthropy.

To counter this historicist prejudice and restore Kant's argument to its proper political power, one needs first of all to note the profound dissymmetry in the outcome of the moral battle, as Kant describes it. Rather than weighting things toward the triumph of the autonomous will over a selfish investment in external circumstances, as critics of his supposed naivete might lead one to suspect, he surprises us by observing *only* a bad outcome. Evil self-interest trumps moral righteousness every time, as the evidence inescapably shows. What Kant's rigorism forces us to confront is not simply the occasional or partial inmixing of self-interested and purely moral motives, but the very subordination of moral, universal law to the imperatives of self-regard. He locates in man a profound malignity that causes him to be bad even when he is good; that is, even as he heeds the moral law, he does so, according to Kant, for self-interested reasons. If we perform some virtuous act, it is to impress others with our virtue; if we decline to tell a lie, it is because we are afraid we might be caught in it, and so on. Moreover, Kant argues, this is not simply true of some of us, or some of the time, but is universally true of all of us, without exception. "The ultimate subjective ground of all maxims . . . is entwined with and, as it were, rooted in humanity itself" (27–28). Radical evil, "the foul taint of our race" (34), is everywhere and always evident in the fact that man devotes his will to the pursuit of egoistic gain. Far from "transcending" the network of his social circumstances, he enmires himself in them, harmonizes with his social surroundings by seeking his own desire in the desire of others, his value in their admiring or admonishing eyes.

In order to mock this propensity of man, Kant had, in the *Critique of Practical Reason,* quoted a satirical poem in which two halves of a couple each wish for the ruin of the other. The sentiment and phrasing of this poem recalls Francis I's account of his battle against the Emperor Charles V: "Oh marvelous harmony; what I want, he wants, too. What my brother Charles wants (Milan), I want, too." There is no mistaking this sentiment, for it is the common motif of all-out and perpetual war that initiates modern struggles for "pure prestige," in which individual subjects and nations seek the absolute elimination of their rivals. Yet what has been obscured by contemporary thought is the fact that this relativization of our desire is no less an incitement to war when we decide not, as in the case of Francis I, to define our wants as the *same* as our brother's, but as irreducibly *different* from his. The celebration of the plurality of cultures and hence the relativity of our desires, is, in Kant's terms, no less an indication of the wickedness and corruption of the human heart than is the coveting of all our brother holds dear. That is, "to each his own desire" is no less dangerous a sentiment than "what I want, he wants, too." For cultural relativists also adopt a heteronomous definition of desire, which supposes it to be determined by the desires of other members of one's own culture. Relativism simply foregrounds the banal truth of every such heteronomous definition of desire: it inevitably encounters an obstacle in the form of another who refuses to prize what we value, who refuses to recognize our worth. These two seemingly opposed positions are also similar in that they both negate the possibility of an autonomous will—one that is not dependent on others—and of ethics itself, insofar as they make what is historically present and true the sole standard of what should be and thus dissolve "ought" in the medium of a historical "is."

GUILT

But how can we, from a Kantian position, condemn historicism's heteronomous definition of will and desire when Kant himself seems to be incapable of safeguarding his own notion of autonomy? Doesn't the concept of radical evil represent the collapse of the very distinction between an autonomous and heteronomous will? Isn't "the foul taint of our race" precisely the fact that our will *cannot* determine itself by itself, but must instead seek motivation in some extraneous content, that desire must always have a pathological incentive?

To be honest, these are not the only questions Kant's position raises at this point. My own description of the dissymmetry between good and bad outcomes blundered through an aporia in Kant's thought without bothering to expose it. You will remember that his fundamental argument, that the principle of evil is not to be found in man's animal or sensible nature, is what obliged Kant to discredit simple observation as evidence of moral wrongdoing. To condemn an act as bad, one has to conclude that it was performed in accordance with a bad maxim; and to reach this conclusion, one would have to look beyond outer appearances to fathom the depths of another's or one's own heart. And yet, as Kant himself insists, this is impossible; one cannot with certainty acquire "knowledge of the basis of [others'] maxims . . . or of their purity" (57). If freedom shields the human heart from observation, makes us inscrutable, it would seem that what Kant *should* have argued is that we can never know whether a particular act is guided by a good or bad maxim. But, as we have seen, he concludes instead that all our maxims are bad, and he condemns all our acts as "*always* . . . defective . . . *always* inadequate" (60; Kant's emphasis). How does one account for the harshness of his judgment, the certainty with which he regards the fact of evil? What makes Kant so sure not only that we always *transgress* the moral law, but also that we are conscious of these transgressions and that we *loathe* them? For, as I have already noted, in distinguishing radical from diabolical evil, Kant argues that the latter is impossible for man, who never elevates his transgression into a universal law, but rather regards his own act as a culpable and loathsome exception to it.

This inexplicable profession of certainty in a place where we expected uncertainty has a definite resonance for readers of Freud, who will discern similarities between the philosopher's argument and the psychoanalyst's description of the superego. Freud, too, regarded moral conscience as "sure of itself," as requiring no confirmation and no justification for the condemnation it heaps on us. A sense of guilt, he says, is "as self-evident as its origins are unknown."[5] Common to Freud and Kant is the unexpected assertion not only that moral conscience is always certain, but that it is, moreover, certain of only one thing: its guilt. And in the arguments of both, this guilty conscience seems to have been allowed to usurp the entire territory of moral action in that it condemns *all* our acts as bad, even and especially those performed by the most virtuous among us. Saving his strongest denunciations for those acts that outwardly appear to be the most moral, Kant responds exactly like Freud's superego, which is most remorseless in its condemnation of precisely those who are the most conscientious about fulfilling their moral duty.

Why should this be so—why would the morally conscientious be subject to the fiercest condemnation? To clarify what is at issue here, let us examine a statement I just made: moral conscience is certain of only one thing, its *guilt*. Is this actually true? Doesn't Kant—and Freud, for that matter—say that what moral conscience is certain of—can neither mistake or escape—is the clear and imperative voice of conscience that bids us obey the *moral law*? Yes, but there is no contradiction here. When Kant says, for example, that "there is no man so depraved but that he feels upon transgressing the internal law a resistance within himself and an abhorrence of himself" (31), he is not arguing that man is conscious of two separate and opposing phenomena: the moral law and its infraction. Rather, he is arguing that our only consciousness of the law is our consciousness of our transgression of it. Our guilt is all we know of the law. This is how Gilles Deleuze, for example, describes Kant's innovation in the conception of moral law: "Kant, by establishing that THE LAW as an ultimate ground or principle, added an essential dimension to modern thought: the object of the law is by definition unknowable and elusive. . . . Clearly THE LAW, as defined by its pure form, without substance or object of any determination whatsoever, is such that no one knows nor can know what it is. It operates without making itself known. It defines a realm of transgression where one is already guilty, and where one oversteps the bounds without knowing what they are."[6] The moral law is, in Kant, purely formal, empty of content; and the voice of conscience, while indubitable, utters neither prescription nor proscription; it says *nothing* to us because it speaks to us in our singularity, as free and autonomous subjects. Addressed to us alone, the voice is that which cannot be exhausted in any phenomenalized language. For, whatever message is imparted completely by language is *transmissible* to others.

And addressed to us as free, yet finite subjects (affected by sensibility), the voice of conscience reveals not only the autonomy of our will—the fact that we can freely determine our actions without regard to creature interests—but also that we are free to choose *whether* to be free or to bow to these interests. As is well known, Kant indicates this double aspect of human will by using two words for it: *Wille*, when he refers to its legislative capacity, and *Willkür*, to refer to the choice of freedom it gives itself. It would be a mistake, however, to hypostatize this distinction by speaking of two different kinds of will. The function of the distinction is to expose the self-limiting nature of human will, the internal impediment that divides it from itself. This internal noncoincidence of human will with itself prevents man from identifying in any straightforward way with his own autonomy. Our moral experience reveals to us not our freedom so much as our failure to be sufficiently free; or, better, our capacity for freedom is suggested to us only through our moral chastisements. Reversing the historicist error—which completely absorbs "ought" into "is," effectively eliminating the former—Kant absorbs "is" (the nature of human will, which is to be free) into "ought." The only way we know that we *can* act freely—that is, that we *are* free—is through the voice of conscience, which tells us that we *ought* to free ourselves from our slavery to external motives. In Lacan's translation, the status of the subject becomes, with Kant, ethical; the subject can be supposed only as capable of subjectification. The Kantian theses regarding the impossibility of identifying ourselves with our freedom and the emptiness of the moral law together seem to suggest that the law makes itself known only in the negative experience of guilt, of not being up to the task of our freedom.

The liberal reading of Kant—which identifies man directly with his freedom and with an unalienated, undivided will—apparently ignores all the textual evidence of the will's internal division in order to fabricate a voluntarist version of his philosophy. But if I do not agree with those who read in Kant's refusal to grant man a *devilish will* a lack of intellectual nerve, this is because I do not believe this refusal condemns to perpetual failure the subject's attempts to realize her moral vocation, that it makes it inconceivable that one could ever become a "good enough" moral subject. I take the denial of diabolical evil to be a dismissal of voluntarism, not as a dismissal of the capacity of the subject to act in such a way as to destroy the very principle on which she is founded. There is a difference, I am arguing, between the principle of one's foundation and the moral law; only the latter resists annihilation. Let us remember that Kant is attempting to make room for a religious disposition that could exist within the horizon of reason, which he takes as having no beyond. There is no other principle—no God, for example—that opposes reason, manipulates it, or guarantees its validity from without. Reason alone must account for the possibility of a certain religiosity capable of surviving in the modern period. As a principle of reason, the moral law similarly admits of no outside. It cannot be opposed by some God, Devil, or Rebel who stands outside it, who would represent a principle of anti-reason or a diabolical will.

Numerous critics have claimed that Kant's moral aversion to the idea of diabolical evil is the same as the aversion he expresses in *The Metaphysics of Morals* toward the idea of a formal trial and execution of Louis XVI. It is not to the simple murder of the king that he objects, but to the idea, which strikes him as inexplicable, of the law's overseeing its own destruction. As long as the murderous deed aims at the man, Kant has no moral problem with it; it is only when regicide aims, through legal procedures, at the principle or rule of law this man represents that Kant's outrage is aroused. In both cases, regicide and diabolical evil, Kant stands opposed to the law's destruction of itself, his critics avow, and this is because he has trouble conceiving a successful moral act that could rise to the level of its duty and overthrow the law.

My point is that these two cases are not equatable. It is only because Kant takes the position that nothing acts on or opposes the moral law from its exterior (there is no diabolical will, in short) that he must (and is thus wrong not to) accept the idea of state suicide through the legal murder of the king as a true ethical act. Acts of state or subjective suicide, that is, of self-destruction, require not that the subject rise above the law of its own foundation, but that she operate on the same level as this law by setting it against itself and thus destroying it from within. The very condition wherein the subject is able to turn against itself and destroy itself is created by disallowing the possibility of diabolical evil. Had he admitted the possibility of a devilish will exterior to (good) will, Kant would have had to maintain that one is always absolutely good or absolutely evil, guided by the principle of good or evil that is one's nature. He argues instead that will can only be good. But to be good here means something different, not to be guided by the principle of one's being, but to have a capacity for perfectibility, to be capable of divorcing oneself from one's own "lawful" position.

LAW AND PUNISHMENT

Because the moral law is empty, does not utter a determinate imperative, ignorance of the law becomes a problem. How do we know whether we have complied with it or not if we do not know what it is? And how do we defend ourselves against such a law if ignorance of it cannot count as an excuse, simply because it is unconditional? This is the territory explored by Kafka, as Deleuze points out. Given that the law itself cannot be put on stage, Kafka takes the approach of phenomenalizing the law in "the extreme specificity of punishments" incurred by its transgression. The law disappears, becomes void, only to invoke scenes of totalitarian bureaucratic terror in which unwitting citizens are charged with transgressions against vague and obscure laws without being allowed either to confront their accusers or clarify the nature of their crimes. This is close to Foucault's picture of panoptic power, in which the law withdraws only to make itself manifest in the prisoners whom it exposes and defines by their deviations from some supposed norm, by their faults and failures, their general subjection to regimes of scrutiny and punishment. The implication, once again, is that Enlightenment notions of moral law, freedom, and will created the inevitable conditions for a voluntary, yet infrangible, servitude to an incomprehensible law.

How, despite his privileging of guilt as the abiding core of moral experience, does Kant escape this picture? And, to return to an earlier point, how does the guilty subject Kant constructs avoid falling prey to the escalating and unending punishments of the superego, so memorably described by Freud? Kant makes a distinction between *guilt* which he sees as infinite (our transgressions of the law being endless), and *punishment,* which need not be infinite (66). Through this distinction he explicitly counsels us on how to *escape* the cruel tortures of the superego or, as he refers to this instance: "the accuser within us, [which is] more likely to propose a judgment of condemnation" (70). "More likely than who or what?" we can't help asking. Is there another judge to whom we can appeal? Kant's warning comes as a surprise. Since the autonomy of the subject depends on his or her refusal to cede moral decisions to an *external judge,* we might have expected this *internal accuser* to be hailed as the instance of judgment on which the subject ought to rely. But Kant says "no"; this judge like the external one is also to be mistrusted. On what basis does a dismissal of these intimate accusations become conceivable; how is it possible to avoid the paradoxical cycle of moral conscientiousness, guilt, and punishment that results from listening to the moral law within us?

To answer these questions, it will be helpful to understand first how the paradoxical logic of the superego *does* follow (though not, as I will argue, unavoidably) from the notions of the *autonomous subject* and the *empty moral law.* For it cannot be doubted that a kind of servitude has historically been consequent on these notions. If Kant's definition of a positive or radical evil has so far accorded very little with our intuitive sense of what it means to speak of *modern evil,* to assert that an unprecedented wickedness has been introduced into the world, here we finally arrive on more familiar ground. We come face to face with the colonialist taste for empire, the Nazi lust for genocide, and casuistry of the bloodiest kind. For, if these modern phenomena do have their source directly in the perversion of our maxims (in radical evil) and in the experience of guilt that accompanies this perversion, they are not evidence that the fate of man is sealed, that he is to be considered as base or unavoidably evil.

Subordinating the moral law to laws of self-interest, we deliver ourselves to our animal interests and to the principles of predation that govern them. Yet, if Kant is correct, if as humans we freely choose to obey our sensible inclinations, then some evidence of our freedom, or of our capacity to resist these inclinations, must betray itself in our actions. If, despite the constancy of our choice of evil or the inextirpableness of our self-regard, we rightfully believe ourselves to be free and thus capable of moral action, then we should expect to find some trace of a surplus of existence beyond our mortality in our acts, which would thereby demonstrate their irreducibility to mere animal behavior.

Salò (1975), Pier Paolo Pasolini's film about Italian fascism, provides some clues as to where one might look for this surplus. In one sequence, that of the "most beautiful ass" contest, the libertines survey a sea of bare bottoms in order to choose the one most pleasing to them. The monotonous anonymity (to our eyes, at least) of row on row of this single, exposed body part helps to establish the parallel Pasolini wants to draw between these sadistic sodomites and Italy's fascist leaders. For these nude, anonymous, and vulnerable-looking bodies recall to mind prisoners in concentration camps, except for the fact that those disposable bodies were always half-starved or dead and rotting. The comely, young bodies in the film are well fed, well formed, and in some fantasmatic sense indestructible; in this scene, for example, they are lit with a kind of silver-screen glow. As the contest proceeds, two of the philosophically inclined libertines conduct a short disquisition on the very subject of this comparison between themselves and Nazi executioners. The first libertine solemnly opines: "The act of the sodomite is the most absolute in the mortality it implies for the human race." To which the second answers, "There's something still more monstrous: the act of the executioner." "True, but the sodomite's act can be repeated thousands of times," the first rejoins. The second will not be outdone: "A way can be found to repeat the executioner's." He need not specify what the executioner's way entails; we know that it is accomplished through the execution of another victim, and another, and another, ad infinitum. Six million and more. Where the allies and cohorts of Hitler pursued the ever receding "final solution" by exterminating an infinite series of victims, the sadistic libertine endlessly tortures the same victim, who miraculously refuses to die or even display on his beautiful body the signs of torture. "Don't you know," one libertine asks the boy with the most beautiful ass, "that we'd want to kill you a thousand times to the limits of eternity, if eternity has any?" It does not, neither for the sadistic sodomite nor for the Nazi and fascist executioners, at least not one that is reachable by them.

For libertine and executioner alike, what Kant refers to in his text as the "totality of this series of approximations carried on without end" (60) always lies asymptotically beyond their grasp; though the severity of the tortures escalates, the act of torture remains "defective," "inadequate," unable to complete itself through the extraction of a sufficient dose of pain. In each case, the futility of the

Figure 5.1 Pier Paolo Pasolini, *Salò—The 120 Days of Sodom* (1975). Courtesy The Museum of Modern Art (N.Y.)/
Film Stills Archive.

torturer's act is attributable to the resistance of the victim. The body of the libertine's victim resists through the persistence of its beautiful form, which escapes any deformation. The body of the executioner's victims, on the other hand, resist through their very formlessness. Philippe Lacoue-Labarthe and Jean-Luc Nancy, in an essay entitled "The Nazi Myth," uncover the fantasy of the Jew constructed by National Socialism, according to which "The Jew has no *Seelengestalt,* therefore no *Rassengestalt:* his form is formless. He is the man of the universal abstract, as opposed to the man of singular, concrete identity. Thus Rosenberg takes care to point out that the Jew is not the antipode of the German, but his contradiction, by which he no doubt very clumsily means to say that the Jew is not an opposite *type,* but the very absence of type, a danger present in all bastardizations, which are all parasitic."[7] Having no form, culture, or nation of his own, parasitic on that of others, the Jew mimics or plagiarizes the identity of those around him and in this way escapes detection. One can thus never be sure one has tracked down the last one. The extermination of the Jewish race then fantasmatically presents itself as a task that stretches out through a limitless eternity, and the "Jewish plot" presents itself not only as secret but as eternal as well, as without beginning or end. But if the victims are indestructible, the wills of their torturers are no less so; they seem to toughen, to assert themselves more insistently, in their attempts to triumph over such impossible obstacles.

Once again, the nagging question arises: is *this* the will Kant was so intent on defending? I think we can see now not only that it is not, but why it is not. As I have already pointed out, Kant describes human will as alienated from itself by an *internal* fracture. But the executioner experiences this impediment to his will as coming from the victim's resistance; only an enemy Other opposes the torturer's unalienated will, checking its otherwise absolute power. Freud used the term *projection* to describe the mechanism by which what is internal to the subject comes to be viewed as imposed from outside, but he was not satisfied that the term adequately described all that was involved in this process. I will therefore suggest another term with which to explain the response to *radical evil*—or the internal fracture of human will—that produces *modern evil.*

That which is missing from the notion of *projection* is supplied, I will argue, by the notion of *subreption.* Through subreption, a supersensible idea, that is, one that can never be experienced, is falsely represented as if it were a possible object of experience. One of the points preached by Kant is that human freedom and immortality are supersensible ideas. To abbreviate this argument, at least as it has appeared thus far: we have so little experience of our freedom that the only experi-ence that allows us to suppose it exists may be our experience of guilt. It is possible, however, to propose a *sensible* definition of human freedom and the immortality of the soul, not in Kant's terms, of course, but in others. It would seem that the de-nial of supersensible ideas would cause the subject to become totally assimilated to its mortality, reduced to his natural unfreedom and finitude. But this is not what happens; as we said, the fact that the subject is free reveals itself in a certain surplus: of fantasy. That is to say, although through subreption the subject is assimilated to its concrete, historically defined particularities (the "blood and soil" of Na-tional Socialism, for example), its freedom and immortality return in the fantasy of progress to infinity (to which National Socialists were not the only ones wholly to commit themselves). Within this fantasy, subjective finitude and failure are effaced by the promises of progress. Death is indefinitely postponed and the temporary checks on the power of human will are denied any ultimate victory. It should be easy to see how this fantasmatic notion of infinite progress sustains the individual fantasies of both the sadistic libertines and the executioners, who hold onto a sensible definition of themselves without surrendering their freedom or immortality. Their fantasies allow them to dream of what Kant calls the "enjoy-ment of ever-increasing pleasures" and a "freedom from evils" (61).

GRACE

The above argument only reintroduces a question previously posed. How can Kant, one of the prime proponents of progress and the perfectibility of man, come to stand for the very opposition to them? This question can confound us only if our notion of progress is limited to that infinite progress promoted by nineteenth-century science. But infinite progress is *not* the one for which Kant reserved his approbation, as *Religion within . . .* makes clear. What causes his disdain rather for that conception of progress is undoubtedly the fact that it is produced through subreption. This is how he states his objection: "conduct itself [defined] as a continual and endless advance from a deficient to a better good, ever remains defective" (60). Why is this so? He has given his answers a few lines earlier: be-cause "the distance separating the good which we ought to effect in ourselves from the evil whence we advance is infinite, and the act itself, of conforming our course of life to . . . the law, is impossible of execution in any given time." In other words, whatever dreams the fantasy of infinite progress encourages, the fact re-mains that its definition of the subject as "ever only a *becoming*" (my emphasis) assimilates us to "our failure ever wholly to be what we have in mind to become" (61, fn.). The notion of progress to infinity anchors us to our mortality, to a temporality that ensures our failure from moment to moment, to an infinity of failure, therefore, and an infinity of punishments.

When Kant urges us to turn a deaf ear to the "accuser within us," who would pronounce too severe a verdict, he is attempting to circumvent the snare that this belief in progress to infinity represented and in which so many around him were being caught up. But the connection between this particular belief and this severe judgment is perhaps not as clear in Kant as it might be; it awaits Freud and psychoanalysis to elucidate their relation. I have already made the point that the internal judge to which Kant refers is strictly equivalent to the superego that, as Freud describes it, heaps blame in proportion to the diligence of our moral efforts, demands greater sacrifices the more we sacrifice. It is only by placing Freud's description alongside Kant's warnings against our modern faith in infinite progress that we begin to see how the paradoxes of the superego spelled out in *Civilization and Its Discontents* relate to those other famous paradoxes of Zeno. Zeno's paradoxes were designed specifically to ridicule the philosophers of Becoming, the paradoxes of the superego exposed by Freud demonstrate that the more we define ourselves as *mere becoming,* the more we place ourselves in the service of a cruel and punishing law of sacrifice, or, as Lacan says, a "dark God": "There is something profoundly masked in the critique of the history that we have experienced. This, re-enacting the most monstrous and supposedly superseded forms of the holocaust, is the drama of Nazism . . . —which only goes to show that the offering to obscure gods of an object of sacrifice is something to which few subjects can resist succumbing, as if under some monstrous spell. . . . [T]he sacrifice signifies that, in the object of our desires, we try to find evidence for the presence of the desire of this Other that I call here *the dark God.*"[8] Lacan's suggestion is that enslavement to this cruel law of sacrifice is *not* equivalent to a heeding of the moral law follows Kant's lead.

That the voice of conscience is heard to demand the sacrifice of enjoyment indicates the extent to which we have subscribed to the historical fantasy of infinite progress, which turns out in Kant's reading to be nothing but a fantasy of infinite deferral. While on the one hand, this fantasy seems to allow us infinitely to defer our own death, on the other hand, experience has shown, it binds us to death by reducing life to the struggle against it. And although the fantasy seems to hold out a promise of infinite pleasure, it in fact requires us always to tithe our pleasure to this promise. In short, the historical subreption that attempted to re-define our ethical vocation as the pursuit of happiness and the cherishing of well-being, or physical life, has brought us the most unimaginable horrors and an undeniable "contempt for life."[9] The eugenic schemes of National Socialism are only the most obvious display of the paradoxical effects of the subreption that has placed us in the thrall of our internal judge.

Yet it would appear that Kant attempts to save us from one harsh judge only to deliver us to another, for he suddenly switches gears and begins speaking of the necessity of submitting ourselves to a second or, more specifically, a final judge. A reference to a final judgment would seem to abort the very possibility of thinking of the freedom of will or the perfectibility of man and therefore to un-dermine Kant's entire project. For, in fact, Kant builds his moral theory on a firm opposition to finalism. A moral or free act is one that is not directed by any end; it is absolutely unconditioned and does good only for the sake of the good it defines through its own realization. Yet Kant also argues that although no end can serve as the *basis* of a free act, it is unreasonable to think that no consequences is-sue from our act, that there is no terminus of our actions. This distinction, noted and discussed above in chapter I, spares reason the absurdity of attempting to construct an ethics that would be indifferent to the consequences issuing from the realization of our acts. In more polemical terms, Kant is not the dupe of that "poststructuralist" or "deconstructionist" turn in ethics which endeavors to dis-courage every utopian idea on the grounds that any practical action is by its very nature compromised. If an act can be considered something other than mere ran-dom or automatic behavior, it must be executed with purpose and must result in some end. To be suspicious of all purposes and all ends is, in the final anal-ysis, to proscribe action as itself unethical. Kant quickly dismisses this position as incoherent.

If Kant advises us then to submit ourselves to a final judge rather than to the condemnation of the inner accuser who finds all our acts defective, it is pre-cisely in order to make room for free, purposeful action. For Kant, this "last judgment" stands in direct opposition to the notion of infinite progress, which serves to belittle all our accomplishments. He does not ask us to await the hand-ing down of this final judgment in some undisclosed future, some ever-deferred moment anon. Nor does he ask us to renounce indefinitely any enjoyment or ac-tion until this ever-deferred moment arrives. He describes us, instead, as the beneficiaries of this judgment *now,* in the present, for it comes as a gift, before any due date, without being earned. It does not depend on the scrupulousness with which we renounce pleasure nor the diligence with which we work to secure a "better tomorrow." The final judgment arrives in haste, prematurely, as a pure gift of grace. It is as if everything up until this point in *Religion within . . .* had been written from the perspective of one submitted to the law of the superego, the inner accuser, and now, suddenly, a new perspective had opened up. The defectiveness of all our actions—never quite good enough, uncompromised enough, to allow us to exonerate ourselves from the charge that we are inescapably, radically evil— all our inadequacies are not negated so much as made up for by this bonus, which comes as from out of the blue. Although from moment to moment we seem to be ill willed, we are all at once, through the "miraculous" intercession of this final judgment, this "surplus . . . over the profit of [our] good works," graced with a "good disposition," or moral nature, "which stands in the place of the totality of this series of approximations carried out without end; [and] makes up for [our] failure . . . ever wholly to be able to be what we have in mind to become" (60, fn.) After all the talk of the incurable perversity in the heart of man, the evil at the core of our nature, Kant now credits us with a moral nature that we can never deserve, and he credits it to us posthaste, "exactly as if we were already in possession of it," even as we are: radically evil (70). This bounty is ours despite ourselves.

Before dismissing this argument as theological vacuousness, it would be helpful to reconsider the rise, throughout the world, of religious fundamentalism. Although this phenomenon is commonly viewed as a reaction *against* modernity, such that the electronic aggression and media savoir-faire of this growing fringe are seen as somehow incompatible with its fundamentalist message, there is in fact no lack of sympathy between a certain belief in progress and religious dogmatism. The more we hold onto a certain notion of scientific progress, the more we secure the Kingdom of Heaven. Having no *naural* limit, in the sense that it is procedurally obliged to seek the causes of causes, the conditions of conditions, without end, reason/science is structurally predisposed to the fantasy of infinite progress and thus disciplinarily devoted to its own failure. The ratcheting-up of self-punishments follows on this. Ironically, then, the attempt to seize life from the perspective of our sensible existence uproots us from life and leads to an indefinite postponement of gratification. It makes self-contempt the only *rational* result of any self-estimate. In a world such as this, salvation can only be conceived as coming from *outside,* beyond reason—and so it increasingly is.

The convocation to a final judgment is designed to dismantle the cruel machinery that sustains such religious dogmatism, for this bonus comes to us not from some place beyond reason, but is rather the gift of reason itself. We are "by nature" moral beings because we are able to overturn our own "nature" through reason. Kant considered moral progress to be not a matter of an infinite, incremental advance from one generation to the next, the forwarding of an agenda defined by those who have come before us and whose aspirations we have inherited, but of that conversion by which an individual subject completely disbands her own sustaining fantasy or desutures herself from her most intimately held beliefs. For, what is grace in Kant's account if not a kind of special dispensation from the law, the superegoic law that binds us to the conditions in which we find ourselves, the circumstances we inherit and the obligations they hand down to fashion the future as an improved version of the past? It is only by the grace of Kant's notion of reason that we are able to disinherit the debts of our past, the heritage that constitutes our particularity.

It would be easy I suspect to denounce Kant's solution as specifically Christian and therefore limited. But just as the notion of radical evil cannot be reduced to that of original sin (despite what many, and not only Kant's contemporaries, may have thought), neither is grace reducible to the Christian idea of God's redeeming mercy. We are not saved in the eyes of the Lord nor saved from sin. The concept of grace does not speak to the question of our moral worth but to that of our moral capability. That is, the concept of grace that emerges from *Religion within . . .* does not unburden us of the imperative to act; it does not dismiss all our acts as inconsequential, inadequate to the saving of our "souls," which task would then remain dependent on the good grace of God. No, grace does not diminish *the act;* it condemns to fruitlessness only *action,* that frenetic type of work that labors to keep things going forward. Grace does not mean that nothing we can do saves us, only God can; it means rather that nothing can by itself determine our act. Or: grace does not save us from sin, it saves us from being caused from without, by our own empirical history.

Kant theorizes this grace, which is bestowed by a final judge, in terms that intersect with an argument Freud will make in *Moses and Monotheism.* This argument concerns the concept of Jewish election, that is, the idea that the Jews are the chosen people of God. This idea appears immediately as an indefensible instance of exceptionalism, but Freud enables us to regard it in a different light. What renders the Jewish belief in the favored status of the race puzzling, rather than automatically comprehensible, to Freud is the fact that it is joined to a belief in one God as the God of all. There are actually two puzzles here: (1) monotheism itself, because a belief in a universal God entails a "sacrifice of intimacy" with one's personal god, who has to be shared "with . . . foreigners"; and (2) the concept of election, which is joined to that of a universal God.[10] It is perhaps because he does not take for granted the notion of the universal that Freud is able to raise the question of its relation to an exception. This puzzlement leads him to discern two different relations between monotheism, or the universal, and the exception, the idea that one people is preferred by God. These differences constitute the distinction Freud draws between the first appearance of monotheism in ancient Egypt and Jewish monotheism.

Here is what Freud says: "In Egypt . . . monotheism grew up as a by-product of imperialism: God was a reflection of the Pharaoh who was the absolute ruler of a great world-empire. With the Jews, political conditions were highly unfavourable for the development from the idea of an exclusive national god to that of a universal ruler of the world. And where did this tiny and powerless nation find the arrogance to declare itself the favourite child of the great Lord?" (65). What is the difference between these two universal Gods, these two forms of monotheism? In Egypt, the God of all people was, we might say, "Pharaonic," that is, it possessed the features of the Pharaoh whose powers it reflected. What was at issue, then, was a *particularized universal*. The spread or progressive extension/universalization of the reign of this God obeyed the logic of imperialistic conquest, which is to say, those people who were gradually included in the "all the people of God" were those conquered or in principle conquerable by the Pharaoh. This type of monotheism, or universal, defined by a specific feature, let us say, "conquerable by the Pharaoh," implies its own exception: the Pharaoh and the original conquering nation that spread itself over or conquered the other nations. That is, the Pharaoh and his original nation are the defining condition of the universal rather than members of it; they could not be included within the universal without destroying it. In short, this universal depends on the mutual exclusion of conquerors and conquered.

The case of Jewish monotheism is entirely different. It is not formed from an exception, an exclusive national god, who then becomes a universal ruler. The universal is thus not particularized, it does not reflect the features of the Jews. It does not possess any other features, for that matter; it is completely without tincture, without character. There seem to be no criteria for belonging to the all that constitutes the people of this type of monotheism; no reason can be given for its formation. What Freud says is, "the problem of the origin of monotheism among the Jews would thus remain unsolved," yet this lack of origin should be accepted as the solution, not as the failure to find one. For, the all must originate out of nothing, or must not emerge from a reason external to it, if it is to avoid being particularized, without limit. But if the all of their monotheistic religion is truly without limit, then the chosenness of the Jews, their election by God, must constitute *an immanent exception,* an exception *within* and not *to* the all.

Let us return to the imperialism of Egyptian monotheism. This characterization is apt not only because the universal it implied reflected the grandiose power of the ruling nation, but also because it was driven to extend itself beyond its own limits, to continue to impose itself on external territories. This is to say that Egyptian monotheism defined itself in a significant way by its limits, which it constantly sought to make up for by extending itself. This acknowledges that this type of montheism was invaded by a primary and paradoxical incompleteness; it presented itself to itself as incompletely inclusive. The all of Jewish monotheism, on the other hand, seems to be invaded by a paradoxical surplus, the surplus of election: while everyone, without exception, without exclusion, can claim this God as his or her own, the Jews are favored among them. Significantly, this surplus affects the category of belonging, since the favored status indicates a surfeit of membership in the all. Everyone is a member, but the Jews are members "more" than the others, since they were elected to membership. Curiously, this surplus does not in any way limit or particularize the criteria for belonging; on the contrary, its only function seems to be to underscore the absence of criteria. Why do I say so? Because the election of the Jews does nothing but deselect their particular characteristics. They are not chosen for any specific qualities or history, except their ability to avoid being reduced to their miserable history or traits of indistinction: their smallness or powerlessness as a nation, the troubled history of their meanderings and travails. That Jews consider themselves favored only exposes their "arrogance" and "audacity," that is, their refusal to allow their history of suffering to define them.

This is the point, mentioned earlier, where Freud's theory intersects with Kant's concept of grace. For, Jewish election and the final judgment in *Religion within . . .* both rescue—or rather, allow the subjects graced by their gifts to rescue themselves from, or maintain a distance toward—the circumstances that surround them. One can never stress too often, however, a point that almost always gets lost: these gifts do not place their subjects outside history, but in the very middle of it, that is, at the point of the real, the opening from which history emerges. Jews defy their history, as Freud remarks, not by rising above it, but by "holding their own in commercial life and . . . making valuable contributions to every form of cultural activity" (91). Freud gradually came to argue that libidinal energy is split from the outset; while much of it is repressed, a small quota remains unrepressed. Though the "scar tissue" of repression blocks the path to the satisfaction of the drive, which must thus look for substitute satisfactions, that is, for satisfactions that refer to or translate repressed ideas, a quota of unrepressed libido operates according to no such strictures. It is pure surplus, pure gift. It can be used without prior conditions, without restriction, for the invention of new attachments to life.

I will close by restating my understanding of how grace functions in *Religion within*. . . . At first glance grace appears to enter the text on the wings of the phenomenon-noumenon distinction. In this case the argument would be: though from moment to moment we seem to be steeped in sin, radically evil, this is only the way things appear from the phenomenal point of view. Grace provides a noumenal perspective, a view from above, of our complete and not merely incomplete, temporally hindered being. What throws this explanation off balance, however, is the fact that the "noumenal perspective," the view from above, is that of our "inner accuser," the superegoic point of view that grace does not represent but, on the contrary, *disrupts*. It is from the perspective of this inner accuser that we seem always already to have inverted the hierarchy between pathological motives and moral law, always already to have obeyed the law for selfish reasons. Grace, however, "descends" on us when we descend from this position to settle ourselves in the finite order of time. At this moment, grace opens up a space in the temporal order itself where things are not yet decided. The subjective experience of this space is the experience of jouissance, of an undeserved, unexpected, and indeed unwanted pleasure that unsettles us from ourselves or, to use Kant's vocabulary, from the autonomous assumption of our disposition, our previous choices of maxims of action. The "spiritual" gift of grace, then, does not lift us out of our finite, bodily being, but "infinitizes" it, invades the body with a deregulating pleasure that awakens it from its corporeal torpor.

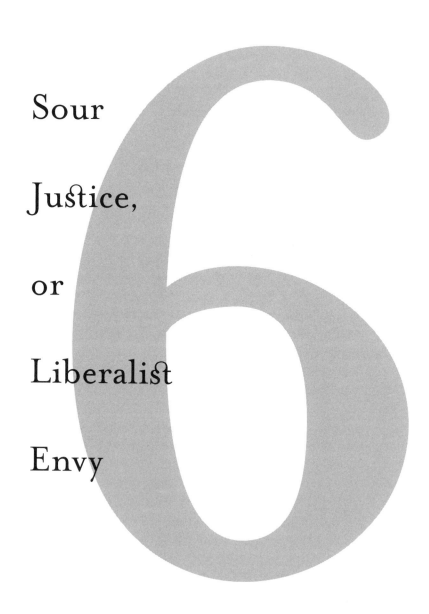

Sour

Justice,

or

Liberalist

Envy

Grant me, for the moment, the anodyne assumption that film noir is, among other things, a compendium of base human emotions, and you will be less surprised by my beginning this discussion of the religious and ethnic tensions that perturb relations in cities such as Jerusalem with a scene from one of the classics of the noir genre. My focus will be on one base emotion and the fundamental way in which it challenges liberal theories of community and justice, raising significant questions about the politics of civility and the "rights to the city." I have in mind the 1944 film, *Laura*, particularly that scene in which the voice-over narrator, Waldo Lydecker, discovers that Laura, the woman whom he has calculatedly transformed into his most admiring devotee, has begun spending her evenings with another man. As he peers up from the street at the drawn shade of her second-story window, Lydecker catches a glimpse of *two* silhouettes—not the lonely one he would have preferred to see. From this moment on he will not rest until he has utterly demolished the career of the man who casts the second silhouette, a painter named Jacoby.

The question before us is this: why does Lydecker set himself on this path of destruction, which will lead him to annihilate not only Jacoby, but also Laura, whom he will later shoot in the face with a shotgun at close range (or so he thinks)? The answer most ready to hand is that he longs for the sort of sexual involvement with Laura that is missing from his relation to her, but which Jacoby apparently enjoys. Nothing, however, could be further from the truth. That Lydecker feels only disgust for such sexual liaisons is unmistakable both from his own comportment toward Laura and from his frequent contemptuous remarks about the earthiness and obvious corporeality of her other suitors. We must take these expressions of disgust at face value, for Lydecker is definitely *not* jealous of Jacoby, he is envious of him. The next question is, of course: what's the difference? Crabb's *English Synonyms* offers this answer: "Jealousy fears to lose what it has; envy is pained at seeing another have that which it wants for itself."[1] Descriptively considered, this distinction isn't bad. Opposing "what it *has*" to "what it *wants*," the definition accurately grasps the fact that jealousy is grounded in the *possession* of a certain pleasure, whereas envy stems precisely from a *lack* of it. Yet one would be wrong to assume that envy's lack can be filled by the possession of that pleasure it is pained to see the other enjoying. As the dictionary entry goes on to remark, "All endeavors . . . to satisfy an envious man are fruitless." Why? Because what he wants and what he perceives as the other's enjoyment are not at all the same thing. And since the envious man does *not* want for himself what the other has, the attainment of that other, altogether foreign pleasure will never appease his desire.

It is no coincidence that the "two silhouettes on a shade," the object of Lydecker's perception, is a cliché. You will miss its meaning, however, if you ascribe this cliché to the film rather than to the character who beholds it; that is to say, it is Lydecker who is responsible for the hackneyed form his discovery takes. If this perception is neither immediate nor fresh, but filtered through a stock image, this is because Lydecker's envious look is not inspired by desire. And yet the window he regards from a cold, dark below is lit with a bright glow, as if a glint of the real shown from the imaginary scene, the sign no doubt of his certainty that the scene displays the image of a complete, closed-off contentment. The pleasure he observes taking place at a distance remains alien to him, turned in on itself. The look with which he beholds this—to him—complete, absolute, and yet incomprehensible pleasure has thus a malevolent potency; it is bitter.

As has been documented, "virtually all languages, ancient and modern," have a term for the "evil eye" that accompanies envy.[2] The feature that justifies this look's being given a distinct designation is its apparent intent to poison or pollute. While every other "mean and hungry look" —of anger, greed, or jealousy—remains focused on harm, concentrated on robbing the other of some coveted object, only the evil eye of envy seeks to steal enjoyment itself. In seeking to leave the other bereft of that which brings him pleasure, those other malicious looks would nevertheless leave the other's capacity for pleasure intact. Not so envy, which wants nothing so much as to spoil the very capacity for enjoyment. "The envious man sickens at the sight of enjoyment. He is easy only in the misery of others."[3]

In the famous judgment of Solomon, it is his discernment of the presence of an evil eye that allows the wise leader to unmask the "false mother." Having just lost her own precious, irreplaceable child, she is still far too bereaved to desire another. What she wants, then, as Solomon sees, is decidedly not the real mother's little "bundle of joy" (that this foul-smelling, puking little package could be the source of someone else's joy must, in actual fact, seem unfathomable to her), but the extinction of the other's maternal satisfaction. For this reason, splitting the child in two is not a compromise she is willing to accept, but the sort of ruination for which she longs.

It is well acknowledged that pleasure is a private matter: "to each his own," we say. But the incomprehensibility with which we encounter another's pleasure is not in itself the cause of our hostility. What must be added to this state of affairs for envy to arise is an obstacle that prevents the envious person from relishing his own pleasure. Some deficit of pleasure must be felt that spoils the pleasure that remains to him, makes it distasteful. When this happens, the deficit can never be made good, never be filled by anything in this world, and the envious person thus begins to regard with malevolence the idiotic passions of others. I have noted that it is the inconsolable loss of her child that initiates the bereaved mother's envy. Turning again to the film *Laura*, we find at its heart a loss that is similarly abysmal. According to the ordinary view, the film depicts a struggle between Lydecker, whose contentments are said to be purely intellectual, and MacPherson (one of Jacoby's successors), whose passions are more corporeal. But if the film were merely about a battle between two positive passions, Laura, the source of the other's enjoyment, would not have been the direct object of a shotgun blast. It is therefore necessary to suppose that although Lydecker does derive the only pleasure he allows himself from intellectual pursuits, this pleasure is never felt by him to be adequate to fill the loss that deracinates all his endeavors. This supposition is confirmed by the film itself, especially the final sequence.

At the outset I identified Lydecker as the voice-over narrator of the film. A question related to this role hangs suspended throughout the film: from where—from what point in the narrative—does he narrate the story that unfolds? The final sequence reopens the question as preparation, finally, to answering it. In this sequence, the location of the point of enunciation becomes a question with narrative consequences. As Laura in her bedroom listens to Lydecker's weekly radio address, she assumes he is in the radio studio and that she is thus at least temporarily safe from his aggressions. We, the audience, can see, however, what she will soon learn: through prerecording his voice has been separated from his body. While his voice is being transmitted from the studio, he is in the next room preparing to murder her. This revelation cues our attention to the critical separation of voice and body that will conclude the film. Shot by the police, Lydecker falls to the floor and with his dying breath utters a simple "Good-bye, Laura."

These are his last living words. But they are not his last words in the film. As the camera lingers on a sprung clock, we once again hear his voice, this time off-screen, speak the film's final line: "Good-bye, my love."

From where do these words come? Not from Lydecker, clearly, as he lies now dead on the floor. The final living words issued from the diegetic space of Laura's apartment and from the visibly wounded body of Lydecker, but these words emerge from elsewhere. The difference between the two spaces is audible in the lack of room tone in the second "good-bye." This suggests that the final line was, like Lydecker's radio address, recorded in a sound studio, not on the film set and thus not from the diegetic space the film creates. In narrative terms, we would locate the place of their enunciation on the other side of death, somewhere beyond the grave. In other words, the film does not close in the dream that is to us life on earth—I am recalling the words Lydecker recites on the radio, "They are not long, the days of wine and roses. Out of a misty dream our path emerges for awhile, then closes in a dream"—but on the far side of it.[4]

Laura is no horror film, and it would be unwise to try to make it into one by mistaking the import of its ultimate positioning of Lydecker's voice-over narration outside time (the sprung clock), outside the narrative space, beyond earthly life. By locating his enunciation beyond the grave, the film gives us insight not into the ontological character of its world, but into the psychological character of Lydecker. It is he who places himself—or, that which is most precious to him, what he most deeply wants—beyond earthly life and all the pleasures it can offer. He speaks and perceives the world as one who is dissatisfied with it, precisely because, by definition, it lacks and therefore cannot give him what he desires. Life for him is as insubstantial as a dream; what he wants is something more profound.

What about Laura? Does he want her? The answer is a complex "no." She is, for him, an idealization, which is to say, she represents not so much what he wants as its unavailability. She is a stand-in for that which is missing from the world and which he therefore cannot touch; she embodies not a positive good, a particular pleasure, but the distance that separates every good that is in reach from the absent one he longs to possess. This is manifest in the very opening line of the film, spoken by Lydecker, "I'll never forget the day Laura died." As the film reveals, however, Laura did *not* die on the day he so vividly recalls for us as the moment of her death. This *premature expression of* mourning betrays Lydecker's melancholic attitude toward Laura, as toward life in general. The melancholic mourns the structurally lost object by allowing it to cast a shadow on the living, which suffers therefore an untimely death. Here we touch on the structural truth of envy: it is always closely tied to the idealizations it both feeds on and feeds. For, envy's unhappiness is the very stuff from which idealizations are contrived. We might even venture the interpretation that the baffling opening sequence—which offers an *image* of MacPherson examining objects on display in Lydecker's apartment, while Lydecker sits, so far unseen, writing in his bathtub, his voice-over narrating the film—demonstrates that MacPherson himself and the other suitors before him are the literary creation of Lydecker, who invents a series of robust, athletic-looking enemies from a feeling of his own emaciated impotence. That is, Lydecker not only destroys his enemies with his pen, but invents them *in order to destroy them.*

Earlier, I justified my excursive reference to *Laura* by commenting that film noir is known above all for its dilation on the baseness of human emotions. These films formed part of a broader speculation on the urban topologies of adjacencies and the dark personal entanglements in which they increasingly issued. Noir films are about the city and the myriad ways in which life in it turns toxic. During the historical period of the genre's development, racial and ethnic tensions were just barely perceptible behind the smog, as one of its causes. The hard-boiled detective, the main protagonist of many of these films, might, for example, be forced to venture into a black neighborhood or jazz club, areas generally skirted by whites, in order to track down some lead. But these parts of town still formed the background; in the foreground of the detective's seedy but still socially acceptable office, the denizens of discounted, unimaginable neighborhoods would stream through one by one, quirky, in some way deformed, but never clearly racialized. It was as if they had been required, by some artistic rule, to doff such tell-tale traits at the detective's door as the price of entering. That this is exactly what was going on is also the surmise of later films of the period and of more recent revivals—think of *Kiss Me Deadly,* which is populated by aural grotesques, or *Blade Runner,* with its visual grotesques—in which the formerly doffed traits are returned to these characters. The gallery of rogues is exposed as a gallery of racial types. Identitarian references began to pile up as quickly as dead bodies.

ENVY AND JUSTICE: RAWLS

But if noir adumbrated envy as the fathomless and bitter source of social rivalries, social and political theorists did not pick up on the clue; they have given no serious consideration to this vice and its injurious contributions to social relations— except for John Rawls, whose benchmark book, *A Theory of Justice,* does indeed pause to examine the place of envy in social life.[5] Because the aim of Rawls's book is to propose, as the title indicates, a theory of the possibility of *justice,* envy—which stands in justice's way—is set aside at the beginning. A neo-Kantian, Rawls wants to locate the conditions of the possibility of justice in human reason and thus brackets those motives of self-interest—such as envy—that cause reason to swerve away from its proper destiny, which is by definition disinterested, rather than selfish. But he can avoid the topic of envy for only so long, since he cannot pretend to be unaware of a significant challenge to the legitimacy of his assumption that envy is a mere obstacle to justice. According to this challenge, articulated most forcefully by Freud, envy is not simply an impediment, but the very condition of our notion of justice.

Freud argues in *Group Psychology and the Analysis of the Ego* that the intensity of envy's hostility is so noxious that it threatens to harm even the one who envies, who thus calls for a truce in the form of a demand for justice and equality for all. That is, envy defends itself against its own invidiousness by transforming itself into group feeling. The esprit de corps cementing group relations is guaranteed by the following pledge: "No one must want to put himself forward, every one must be the same and have the same."[6] From this Freud draws the radical conclusion that "Social justice means that we deny ourselves many things so that others may have to do without them as well, or, what is the same thing, may not be able to ask for them. This demand for equality is the root of social conscience and the sense of duty."[7]

Freud's conclusion blasts at the foundations of the theory of justice Rawls lays out; he must, therefore, deal with it head on. How does he do so? First, he argues that the notion of equality Freud targets is different from the one he, Rawls, proposes: an equality that is "bound in the end to make everyone including the less advantaged worse off" (538) may be *one* kind of equality—specifically, the one implied by strict egalitarianism's insistence that all goods be equally distributed—but it cannot be accepted as a definition of equality, as such. Rawls believes he is protected from the charge that his theory of justice aspires to equality in Freud's sense because his theory respects "the plurality of distinct persons with separate systems of ends" (29), that is, he rejects utilitarianism's false notion that we all desire the same things and argues instead that individuals have—and have a right to have—different desires. As we will see presently, however, Rawls does finally allow one common desire to sneak back into his theory, and even to assume a primary place there.

Rawls begins by focusing, as Freud did, on the emergence of envy among siblings, in the nursery. He speculates that Freud may have inaccurately described what goes on in this ur-scene of envy; rather than the nonmoral feeling of envy, sibling rivalries may actually exemplify legitimate moral resentment about being unfairly denied one's due share of parental attention and affection. The siblings may vie with each other, not out of a feeling of impotence or a lack of self-confidence—the roots of envy, in Rawls's view—but out of a confident conviction that their claims to their parents' affection are equally valid, that is, out of feelings of fairness and self-worth. By redescribing the nursery scenario in this way, Rawls intends to distinguish Freud's notion of equality from the one at stake in his theory of justice and thus to reclaim the scenario for his theory. His redescription implies that the siblings do not have the *same desire,* but instead want their *different desires* to be recognized by their parents. Rawls thus avoids strict egalitarianism's demand that equal shares of goods (or: the good) be distributed to all in favor of a demand for equality of opportunity and recognition. His belief is that this demand is a demand for justice and that this notion of justice is immune to Freud's accusation that it springs from an illegitimate feeling of envy. But all Rawls has done is inverted Freud's argument: a now legitimate or what he calls "benign" feeling of envy is argued to derive from a now primordial notion of justice.

Rawls's first mistake is to assume that Freud's notion of envy implies a desire for the object of another's desire. The affect of envy is not a matter of desires or an appeal to others for recognition, but of jouissance, which seeks no such validation. Just as Lydecker is envious without wanting what Laura's other suitors want, so, too, according to Freud's theory, may siblings in a nursery find enjoyment in different things and be envious still. In fact, in order to be sure one understands what envy is, one would do well to perform a little thought experiment by adjusting slightly that nursery scene which is the locus classicus of the evil eye: the beginning of *The Confessions,* where Saint Augustine notes the look of bitterness on one brother's face as he beholds his sibling nursing at their mother's breast. Now, you mustn't imagine that the envious brother fears the enviable other is sucking at a source that may run dry, thus leaving him, the next in line, thirsty. Augustine makes it clear that this source is a "richly abundant fountain of milk" and able, presumably, to accommodate both.[8] But no amount of milk and no amount of recognition will temper the bitterness that arises. You will understand the point better if you imagine the envious brother to be a bit older than the nursling and therefore greedy not for breast milk, but for something more suitable to his age—something cold, from the fridge: a coke, perhaps. As he regards his younger brother, he is nevertheless overcome by an envy that eats him up inside. Why? Because no matter how much pleasure he gets from a refreshing glass of cold coke, he worries that his brother may get more from that trickle of warm milk, for which he, the elder, has long ago lost his taste. It's not the object—the milk—he begrudges his brother, it's the satisfaction.

That, in its most compressed form, is the point: envy envies satisfaction, enjoyment. This odd fact is the source of the excess cruelty with which envy is invested. For if one simply envied an object, one could devise strategies—even vicious ones—to steal it away from another. But no strategy can ever be devised to take back the *pleasure* of which we feel we have been robbed if the source of that pleasure—which is in the possession of the other—is unappealing to us. No strategy but one: destroy the other's ability to take pleasure, to enjoy. This can be done either by annihilating the other, in which case we submit ourselves to a battle whose fatal consequences we cannot be sure of controlling, *or* by demanding equality, in which case we submit ourselves to the same proscription on enjoyment to which we submit the other.

Since the psychoanalytic picture of envy does not depend, as he assumes, on denying the uniqueness of individual pleasure, Rawls cannot claim to have corrected Freud's view by insisting himself on this uniqueness. He thus fails to provide himself with a new basis for simply inverting the priority of envy and the demand for equality. The argument about the *differences* between desires is just so much stage business that will distract us, if we are not attentive, to what is really going on, that is, to Rawls's attempt to insinuate equality as the cause of envy, rather than the reverse. But this unfounded and faulty premise cannot be slipped under the radar of Freud's corrosive critique. On the contrary, it places itself, along with the whole theory of justice as fairness, squarely in the latter's path and betrays the theory's own envy-tainted origins. How so? In his reinterpretation of the nursery example, Rawls contends that the siblings' supposedly envious demands are in fact demands for "the attention and affection of their parents, to which . . . they justly have an equal claim" (540). In other words, they are bids for recognition from a parental other deemed capable of granting it. But such bids are precisely what Freud's theory of the envious origins of the demand for equality have prepared us to expect. The reversal of hostile feelings of envy into the social feeling of equality and community can take place, Freud says, only through the mediation of an other who is not a member of the group. "The necessary precondition" for the formation of a sense of community "is that all [its] members should be loved in the same way by one person, the leader." He later adds, "The demand for equality in a group applies only to its members not to the leader."[9] What has happened here to make Rawls's scenario conform so closely to Freud's? The notion of a universal desire—which the political philosopher had denied, in one form at least, to utilitarians—has resurfaced in the form of a universal desire for recognition from the same parental figure.

In his mostly astute essay on "The Strange Destiny of Envy," John Forrester takes Rawls to task simply for refusing to cede Freud's point that a base passion such as envy could be the source of such lofty and rational ideals as equality and justice.[10] This reduced charge miscalculates the extent of the damage done by Freud's argument. Rather than gold from ore, as Forrester assumes, the proposal that envy is transformed into a demand for equality extracts vinegar from sour grapes. Instead of simply supplying the demands for equality and justice with an ignominious but still triumphant history, Freud thoroughly discredits them. Any political program structured according to their demands will thus be subject to his reproach, and this is what Forrester does not see.

Two questions: first, what is Forrester's error and, second, what is Rawls's? Forrester goes wrong because he fails to question the relation between the superego and ethical action, assuming implicitly that the function of the first is to rally the second. What the superego rallies, rather, is a pinched and nasty moralism, such as is described in Freud's myth of the overthrow of the primal horde by a fraternal society. According to this myth, evidence of the repressed murder of the single *exception* to the fraternal order—the priapic patriarch—returns in the brotherly taboo against the slightest trace of *exceptionalism*. Differences are from this point denounced, abhorred, as is every form of jouissance that cannot be conscripted into the anti-exceptionalism of the fraternal cause. Again, the rule is: "everyone must be the same and have the same." This is a superegoic injunction; it must not be confused with an ethical command.

Rawls's error is not to see that his image of brothers demanding validation of their unique desires is nothing but a bad faith version of Freud's myth. The desperate fiction of incommensurable desires submitting themselves to a common measure scarcely disguises its own absurdity. As psychoanalysis teaches, one has to limit the Other's knowledge to make room for jouissance, or: jouissance flourishes only there where it is *not* validated by the Other. Turning this around, one could say: out of a number of unique desires it is impossible to construct any big tent, any subsuming whole, that would not quash the differences themselves or increase hostility toward them. This is the poisonous pellet in Freud's theory of group formation to which Lacan drew our attention in various ways, but never so vividly as in his characterization of the utilitarian project as the misguided attempt to cut enough holes in a piece of cloth for a number (the greatest number!) of people to stick their arms and heads through it.[11] Any social theory that includes a reference to jouissance, as it must, will find that no single cloth will be sufficient to cover all desires. In the words of Willie Stark, in Robert Penn Warren's *All the King's Men,* every piece of cloth will be as inadequate as "a single-bed blanket on a double bed and three folks in the bed and a cold night. There ain't ever enough blanket to cover the case."[12]

Opposing utilitarianism, Rawls raises what he takes to be a fatal objection to it, in effect protesting, "But, Mr. Bentham, my good is not the same as another's . . . and your principle of the greatest good for the greatest number [thus] comes up against the demands of my egoism."[13] In other words: I want what *I* want, not what my neighbor deems desirable. But my egoism is quite compatible with a certain altruism: I am content to allow the other what *he* wants. The problem with this bad faith version of the egoistic demand for equality is its tendency to run afoul of the Other, who is more often than not suspected of not being as altruistic as the one who formulates the demand. That is, the problem always stems from our uncertainty about the Other and thus our fear that she will not do what is right and allow *me my* desire. I am willing to place myself behind a "veil of ignorance," to abstract myself from my pathological self-interests in order to determine what is fair, but I do not know what she is doing behind her *burqua.* In raising his egoistic/altruistic objection, Rawls does not avoid utilitarianism, I would argue, but articulates a more clever version of it. What corrals his theory, maintaining it within the expanded field of utilitarianism, is his commitment to normative judgment, to a measure or standard of pleasure, which is the inevitable consequence of his insistence on "parental" recognition. Ignorant of the structure of pleasure—which, as Freud taught, is only ever partial, never complete—and believing naively that complete satisfaction is attainable by anyone who, unimpeded by bad fortune, sets about realizing a rational plan (409), Rawls is not well positioned to see that the need for recognition of one's desire is also the occasion of envy.

As a Kantian, however, Rawls does admit that a consideration of pleasure is crucial to a theory of ethics. Though we have seen how his image of siblings seeking affectionate recognition of their differences is disqualified under Freud's concepts, we may therefore want to know how it fares under Kant's. Despite his reputation as a cold rationalist, Kant well knew that a purely abstract moral law had no chance of receiving a hearing from an embodied subject. This is why he wrote the third *Critique:* to heal the gap that had erupted between reason (as he had so far theorized it) and pleasure, to show the indispensible role aesthetic pleasure, specifically, plays in the practical use of reason, that is in an ethical, or free, act. The difficulty is in understanding just what this role is. What does it mean to say, as Kant does, that aesthetic pleasure is prompted by beholding a beautiful object, an object which symbolizes our morality?[14]

The first answer to come to mind is that the beautiful object represents the end that the ethical act strives to attain. This teleological answer is wrong, of course, in Kant's terms. For if an ethical act is free, it cannot be guided by anything but itself. It cannot, then, be guided by an external goal, since this goal would become the *basis* of morality, that on behalf of which the act was undertaken. Such an act would not be free, but would be bound by the idealized vision it served to realize. External to will, an independent goal cannot claim any basis in moral law. Nothing guarantees, therefore, that the goal is freely chosen and is not concocted out of self-interest. It is this antiteleological argument that is at the root of the "postmodern" condemnation of master strategies, masquerading as benevolent, which would solve urban problems by imposing "just" and "proportionate" schemes over vast territories, in order to create "ideal cities." Such strategies, which start with a whole that they then proceed to carve up, are doomed to fail; naively taking the whole for granted rather than questioning its possibility, they soon run into the single-bed blanket problem: it is always "too short and too tight for a growing humankind."

BEAUTY AND JUSTICE: SCARRY

Once this visionary answer to the question of the role of the beautiful is rejected, an alternative is ready to step forward. According to this answer, the beautiful object does not represent a goal to be sought after, but is, rather, that which *incites us to abandon our selfish goals.* An example of this argument can be found in the recently published (and beautifully written) *On Beauty and Being Just,* by Elaine Scarry. Beauty, Scarry maintains, is always a call for distribution; it exerts on us a pressure to surrender our imaginary position at the center of the world and to extend our regard laterally, to others. Beauty gives us an "opiated" sense of "adjacency" and thus prepares our sense of justice. Beautiful things, she opines, "act like small tears in the surface of the world that pull us through to some vaster space; . . . so that when we land we find we are standing in a different relation to the world."[15] Concurring with the belief that it is "fraternity" and equality that "[underwrite] liberal theories of justice" (95), she embraces what she refers to as Rawls's "widely accepted definition . . . [of] fairness" as the "symmetry of everyone's relation to each other" (93). Similar in many respects to the first definition of the role of beauty, this one, articulated by Scarry, is nevertheless, as I stated above, distinct. Whereas the first presented the beautiful as a goal to be achieved, the second presents it as a salutary fiction that boosts the spirit of ethical will and persuades us to believe in the possibility of justice and in the reality of moral law. Before accepting Rawls's revamped nursery scenario as just such a compelling fiction, however, one must note that this second definition of beauty stands condemned on the same grounds as the first: it believes the unbridgeable gap between subjective happiness and the public good of the community can be healed through public recognition.

But if both definitions of the role of beauty have a certain staying power, even among some who attempt to think in the Kantian mode, this is because each answers to some fundamental argument of Kant's theory. The first attaches to an understandable reluctance to surrender the notion of purpose altogether, for, as Kant insists, "in the absence of all reference to an end, no determination of the will can take place in man. . . . [H]ow the question, *'What is to result fom this right conduct of ours'* is to be answered . . . cannot possibly be a matter of indifference to reason."[16] A will that envisions to itself no definite goal is incapable of achieving *satisfaction,* Kant remarks. The second definition of the role of beauty, on the other hand, thrives on his insistence that the pleasure one takes in beauty depends on a sense of harmony, of fitness and balance, which is occasioned by beholding the beautiful object. These attributes describe, Kant argues, not the object itself so much as the faculties of the beholder, which are on this occasion in accord.

Scarry's argument revolves around this aspect of balanced symmetry, which she promotes as the essential attribute of beauty, and she finds confirmation of her view that this attribute is the sine qua non of the beautiful in, for example, Aristotle's depiction of justice as a perfect cube, equidistant in all its parts; in the spectacle of trireme ships, which she claims nourished Athenian democracy; in public parades, in which a plurality of classes and "genders" move in concert and on an equal footing. But if all these beautiful things function not as ends to be achieved, images of ideal societies to be realized, neither do they serve merely as inert analogies for political fairness. One is heartened to observe Scarry begin to take her distance from others who argue from analogy, who see in the symmetry of beautiful things a mere formal similarity to the symmetry of relations of moral fairness. Her bolder claim is that aesthetic symmetry encourages and helps to bring about the actual symmetry of just relations. Insofar as it conceives the beautiful image as something that actively impels us to act, to create something anew, this position is clearly more attractive, if ultimately inadequate. By insisting that the beautiful object compels us to bring into being the second term of an analogy—the justice that would be analogous to a beautiful, symmetrical image—Scarry invents something akin to the notion of the half-said, by which Lacan interpreted Kant's categorical imperative. The imperative is only half- and not fully said, because it requires an actual act to complete it. There is no fully stated law that is then followed by an obedient and actualizing act; rather the act retroactively consitutes the half-stated law. But because Scarry makes no such provision for retroaction in her scenario, the act she wants the will to undertake seems less one of creation and more like mimesis.

And this is to say nothing of the fact that the privileging of balance and symmetry betrays a disappointingly conservative notion of the aesthetic object. Noting that the current denigration of the beautiful is the result of an unfavorable comparison with the sublime—a comparison Kant initiated with his division of the aesthetic into these two categories, the first "feminine" and small, the second "masculine" and great, or powerful—Scarry reminds us that this division is neither long-standing nor uncontested. This useful reminder prepares us for a full-scale redefinition of the beautiful, one that would include the forceful and perturbing aspects of the sublime. How does Scarry carry through on her implied promise? She attempts to conceptualize the beautiful both as "pacific"(107) in nature *and* as having an agitational force that is able to engage the passions of the will. If the beautiful incites the will, however, what does it pacify or calm? One might be tempted to answer, as Lacan does, that it "pacifies the gaze," it causes us to lay down our gaze. Scarry does not say this; and this would, of course, be fine if she offered some alternative, but she does not. We find in her book no theory of envy and enjoyment—which in Lacan's theory incite the gaze that requires pacification—nor of anything in its stead. What it is that needs pacification is therefore left vague—is it our feelings, perhaps?—and the means of pacification, balance and symmetry, are dependent on a similarly vague, or unarticulated, physiological notion of what sort of composition is best suited to soothing the eye or calming our look. But why would a soothing of feelings—and which feelings?—lead to just action? If we have no notion of what is to be soothed or why, we cannot judge the appropriateness of the solution. Indeed, although Scarry speaks of the *beauty* of balance and symmetry, one is as likely to be horrified by them: a harmonious whole with all its parts snuggly in place can just as easily describe the architectural plan of a police state, rendered as all such plans are from a transcendent point of view.

Despite my criticisms, Scarry's moving book must be admired for its sustained attempt to take seriously Kant's enigmatic formulation: beauty symbolizes our morality. It is the word *symbolizes* that has got everyone stumped. It leads us astray by causing us to look for a representation of the will or of what will has the power to bring about. What if, however, there were a type of symbolization that did not function to represent something, but that made nothing appear? What if the beautiful were not a representation but, in Lacan's vocabulary, a *semblant,* an *apparent* nothing or that which made nothing appear? This raises a further question: why would nothing incite an autonomous or ethical will to action?

Kant is often accused of formulating a notion of desire that remained issueless, a will that was without hope since we could never be certain that it had ever succeeded in acting freely. In truth, Kant was himself sensitive to this problem. A practical use of reason has still to be reasonable, that is, it has to have some cause to believe in the chances of its own successful realization, despite the fact that moral, disinterested acts are as a rule less likely to be rewarded with success than conniving or calculated ones. Since Kant's notion of reason disallowed any guarantee of heavenly reward, and market and social forces were increasingly valorizing acts of cunning, ethical will stood, at the time Kant wrote, in sore need of motivation. What reason then could Kant give to practical reason to believe it had any place in the modern world, to believe that this world did not itself conspire against it? In Dieter Henrich's thesis, Kant's solution was to argue that along with moral will there arises spontaneously a "moral image of the world," that is, an image of the world as not indifferent or opposed to acts that are ethically motivated.[17] This moral image—which is the *cause* of ethical action, which makes it reasonable to act unselfishly—is not to be confused with a belief in the existence of God. It is rather an image of the world in which moral will is a genuine—that is to say, an integral and constitutive—part. Not a world *against* which the autonomous subject stands, ready to do battle with it, but *in* which the subject finds a place for himself, though one that can only be described as supernumerary, since the subject does not fit into the purely natural scheme of things.

If the subject is able to envision for herself this admittedly supernumerary place in the world, this is because she locates in the world an empty place, one occupied by precisely nothing. The surplus of the subject requires this deficit of the world, which, by this very incompleteness, is revealed to be incapable of realizing itself on its own. What we have here in Kant is not a structure of opposition in which subject and world face off against each other, but an envelope or topological structure in which the subject appears twice, first, as subtracted from and second, as added to the world. The role of the beautiful in this structure is to represent the nothing in which will is able to trace its own reflection. The semblant does not, then, incite will to create symmetries among people or insist on their equality; it incites us to create, purely and simply. What's wrong with the rigidly formal definition of justice as fairness is that it ignores, as I have argued after Freud, the concrete reality of pleasure, which not only actively resists symmetrization, but turns lethal under its constraint. This is not to imply that ethics comes down to either fencing pleasure in so it won't wander into the neighbor's space, or liberating pleasure so that it can roam where it will. Such spatio-economic proposals for the ethical partitioning of pleasure are based in a still too naturalistic conception of pleasure, in something that is much closer to need.

It has often been remarked that liberal theories of ethics seek merely to provide equality of circumstances and opportunity to all and to protect all subjects from natural harm. Ethics is thus reduced to a guarantee that everyone will have the basics to sustain "bare" life. Rawls, aware of the limitations of such a project, attempts to go beyond it by advocating the recognition of individual pleasures. But he does so while adhering to a notion of pleasure that scarcely distinguishes it from a material good. He thus fails adequately to understand that once pleasure is denaturalized and shown to be constituted by a detour through the field of the Other, its equitable distribution is no longer an appropriate or feasible goal. The problem should not be posed as one of distribution, but of deprivation, instead. That is to say, the problem is no longer to ensure that everyone has an adequate portion of the pleasure she wants, but to ensure that she wants it in the first place. Arising in the field of the Other, pleasure arises alongside our uncertain relation *to* the Other. What does he expect of me? Who does he think I am? Since the surest way of guaranteeing that the Other recognizes us for ourselves, or that he acknowledges our desire, is to make our desires his, we end up depriving ourselves of our own pleasure, choosing instead, for the sake of a more pacific relation to the Other, to invest our pleasure in his (lost) cause. The problem with pleasure is any of the countless reasons we invent to forsake it. What we find most difficult is hanging onto and enjoying the pleasure we have. It is this dissatisfaction we thus impose on ourselves that leads us to demand the same dissatisfaction of others.

THE "AXIOM OF EQUALITY"

If the psychoanalytic critique forbids a single Jerusalem solution, so too does it forbid talk of a shared Jerusalem, which would partition its people and their pasts "fairly," through a beautiful, symmetrical scheme. There is no whole, no all of Jerusalem to be shared, because there is no big Other to recognize and bestow affection equally on all its citizens. This is to say, there is no external norm that can be imposed on the territory. For this reason, equality as a program has to be scrapped. At the end of "Philosophie et politique," however, Alain Badiou makes an intriguing distinction between a "program of equality" and an "axiom of equality." The latter, he says, disengages equality from its "economist connotations" and restores it to its "subjective trenchance."[18] One imagines that by "economist connotations" he has in mind those considerations of "fair distribution" that form the staple of liberal theories of equality, up to and including Rawls's and Scarry's. A program of equality is as clearly destined to defeat as is the goal of reaching infinity starting from a finite point. As we know, infinity will never be reached—no matter how much time passes—within a finite space. A program of equality is similarly absurd insofar as it attempts to secure recognition for pleasure while pleasure essentially depends on the subtraction of the Other's recognition—or, *has* historically depended on this subtraction since the beginning of the modern period when happiness acquired a *subjective* status and the accord between individual happiness and the common good, which Aristotle had taken for granted, was no longer assured, when indeed subjective happiness and the public weal came, by definition, into conflict. In the modern period, the paradox of pleasure, its demand for recognition coupled with the impossibility of receiving it, could be said to have been added to the list of Zeno's paradoxes. As Zeno demonstrated, the only way out of such paradoxes is via the axiom. One must, for example, begin axiomatically from an assertion of movement since the attempt to produce it through an exhaustive description of the static points that compose it merely causes it to disappear and is thus demonstrably doomed to failure. One must start from the notion of infinity because it is impossible to introduce it by the path of the finite. And one must begin with an axiom of equality rather than foolishly trying to bring it into being through some Other who would recognize and validate individual pleasures.

The axiom of equality functions basically as Scarry wants balance and symmetry to function: it incites will to create in reality the "second half of the analogy" whose first half it is. Or: the adoption of the axiom of equality ensures that we will not be indifferent to the consequences of our actions, but will seek to protect the equality of all through political action. The difference is that, unlike Scarry's balance and symmetry, Badiou's axiom does not project an image of a just society as one where conflict would or could ultimately be resolved, where dissent, in effect, would be silenced and everyone would know his or her place. In brief, the axiom of equality does not imagine a just society as one in which balance and symmetry reign.

Throughout his teaching, Lacan referred several times to "The Prisoner's Dilemma," a logical puzzle out of which he essayed to compose a kind of "Group Psychology beyond the Ego."[19] In this puzzle, each of three prisoners has either a black or a white circle attached to his back. In other words, the game begins with each player placed behind a "veil of ignorance." Operating with the knowledge that the prison warden has five circles, three white and two black, to work with—that is, knowing that two circles have been withdrawn from play—each prisoner must determine from the evidence of the circles he is able to see on the backs of the other two whether he is himself a black or a white. The prisoner who figures this out first will be freed. Had there been five prisoners and five circles, or had two of the prisoners been given black circles, this fateful game would have presented little problem. One prisoner could have discerned at a glance from the evidence of the others his own identity. These prisoners, however, have all been given white circles. By putting some circles out of play, and precisely those that would have allowed a simple opposition to enter into the calculations, this game approximates the differential situation of social signifiers, which never constitutes a totality. That is to say, it is never possible, solely on the basis of an assessment of my relations to others, to define myself completely. It is always the signifier of my own unique identity that is missing from the set. It would seem then that Lacan's prisoners could remain permanently stalled, with none able to win the game, since there will never be a moment when knowledge can be accumulated to the point that certainty as to one's own status emerges. Realizing, however, that the differential relations with his fellows are insufficient to determine his true identity, and that while he waits passively for this information to be reflected back to him, the others have time to act and thus precipitate an alteration of the situation, each prisoner feels compelled to act "prematurely"—in the absence of any cognitive certainty—and to determine by his act his own truth. At the end of the apologue, each of the three prisoners is freed, because each verifies, not simply on the basis of what he learns, but also through his own act of passing through the door, that he is white. Each, in other words, produces his "whiteness," which is to say, his *anonymity*, by refusing to allow himself to be defined by others and by *acting* to block this possibility.

One could well imagine a different outcome. The prisoners, unsure of their own identity and fearful of what the others might do to alter the situation, could have entered into an unconscious, pleasure-denying pact in effect to maintain the hell of the status quo. According to this pact, the current wary habits of each of the prisoners would have been routinized and prolonged to form the hardened, time-tested shell of an imaginary identity. It would be as if some transcendent point had simultaneously been added to the game—some prison warden been given just enough circles to identify each of the prisoners with his own separate badge—and from this point the prisoners' actions were overseen and were expected to continue unaltered. No one would exit this game, which would be played indefinitely.

Jerusalem is a city too full of sacred places, too full of ancestral dead, to make living there easy. Life is continuously sacrificed to the past and to the ancestral others by whose dreams the living judge themselves, measure and validate themselves. If the city is to become livable again, it will have to learn *not* how to divide itself up, but how to make nothing appear. Jerusalem's fiercest battle is not between religious and ethnic groups, but between the sacred and the semblant. So far, unfortunately, the sacred seems to be winning.

The Strut

of Vision:

Seeing's

Corporeal

Support

If anything has stirred American academics in the last several years, it's the much-trumpeted observation that bodies matter. This observation has produced a veritable cornucopia of corporeal kinds: volumes have been written and compiled on all sorts of bodies, categorized by function, differentiated by class, race, and gender, meticulously scrutinized in all the nooks and crannies of their differences from some abstract, idealized form. This *un*airbrushing and proliferation of bodily forms harbors the belief that it was a misguided focus on the signifier that led us down the ideologically retrograde path of decorporealization. Analysis of our world as a system of signifying relations yielded, we are told, merely ideal subjects: absolutely abstract, detached from bodies and all their powers, limitations, and demands.

The current revenge of the body, or of interest in the body, is seen as a revenge against the soma-denying power of the signifier, and as such has taken two forms: either it condemns the semiotic project by turning away from it toward the biological or life sciences, or it extends the project by adding the body to the list of the signifier's effects. As the recent barrage of books on embodiment testifies, however, neither this simple condemnation nor this simple addition is capable of producing any real knowledge of the body as component of our human existence. The reason for this, I would argue, is that rather than forcing a fundamental rethinking of the nature and operation of the signifier, the introduction of the body into current discourse has left the signifier undisturbed, whether by rejecting it or by putting it to the new task of accounting for the body's *construction*. Simply stating that "bodies matter"—as though one need only revenge or answer their neglect—these studies have so far buried the crucial *question*: what's the matter with bodies? Why do they suppurate (for that's the word for it) so much trouble for themselves? Why does human embodiment manifest itself as a pitched battle between our bodies and our biology, such that it would be a mistake to take them as synonymous? To be embodied means, of course, that we are not just anybody, but *this* body *here*. But why is it that our corporeal particularity displays itself in such peculiar cravings: why do we find ourselves constantly overeating or starving ourselves, cutting up other bodies into little pieces or prostrating ourselves at another's feet? In other words, why, even in their "basic" pursuits of nourishment and sex, are human bodies given to compulsion, inhibition, sadism, idealization? Animals have bodies, too, but not such exotic pleasures, such perverse tastes. Their instincts, like our drives, are a kind of nonconscious knowledge of what they must do. The difference is that instinct, which suits animals for survival, are determined by nature, whereas drives, which are determined neither by nature nor culture, often jeopardize survival. Yet, it would be a mistake to confuse drive with will or whim, since drive does not appear to be at the disposal of the conscious subject; on the contrary, it exerts an unrelenting, internal pressure that mere will is unable to oppose and the body is unable to escape.

Though the concept of drive pays heed to what is often called the human body's *perversion* or deviance from the natural order, only bad faith would prevent us from admitting that the notion of a nonnatural body is a contradiction in terms and therefore untenable. A body is clearly a part of nature. If one wants to hold onto the notion of drive (and psychoanalysis has given us many reasons to do so), the only way to avoid contradiction is to assume that the notion implies not an overriding so much as a redefinition of nature. This is precisely why, of all Freud's notions, that of the drive has had the least success in attracting supporters; it obliges a kind of rethinking that only the boldest of thinkers would dare to undertake. The question one must ask is: how does drive determine human embodiment as both a freedom from nature and a part of it? In sum, the conviction that bodies matter does not exonerate us from having to ask this fundamental question: what is a body?

However much we have learned about the body in recent years, we've learned next to nothing that would lead us to pose, let alone answer, such a question, nothing that would cast light on the "perversions" of human embodiment.[1] Let us settle on one example of this problem, that provided by the notion of the embodied *observer*. In the late 1970s, it is true, the film-theoretical attempt to analyze vision as a signifying practice did produce a subject that no body could be: a monocular subject of pure, abstract seeing, who occupied no space, was subject to no temporal fluxuations, and laid claim to no sexual identity, except—notoriously—by default. In *Techniques of the Observer,* Jonathan Crary challenges this description of the film spectator by mounting a historically informed argument against it. At the end of the nineteenth century, he tells us, the observer suddenly acquired a body, one that took up space, changed over time, and could be examined in all its contingency by empirical science. Unlike the earlier, abstract observer—which was configured and instantiated by the camera obscura and the geometry that informed it—this corporealized observer had more than a merely ideal existence. The aberrant perceptions of its all too human eyes—retinal afterimages, light distortions, blurring, and the like—that is, perceptions constituted *by the body itself,* were no longer dismissed as carnal errors requiring rational correction, but were instead taken seriously as positive phenomena in their own right—the better to be put to use by a developing capitalism.

Although the argument for such a shift from an anti-optical or geometrical model of vision to an optical or physiological one is amply documented, there is more than sufficient reason to doubt its fundamental soundness. Let us begin with the general argument that the transition from a geometrical to a physiological model signals a transition from an abstract to a corporealized observer. The support given for this argument is mainly of the following commonsensical sort: since the camera obscura was constructed around a single point of projection whereas the stereoscope was constructed around two, the first must have been aimed at the mind's eye and the second at the actual eyes of the embodied subject. Or: since geometry is an abstract science, it supposes an abstract subject, whereas physiology, which studies the body, supposes a carnal observer. From these sorts of assumptions, a guess as to what Crary means by embodiment is a simple affair. In the Cartesian vocabulary that Crary cites, it means that the observer is *res extensa* and not merely *res cogitans,* that is, the observer is an extended substance rather than a purely thinking or seeing thing, a cogito; in nontechnical language, the observer, whatever else it may be, *is* matter, a bounded, finite thing interposed between other things, and as matter it impinges necessarily and meaningfully on vision in ways that can be physiologically studied and manipulated. I do not doubt that physiological science held such a notion of the body; what I doubt is its veracity. Additionally, I would question the broad assumption that this notion represented a more materialist account of vision; in fact, it can be easily shown that it is decidedly more *abstract* than the geometrical account.[2] Anyone who needs convincing should treat himself to reading about the wild shenanigans of these physiologists, who kept coming up—despite themselves, one imagines—with reasons for embracing the blind man as the only proper subject of their experiments, and constantly found themselves in cahoots with spiritualists, vitalists, and other such positivist dupes. In any case, what is most striking about these experiments is their incapacity and unwillingness to distinguish the facts of human and animal embodiment.

Crary does not blink, one notices, when he cites the passage from the *La dioptrique* where Descartes, in the process of describing the construction of a camera obscura, asks his readers to imagine an eye—it could be the eye of an ox, he adds parenthetically—at the lenticular[3] entrance to the darkened chamber. To this offhand remark Crary offhandedly responds, "this only indicates that for Descartes the images observed within the camera obscura are formed by means of a cyclopean eye, detached from the observer, possibly not even a human eye."[4] That is, since the eye at issue here is not a physical one—insofar as it is the cogito, pure seeing or thinking that counts—the eye's actual characteristics are irrelevant. The problem is, however, that when Crary later examines the physiological model of vision, we cannot help recalling this passage from the *La dioptrique* and its Buñuelian sleight of hand. For, in the later optical experiments, all indications are that the human eye that was the object of its study might just as well have been the eye of an ox.

One of the conditions of the possibility, and also one of the greatest errors, of the "life sciences" introduced in the nineteenth century was their improper equation of stimuli that had radically different origins and natures. It was psychoanalysis, rising up to take issue with these sciences, that would eventually untangle them for us. To this end Freud would complain, "a dryness of the mucous membrane of the pharynx or an irritation of the mucuous membrane of the stomach," that is, the physical manifestations of thirst and hunger in the human body, are treated by these sciences on the model of "a strong light fall[ing] on the eye,"[5] even though the pangs of human hunger and thirst need have nothing to do with the presence or absence of food in the stomach or moisture in the mouth, and how well one sees may have nothing to do with the intensity of available light. These two types of stimuli—those with a purely physiological source and those that originate in the drive—cannot, however, be distinguished merely by determining whether they originate externally or internally; what differentiates them rather are the concepts of cause required to account for them. Whereas physiological stimuli and the responses to them are governed by simple scientific laws, or regularities, drive stimuli provoke responses not calculable in advance. This is not to say that the latter do not enter into causal relations, but that these relations are "more complex," as Freud said; or, as Lacan would later argue, in the drive cause and effect are not welded together to form one principle as is the case with the fixed and stable relations that bind stimulus to response.[6] The latter are governed by scientific law, whereas drive stimuli arise where a gap in the law is to be found. To illustrate, Lacan invokes an image of the crushed body of a suicide lying on the pavement. This image would undoubtedly prompt different causal explanations depending on whether the investigator was a physiologist or a psychoanalyst. That it is only a human body that is ever suicided would not enter into the considerations of the physiologist, whose explanation would most likely give more weight to the force of gravity than to the pressure of the drive, though the latter is surely the more relevant fact of this suicide's embodiment.

The fundamental error of *Techniques of the Observer* is, I am arguing, its unthinking acceptance of the mind/body dualism of Cartesian philosophy. It is this dualism that grounds the distinction Crary makes between the geometrical model of vision, which supposedly disregards the body entirely in favor of abstract consciousness, and the physiological model, which reduces the body to its empiricist definition. This history presents us with a false choice between no body at all and what we might call the "abstract body" of the nineteenth-century life sciences, since it lacks both generic (that is, human) and individual specificity. This choice precludes the possibility of Crary's coming to terms with the corporealized vision of a human subject, insofar as this subject constitutes a direct challenge to that dualism. But if his initial error ultimately leads him to misjudge the nature of the corporeal observer, it also causes other problems along the way, including a throughgoing misrepresention of that geometry which informs Renaissance perspective and its "universalist" claims.

This is not to say that this misrepresentation originates with Crary. Since the point of his argument is not to challenge film theory's analysis of Renaissance perspective as that which set in place an abstract observer, but to question the hegemony of this model of vision beyond the late eighteenth century, he accepts without question film theory's analysis and mistakes. As is known, film theory attempted to prop up its notion of cinematic visuality on the analysis of the gaze that Lacan offers in *Seminar XI: The Four Fundamental Concepts of Psychoanalysis*, though the reading of Lacan it produced was so severely flawed that it ended up taking a position completely at odds with his. Where film theory and Lacan diverge, Crary follows the former, often strengthening its argument. This is the case, for example, on the question of the observer/spectator's placement vis-à-vis the visual field. Crary works diligently to secure a rigorous separation of the observer from the observed. Essentially he argues that the geometrization of vision places the observer not only *outside* the body, but *outside* the visible world, as well, whereas the physiological model places the observer *within* the world and *within* his body. Relying on these "age-old assumptions"[7] regarding the simple exteriority of body and world, which could then be placed, like boxes, inside and outside each other, Crary interprets ideologically the textbook argument that states that Renaissance painting introduced a visual objectivity that quickly displaced the subjectivity of medieval painting. He and film theory interpret this objectivity as a *misrecognition* fostered by the belief that the observer could indeed transcend his or her body and world and thus truthfully comprehend it.

   Lacan does not dispute the textbook argument concerning the Renaissance invention of painterly objectivity; but he interprets objectivity in a different way. This difference is plain in statements such as this: "the geometral dimension enables us to glimpse how the subject who concerns us is *caught . . . in the field of* vision" (SXI, 92). That is to say, Lacan argues that Renaissance painting places the spectator *within the image,* not outside it, as Crary contends (though, as we will see, this situation of the spectator in the visible field is absolutely dissimilar to the situation described in the physiological model). Giving full weight to the name by which this model of vision is commonly known, Lacan argues that it shows that all we see, we see from a certain *perspective.* In fact, the relevance of his lengthy discussion of anamorphosis is to focus attention on the *impurity* of the painting's visual field, which consists not only of *what the spectator sees,* but also of a gaze and a vanishing point, which is nothing other than *that which the spectator contributes to what she sees.*[8] This does not mean that Quattrocento painting rendered the spectator visible or transparent to herself in the manner in which Descartes's ideal observer became transparent to herself. If the spectator is pictured there in the painting, she is not grasped as coincident with the thought she has of herself, but as someone who is looked at from a place other than the one from which she sees.

   That Lacan's extended disavowal of the supposed similarity between Descartes's abstract observer and the observer of Renaissance painting should have fallen on such deaf ears among film theorists is no surprise. The missed encounter can perhaps be chalked up to the fact that film theorists mistook anamorphosis for an occasional rather than a structurally necessary phenomenon, or, more generally, to the notorious difficulty of Lacan's paratactical style. But if the particulars of his argument were not immediately clear, its context is unmistakable, and this alone should have sent up warning flares to those intent on nailing down the Cartesian lineage of his supposedly abstract observer. For, these sessions on the gaze are no diversionary foray into the territory of art criticism; they are, rather, an attempt to develop one of the fundamental concepts of psychoanalysis: that of the drive. Lacan proposes that Renaissance perspective provides the exact formula of the *scopic drive,* that is, it gives us the formula not of abstract vision, but of embodied seeing. As I noted above, the concept of the drive is the vehicle by which Freud collided head-on with Cartesian dualism, the means by which he strove to account for the facts of an incarnate subjectivity. Consider once more the definition he gives of the drive in his essay, "Instincts and their Vicissitudes": "[drive] appears to us as a concept on the frontier between the mental and so-matic, . . . as a measure of the demand upon the mind for work in consequence of its connection with the body."[9] This demand (which is precisely *demand* in the Lacanian sense) is that call for a more complex response from the corporeal sub-ject (which is to say, the subject as such of psychoanalysis) than any that could be accommodated within a physiological, stimulus-response model of investigation.

But what is it that *justifies* this argument? What allows one to state that geometrical perspective provides a formula for the relation of the *corporeal* subject (not the purely rational subject) to the visual field? To answer this question, it is first necessary to distinguish *artificial perspective,* which emerged in the sixteenth century out of a revolution in geometry, from its predecessor, *natural perspective.* Whenever this distinction is overlooked, confusion results, as happens in Crary's and film theory's account of Renaissance perspective.

> *What is that thing which does not give itself, and which if it were to give itself would not exist?*
> *It is the infinite!*
>
> —*Leonardo da Vinci*

It is a commonplace to say that Renaissance painting introduced infinity into the visible world. But one needs to specify, beyond this platitude, which infinity it in-troduced.[10] Without explicitly saying so, and while seldom using the word *infinity,* Crary seems to assume that what is at issue in paintings of the Quattrocento is *poten-tial infinity.* Citing two paintings by Vermeer, *The Astronomer* (1668) and *The Geographer* (1668–1669), as paradigmatic illustrations of Renaissance perspective, Crary ar-gues that the two observers depicted in them "engage in a common enterprise of observing aspects of a single *indivisible* exterior. Both . . . are figures . . . for the au-tonomous individual ego that has appropriated to itself the capacity for intellectual mastery of the *infinite extension* of bodies in space" (42–43, emphasis added). Missing the point of Renaissance perspective, Crary here describes not an infinite, but a finite space. Why do I say so? I will try to answer this question after making a few general comments about the central concern of Renaissance perspective.

If Vermeer's paintings are granted a paradigmatic status by Crary this is because they focus thematically on the measurement or mathematization of the material world, which is arguably the major project of the Renaissance. The geometrization of vision is thus considered to be part of a more general quantification of the world, which began to prepare the way for a money economy based on exchange value. It is necessary then not only to attend, as Crary does, to the impact of capitalism, at the start of the nineteenth century, on our notions of vision, but also to observe the development of the imbrication of vision and capitalist quantification in the sixteenth century. Just as capitalism would be incapable of eliminating the need for use value in order to sustain the universalization of exchange value, so too was the mathematization or quantification of the world unable at an earlier date to eliminate the demand for Quality. This is not to say that the quantification of the world would not be complete; it was. But while the *place* of Quality in the modern world was suddenly eliminated, Quality itself lingered on, through the demand for it, as that thing which no longer had a place. And it would make its return in some fleeting, phantom form or other, just as it did later in the fleeting and precarious fetishization of commodities, to cite one of the most obvious examples.[11] Erwin Panofsky, who failed to reckon with the curious persistence of Quality, the unsituatable place of it, in the Renaissance, wrote in "Perspective as Symbolic Form" one of the most consequential and fundamentally wrongheaded essays written on the subject of Quattrocento perspective. The "symbolic form" of the title links perspective to the conquest of the world, to the knowledge or "intellectual mastery" (Crary) of it, through the symbolic forms that turned the world into a representation. The trouble is, the projective geometry on which this form of perspective relied was organized not as a search for knowledge, but, on the contrary, for truth, which pierces a hole in the surface of knowledge. Projective geometry was invented to seek out what eluded representation, what no longer had any place in the quantified, represented world. This does not mean that it sought to *represent* what was plainly unrepresentable, but that it sought to *demonstrate through its procedures* the existence of it.

With this in mind, we turn back to the discussion of the place of infinity in Renaissance painting. Since, as is known, this painting participated in the larger project of recentering the world on man, rather than on God, the infinity

introduced at this time depended on the demolition of that other infinity which figured man's asymptotic approach to God. If infinity were only that point on a never
reached horizon which marked the limit between the finite, sublunary world and
an eternal, heavenly space, painting would have still retained God as its *center,* even
if its *subject* would now be the finite space that dwelt some distance from this center. Yet the space Crary describes seems to be infinite only in this latter sense. By
referring to the space surveyed by the geographer and astronomer as a "single indivisible exterior," he declares it to be an irreducible, an uncomposed, continuous whole rather than an aggregate built up of parts. The finite operations of
measuring and surveying, while ostensibly claiming cognitively to conquer this
exterior space, unwittingly expose their own futility. For, it is these operations
that cannot be brought to an end and that thus inscribe a negative sort of infinity, which is often called *potential,* but which Hegel, using a more derogatory term,
called *spurious.* Rather than manifesting the *grandeur* of thought (or, in Crary's
phrase, the "autonomous individual ego['s] . . . capacity for intellectual mastery"), it is evidence of a "superstition of the understanding," or *deficiency* of
thought: an incapacity to conclude an operation defined by a limit that is structurally unreachable.

    What I wish to argue is that Crary's analysis seems to suppose that Re-
naissance perspective is underwritten by the classical, or Euclidean, geometry that
informed the construction of the camera obscura. (Crary waffles on the question
of what the similarities between the camera obscura and Renaissance perspective
were, choosing sometimes to treat them as virtually the same, sometimes admitting that they were not entirely coincident. But he never once mentions the fact
that they were informed by two distinct geometries.) This geometry—which was
exclusively concerned with the size and shape of figures, not with space—dealt only
with finite points and finite and flat spaces, never with infinity, a notion it re-
garded with open disdain. Since the Good was conceived by the Greeks as finite
and definite, being infinite could only be seen by them as the mark of *privation,* as
the absence of a limit or a lack of definition, rather than as perfection. Infinity
was not something *actual,* but a measure of our ever-deferred encounter with a
limit. Indeed, even the notion of potential infinity was accepted begrudgingly, as
a way of protecting both geometry and philosophy from having to accommodate
infinity as a positive notion referring to an actually existing thing.[12]

    Renaissance perspective was not based, however, on the classical geom-
etry of the camera obscura, but on projective geometry, whose principles were
succinctly set out in a twelve-page treatise by Girard Desargues, published in

1636. The title of this treatise immediately reveals a contradiction between the claims projective geometry makes for itself and those made about it by Crary and others; here is the title: *Example of one of S.G.D.L.'s general methods concerning drawing in perspective without using any third point, a distance point or any other kind, which lies outside the picture field.*[13] Plainly, and contrary to what many theorists have argued, the method informing Renaissance perspective operates without referring to any point outside the picture plane. It does not depend in other words on the eye of some supposed *external* observer, placed at a measurable distance from it. Instead, the field is organized solely around a point *internal* to the painting.

It is not just this lack of reference to an external observer that separates projective geometry from its predecessor. A discussion of some of the other differences between them will enable us to account for Renaissance painting's repositioning of the spectator within the visual field rather than outside it. In the older, Euclidean geometry, parallel lines are defined in a negative way as *lines that do not meet.* Under certain circumstances, of course, when an object is viewed from a distance, they *appear* to meet, but this appearance is read as an illusion created by distance and not confused with fact. Thus, both in its definition of parallel lines and in its correction of optical illusion, this geometry remains tied to our basic intuition about such lines, to the way we ordinarily imagine or represent them to ourselves. Projective geometry, on the other hand, jettisons intuition the moment it redefines parallel lines positively as *lines that meet at infinity.* For, not only does this definition cause infinity to come into being as an actual thing (rather than a kind of "and-so-on," indicating that the drawing of parallel lines has to be carried on indefinitely), it also causes the distinction between parallel lines and all others to disappear. It can now be said of *all* lines that they intersect another line at one and only one point. This new parity between parallel and all other lines has a surprising result: lines and points suddenly lose their hierarchical relation (in classical geometry, a point is a more basic unit than a line, since a line is defined as being made up of points) and become, for the first time, equal. The principle that posits this equality, called the "principle of duality," states that it is possible to substitute *point* for *line,* and vice versa, in *any* valid statement regarding their relation, without altering the validity of that statement.

The principle of duality has revolutionary consequences for geometry, but what needs to be noted for our purposes is simply this: projective geometry represents a break—or, better, liberation—from intuition which grounds classical geometry. Beginning with its positing of an actual infinity—a point that can be neither directly experienced nor represented, but which is nevertheless proved *actually* to exist—projective geometry established itself as radically anti-intuitionist. Unlike the earlier geometry, this one never conceived itself as a method for mapping the visible world, that which it was possible to see; instead it was a method for demonstrating the existence of what it was not possible to see, that which vision must renounce in order to see. The purpose of classical geometry was to assist in the drawing of objects on a two-dimensional surface with as little visual distortion as possible; it was intent on preserving the actual object's *resemblance,* or visual similarity, in the drawing. Projective geometry, on the other hand, was intent on studying the transformation of objects under projection in order to determine what remained the same throughout the process; it sought to preserve the consistency of the object, not visual similarities. Parallelism is not one of the properties that is preserved under projection, since deployment of this method results in the intersection of *all* lines at a point, called in painting the *vanishing point,* and the formation of a line across the painting, called the *horizon.*

Now, if one were to maintain that the vanishing point and the horizon line marked places where parallel lines *appear* to intersect, one would entirely disregard the method of their production and would once again efface the critical differences between Euclidean and projective geometry. As stated above, since this method is not designed to investigate the visual properties of objects, it does not produce, nor intend to produce, a purely optical space. The vanishing point and horizon line that emerge in these paintings are not to be taken, therefore, as illusions of perception, as objects we mistakenly see. They inscribe the eye of the viewing subject, which has been *projected* from elsewhere *into the visual field.*

Renaissance painting requires that we read it as other than a flat surface. We have been encouraged to comply with this requirement by reading the space depicted there in terms of verisimilitude, that is, as the creation of an *illusion of depth* by the receding of parallel lines toward a point—the vanishing point—in the illusory distance. This is, Lacan argues, the wrong way of looking at it. If the space of the paintings is not flat, it is because it is shaped, rather, like a torus or an envelope that folds the eye of the observer back into the field it observes. Through Renaissance perspective, the observer is topologically inserted, or projected, into the observable space, where it becomes visible in the world. This means two things, primarily: (I) the observer at stake in Renaissance perspective is not simply an abstract position from which the visible world is viewed, but an embodied position on view; and (2) Renaissance painting is not a matter of verisimilitude, of accurately representing the world, but a device for demonstrating the unobservable truth about the emergence of vision itself, how it comes about.

It is in *Seminar XIII: The Object of Psychoanalysis* that Lacan again takes up the problem of the spectator to which he devoted so much attention two years earlier, in *Seminar XI*, where he still tries to explain Renaissance perspective through the two-dimensional drawing of the intersection of two visual pyramids. In the later seminar, Lacan abandons the last vestiges of geometrical intuition to which his earlier discussion still remained minimally indebted. Belatedly taking note of the fact that Renaissance perspective depends specifically on projective geometry, he describes the latter as "logically prior to the physiology of the eye and even to optics" (that is, to any consideration of the propagation of light or the problem of resemblance) and states categorically that this geometry gives us "the exact form . . . of what is involved in the relation of the subject to *extension.*"[14]

If the theory of Renaissance perspective advanced by Lacan is confused with others that locate the subject at an ideal point, outside and thus transcendent to the visible world, this is only because Lacan's own argument is ignored. That the subject of vision is not ideal but corporeal is made explicit by this punning reference to the question of that subject's extension.[15] *Extension* is the term Descartes used to refer to material substance (including the body) in contrast to thought. The thought/extension dichotomy in his theory was supposed to guarantee the independence of each term (pure thinking on one side, corporeality on the other), but Lacan argues that the Cartesian notion of extension has thought's fingerprints all over it. That is: material substance is thought as homologous with thought, which means that the former, scarcely independent from the latter, is endowed by Descartes with a covert ideality. Moreover, Lacan argues, if thought is able to think material substance, including the body, as homologous with it, this is because thought already thinks itself as having the finite, limited form of the body, and thus a kind of extension. This does not indicate that thinking is corporealized in any real sense; it indicates rather that the the body, extension, amounts in Descartes to nothing more than an *image* of the body. The Euclidean geometry (which is metrical) that informs Descartes's speculations is capable of taking the measure of only an *imaginarized* body, not the body as such. If we are interested in knowing something about this other relation between the subject and its body, Lacan's argument suggests, we must turn away from the Euclidean assumptions of Descartes's argument and look to the principles of projective geometry.

The lectures of *Seminar XIII* devoted to perspective open with a fundamental question to which Lacan then looks to projective geometry for an answer: "What precisely is this subject, this place necessitated by the constitution of the objective world?" We have determined that this "place" of the subject is the point of infinity (or vanishing point), projected into the world, not located outside it. Although this space is subjectively constituted, it is defined in some nontrivial sense as *objective.* The apparent paradox of this position does not spring uniquely from Lacan's text. Renaissance painting, we recall, is defined in the same paradoxical way, both as perspectival *and* as the invention in painting of a visual objectivity. Painting's precocious visual introduction of this paradox would thus precede by centuries its philosophical exploration; for, it was only in Kant that the dependency of the objectivity of the world on the subjectivity of the subject would come into philosophical focus. Notwithstanding the common caricature of his position, Kant did not hold the skeptical view that we have access only to subjective appearances, but advanced rather the more compelling argument that through a process he called "transcendental synthesis," the subject constituted a world that was not arbitrarily or *simply* subjectively ordered, but objective. The analysis of Renaissance perspective by Lacan ought to be taken, then, as his opening question implies, as an attempt to make sense of this Kantian notion of objectivity.

But why should psychoanalysis have anything to say about the philosophical problem of the objectivity of the world? The answer is: because the problem came knocking directly at psychoanalysis's door, without philosophical mediation, initially as the problem of hallucinatory satisfaction, most floridly, as the deliria of psychotics. Freud thus had to be able to explain how the "objective" thoughts of most subjects differed from the "subjective" ones, the deliria, of psychotics and newborns, who suffered from a lack of reality. We know that Freud first sought an answer in the agency of the ego and that this answer was expressed in Kantian terms: it was to the *synthetic* function of the ego that he looked to restore objectivity to a psychical system potentially overwhelmed by delirious thoughts. But the ego did not turn out to be up to this task, for as the study of narcissism would reveal, the ego is mired in the same muddy waters it was meant, originally, to titrate. It could not for this reason contribute to the constitution of an objective reality, quite the reverse. At this point in his work, Freud turned his focus from the ego to the drive ("On Narcissism" was written in 1914; "Instincts and Their Vicissitudes" in 1915) to find an answer to the question of reality.

One of psychoanalysis's deepest insights is that we are born not into an already constituted world that impinges on our senses to form perceptions, but in the wake of a primordial loss; it is not, then, our relation to the *order of things,* but our relation to *das Ding* that decides the objectivity of our reality or its collapse. In Freud's commonly cited but imperfectly understood formulation, objective reality is not where we find objects, but where we refind them. By *object* Freud meant something distinct from a hallucination, but by qualifying objects as *refound* he declined to sever reality completely from the pleasure with which hallucination was associated. *Das Ding* is roughly equivalent to the maternal body, more specifically to that experience of pleasure it once provided, though Freud maintained from the very beginning that this maternal object has no existence anywhere before it is lost.

In short, psychoanalysis does not take reality or the world for granted, but asks how the subject comes to constitute and thus "have" a reality or world. This constitution becomes precarious not only because it has to be accounted for rather than assumed, but also because the loss out of which she is born disposes the subject *not* to form attachments to external objects, but to pine for the lost one. Relocating the agency of reality's constitution from the ego to the drive, Freud rethought the role of the body and pleasure in the formation of worldly attachments. While the ego was conceived, in Freud's words, as a "projection of a bodily surface" with which the "I" of the subject coincided and, from there, confronted the world, the drive led to a new conception of an embodied subjectivity wherein the subject and its world were less separate than elaborately intertwined.

This description is obviously too sketchy, but as a quick check of its validity, one might consider the psychotic, who offers proof of its contrary. For, although psychosis is commonly said to entail a *loss of reality,* it is clear that it entails a *loss of the body* as well. The psychotic, whose corporeal experience is reduced to only two dimensions, *has no body* to speak of, just a kind of frame or bodily surface. Victor Tausk's brilliant documentation and analysis of the typical "paranoia somatica" or delusions of the "influencing machine" prevalent among psychotics showed conclusively that the psychotic's attempts to cure himself of his affliction consisted not only in the cursory and delusional "miracling up" of an ersatz world, but also in the "miracling up" of an ersatz body, a machine body made up of "boxes, cranks, levers, wheels, buttons, wires, batteries" through which the psychotic seeks to reattach himself to the world.[16] It is clear from this analysis, and from the hints Tausk takes up from Freud regarding the critical nature of the symptom of hypochondria, or "body trouble," among psychotics, that the one, reality, does not fail without the other, the body. The link between reality and the body is an essential datum of psychoanalysis, which nowhere lends support for a transcendent or noncorporeal constitution of reality.

No doubt Lacan had the wobbily edifices of the psychotic in mind—but he must also have been thinking of those of the perverts and neurotics, whose tics, paraplegias, catarrhs, and other self-inflicted wounds bore witness to their own efforts to maintain their grasp of reality—when he charged: "Compared to Freud the idealists of the philosophical tradition are small beer indeed, for in the last analysis they don't seriously contest that famous reality, they merely tame it. Idealism consists in affirming that we are the ones who give shape to reality, and there is no point in looking further. It is a comfortable position. Freud's position, or that of any sensible man . . . is something different. Reality is precarious. And it is precisely to the extent that . . . it is so precarious that the commandments which trace its path are so tyrannical."[17] You might be tempted to think that Freud's observation trumps others because it had the advantage of the clinic behind it, for it was to his clinic that all these botched bodies with their patched together realities betook themselves one by one, seeking help. But Lacan's allusion to "any sensible man" surely implies that the precariousness of reality ought to have been visible even to someone whose human commerce was strictly limited to dinner parties in the small town of Konigsberg. Freud opened our eyes to the fact that even for the most reasonable of us reality's foundations are necessarily shaky—despite Kant's careful and truly admirable attempt to lay the bricks of his famous architecture just so. No transcendental synthesis is capable of locking our reality fully into place, a fact at which Kant's theory itself seems to hint.

The question of reality's instability, it is becoming plain, is not only a matter of the difficulties of forming worldly attachments in the first place, but of a lingering instability that persists even once they are formed. To get to the heart of the problem as Lacan sees it, we begin by noting that his position on the precariousness of reality seems to set him apart, finally, from his close friend and colleague, Maurice Merleau-Ponty, whose work, especially *The Phenomenology of Perception* and the posthumously published *The Visible and the Invisible,* is admiringly cited in the sessions on the gaze in *Seminar XI.* Between the two friends there is much common ground. Like Lacan, Merleau-Ponty adamantly insisted that vision could not be divorced from carnality. The corporeality of the observer enters into, structures, the act of seeing. In Merleau-Ponty's signature notion of the "flesh," one can plainly discern the "uncolonized" or "inhuman" dimension of the drive, which tears holes in the tamed or socialized body, lacerating the projected surface of the body-ego image and causing the field of vision to be haunted by what remains invisible in it, by the impossible to see.

One is additionally struck by the similarity between the recurring figure of the chiasmic intertwining of vision and viewer, sensible and sensing being, touched and touching flesh, each folding or wrapping itself over the other, in Merleau-Ponty and the description of the envelope stucture of Renaissance painting in Lacan. Lacan even pauses to refer directly to one of the working notes appended to *The Visible and the Invisible,* in which the topology of the chiasmus is represented by the metaphor of the inside-out finger of a glove. Here is part of that note: "Reversibility: the finger of a glove that is turned inside out—There is no need of a spectator who would be *on each side.* It suffices that from one side I see the wrong side of the glove that is applied to the right side, that I touch the one *through* the other (double 'representation' of a point or plane of the field) the chiasm is that: the reversibility— . . ."[18] The eruption of the gaze into a Renaissance painting is analogous to the protrusion of the glove's fur lining when the leather finger is reversed, turned inside out. But where Merleau-Ponty is trying to expose the continuous lamination of the chiasmic terms, which would allow the viewer to bathe in the warmth of the gaze, Lacan forcefully delaminates the eye, or field of vision, from the gaze, renders the two radically disjunct. Only the artificial device of projective geometry forces the gaze to appear in the visible plane; eye and gaze eclipse each other in actual life. It is the very antinomy of these terms in Lacan's analysis that unsettles the objective field of vision.

As a result, the objectivity of the visible world, will be described differently by Merleau-Ponty and Lacan. For the former, objectivity means primarily that the visible has a certain depth, that is to say, a "behind," which, though it may be obscured from sight at any given moment, is nevertheless potentially visible to others or to ourselves at another moment. These other views "round out" objects, give them facets other than the ones we currently see. In Vermeer's *The Geographer,* for example, the geographer's body is turned almost completely toward the viewer. We do not see his back, nor do we see the whole of the armoire in front of which he stands, blocking our view. Yet we read the painting *as if* the geographer had a back and the armoire a base, which is simply, owing to our perspective, obscured from sight. Objectivity is here derived from the assumption that the existence of others, who see aspects of an object that are hidden from us, *confirm, supplement,* help *stabilize* our view. Lacan takes a different position, as we shall see in the next chapter. Aligning himself on this issue more with Sartre than with Merleau-Ponty, he emphasizes the way the Other's gaze destabilizes our reality, causing it to tremble at its base. When the gaze appears, vision is annihilated.

Let us return to the discussion of Renaissance perspective and geometric perspective, which we left only half-finished. The viewer, or the eye, we said, is projected into the visual field to become a spectacle. The vanishing point marks the place of the viewing subject. At the same time, a second point also becomes perceptible: the distance point, which designates "the spot on which the painter placed himself, at least ideally, to represent [what he painted]—*a ritrarlo* . . . to take its portrait, feature by feature."[19] This is the point Lacan designates as that of the gaze. As he remarks, since projective geometry concerns correspondence, not measurement, the point of the gaze is not determined metrically. What matters simply is that some distance, any distance or interval is marked in the painting as separating the two points: the vanishing point or viewing subject and the distance point or gaze. Why is this? What finally is the purpose of Renaissance perspective, what does it seek to do? It seeks to capture in the scopic *perceptum* the *percipiens.* Here, Lacan does not refer only to the appearance of the eye of the viewer in the scene, but also to the appearance of the gaze in the visible world. In the normal course of things, the gaze is not visible, for the subject separates himself from it in order to see. Through projection, however, there appears in the *perceptum* not only the look we direct at the painting, but the one it directs back at us. If the painting can look back at us, this is only because we are able to withdraw or step back from it, to put some distance between ourselves and what we see. This in turn implies that the *percipiens* or perceiving subject cannot be represented as a mere point, a static and abstract position, but is representable only as the interval or gap separating the point from which we see and the one from which we are seen. It is crucial to note, however, that the second point, the one from which the gaze looks back at the one that looks, is not locatable precisely, as a point, for this would have the effect of reducing it (like the vanishing point or place from which we see) to a part of the *perceptum.* The gap between the two points (one locatable, the other not) is demonstrable then only as a slight gap or interval within the *perceptum,* the painting itself. A minimal difference or otherness disclocates the painting from itself, some distortion or anamorphosis delaminates, peels the painting away from itself. Against all the false wisdom of the standard textbooks, from Panofsky on, wherein Renaissance paintings are described as attempts to represent distance by creating the illusion of a deep three-dimensional space on a flat surface, Lacan is saying that these paintings demonstrate rather the existence of that pure distance which separates the perceiving subject from herself. This distance, which is necessary for representation to be possible at all, defines not the abstract subject film theory set out to deconstruct, but the embodied subject of the scopic drive.

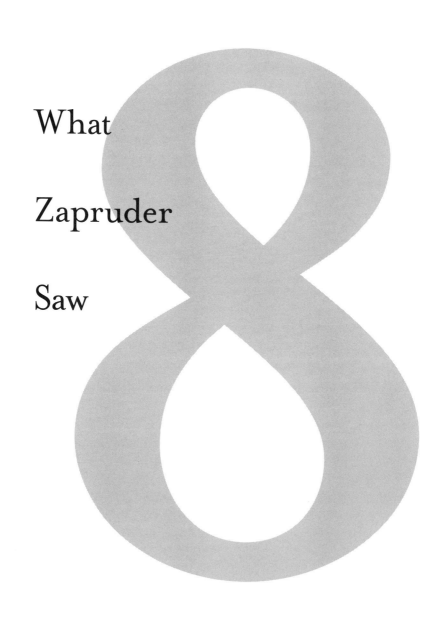

What

Zapruder

Saw

On November 22, 1963, as John F. Kennedy's motorcade drove through downtown Dallas, Abraham Zapruder lifted his 8mm camera to his eye and prepared to turn the ceremonious public event into his own home movie. For the next twenty-six seconds he stared steadily through the viewfinder. The result as everyone knows was a catastrophically aborted film that recently sold for an exorbitant price rivaling and surpassing any garnered by the masterworks of modern art that were auctioned off in the last several years on an especially avaricious art market. Yet even as newscasters drew the monetary comparison, they denied its validity by appraising the value of Zapruder's film not in aesthetic but in evidentiary and historical terms. The footage of the Kennedy assassination recorded a traumatic memory, a wound, as yet unassimilable in the narrative of our nation; this 8mm memory would thus be digitally restored not as a work of art but as a document to be entered into the national archive.

Against this backdrop, the remarks Pier Paolo Pasolini makes about the film—of John F. Kennedy "falling and dying on the seat of a black presidential car, in the weak embrace of his American petit-bourgeois wife"[1]— have a jarring effect. Not only are the preservationist imperative and reverential tone absent from his remarks only to be replaced by his unsentimental description of the action, but the film itself seems to be hauled in, as if arbitrarily, to illustrate an aesthetic argument that in effect impugns the film's evidentiary value. The essay in which Pasolini makes his comments, "Observations on the Long Take," is a brief intervention in the long take versus montage debate that once seemed so pressing to theorists of cinema. In his essay, Pasolini comes down strongly on the side of montage, invoking the Zapruder film, which he chooses to describe as "the most typical long take imaginable," as a counterexample. One cannot help being nonplussed by this marshaling of superlatives toward such a narrowly aesthetic, even technical, end.

Pasolini's thesis is the following: montage is superior to the long-take method of filmmaking because montage punctuates the present tense native to cinema with a kind of cut or "death" that gives meaning to the filmed material. The intervention of this cut allows the filmmaker not simply to juxtapose the bits of film he is assembling, but to coordinate them. The point of this distinction is to condone montage not as a mere mechanical device for assembling raw filmic material but as a means of constructing a point of view—hence, a subjectivity—in relation to which all the images will be ordered. But whereas in films built up through montage, death, in the form of the cut, bestows meaning on the actual, profilmic material (just as, Pasolini says in an absurd simile, a man's death retro-actively gives meaning to his life), in the long-take Zapruder film the situation is reversed: the actual, profilmic death of Kennedy is stripped of meaning precisely because it is filmed *without a cut*. As the only footage of the event, the image of the assassination cannot be coordinated with any other point of view, "that of Kennedy [or] Jacqueline, that of the assassin himself [or] his accomplices, that of those with a better vantage point . . . etc." As a consequence the film remains un-relievedly in the present tense, "aleatory, almost pitiful," and the action recorded in it becomes "almost incomprehensible," virtually meaningless. According to Pasolini's argument, however, the problem is not that the assassination foot-age cannot be coordinated with any *other* point of view, but that without this co-ordination the footage by itself has *no point of view,* properly speaking. Pasolini distinguishes the point-of-view structure created through montage, and the subjectivity belonging to it, from a different, attenuated or reduced form of sub-jectivity that is rendered by the long take. Moreover, whereas montage produces an objective image, the long take fails to achieve objectivity and remains merely subjective. In the long take, in other words, the "reality effect" endemic to cine-matic representation looses its footing and starts to falter.

That the objectivity of reality is not in conflict with but dependent on the subjectivity of an "incarnate" (Pasolini's word) subject is neither an unim-portant nor an unfamiliar argument; Kant first formulated it as the heart of his philosophy, though some have said he paid little attention to the subject's corpo-reality on which Pasolini insists. It is difficult, however, adequately to compre-hend Pasolini's filmic version of the philosophical argument, not just because of the brevity of the essay in which it is stated, but also because the simile it establishes between montage and death is troublingly opaque. Inasmuch as it is absurd on its face to say that life has meaning not in life itself but only retroactively in death

(Pasolini himself admits that he is speaking "poorly" here), we are tempted to view the references to death that crop up in the discussion of montage as misplaced, terminological tumbleweed blown over from the allusions to the Kennedy assassination with which the essay began. In other words, the association of montage with death appears at first to be a rhetorical echo-effect of the opening references to the President's actual death recorded by Zapruder. And yet Pasolini's bizarre thesis moves in exactly the opposite direction: *Kennedy's actual, senseless death is,* in some yet to be specified way, *an effect of the disavowal of montage.*

With an essay this elliptical, it helps not to be a naive reader—or viewer. If despite its underelaboration, the essay still rings true, this is because the central paradox it stammers to describe is already known to us from our own filmgoing experience. The objectivity of cinematic representation is obtained by suturing a series of point-of-view shots, filmed over the shoulders, or spatially related to the various characters in the narrative, with the remarkable result that all the different views somehow form a coherent and objective reality. But our experience also alerts us to a detail that Pasolini leaves out: included among the various shots that can be attributed to some point of view, there is a scattering of shots that, unassociated spatially with any particular character, cannot be attributed to any point of view. They seem thus to come from nowhere—not even, and this is an important qualification, from an omniscient observer, since *there are no objective shots in cinema.* Cinematic objectivity is constructed in the absence of any object shots.

A question arises: what is the difference between the two non-point-of-view shots just mentioned, the *unattributable* and the *subjective* shot? An unattributable shot appears to be neutral or empty of subjectivity because, as was said, in contradistinction to the point-of-view shot, it is not filmed from a space that is proximate to, partially includes, or is spatially associated with a character, but from a space unaffiliated with any particular person. Sometimes, however, the apparent absence of any spatial affiliation may simply be due to the fact that the shot is filmed from the exact position of the one who is looking; in which case the shot would be a subjective one. There is thus a formal similarity between unattributable and subjective shots, which is even exploited by Hitchcock in several films when he suddenly reveals that what the spectator has assumed was an unattributable shot is actually being filmed from the position of some demonic character—or bird.[2] All at once the shot "deteriorates" into an "optical point-of-view" or "subjective" shot.

The main point I am making is that although the distinction Pasolini tries to uphold between montage and long take appears to come down to a distinction between a series of interconnected point-of-view shots and an extended subjective shot, this summary will not suffice. The objectivity he associates with montage cannot be built up exclusively from point-of-view shots, but must include some unattributable shots as well. When Pasolini begins to explore the development of a free indirect style of filmmaking, he will make visible those kinds of shots that I designate as unattributable; but he will associate them exclusively with this style. I agree that these shots are foregrounded by this style of film, but insist that they are present in an unstressed form in standard filmmaking.

In order to emphasize the subjectivity of the supposedly documentary style of the assassination footage, Pasolini accuses Zapruder of not having selected his camera angle, of having simply "filmed from where he happened to be, framing what he, not the lens, saw"(3). The limited or attenuated form of subjectivity associated with Zapruder's subjective long take goes hand in hand with an inability or refusal creatively to *choose* a camera angle, with an acceptance of the position in which history happens to have placed him. Ironically, this reasoning describes the *subjective spectator* as a mere *passive recorder of events*, a mere *object*, or a *slave of history* who forfeits, as a consequence, all claim to objectivity. To attain the form of subjectivity that Pasolini associates with montage requires the addition of a lens. This is the second irony; the quasi-transcendence of one's historical circumstances here depends not, as one might have expected, on a voluntarist leap beyond one's historical positioning into some "abstract and nonnaturalist point of view," but on the addition of some material device: a lens or a camera and tape recorder. The final puzzler is that the picture one might spontaneously form of a spectator standing behind this lens or camera simply does not work as a translation of Pasolini's point, since "what the lens sees" (as opposed to what Zapruder subjectively sees) is rendered through point-of-view shots (in which the one who looks is often included). The lens that produces objectivity must be imagined to be not in front of, but *behind* the spectator. In other words, the filmmaker would have to be a part of the world he viewed through the lens. It is as if the reference to this lens were an attempt to reintroduce a complexity into the argument that the suppression of the reference to unattributable shots excised.

Given these revisions—which stress the strong link between the long take and the subjective shot—a sequence from one of Pasolini's own films, *Salò*, in which a series of subjective shots is deployed to chilling effect, invites our attention. I propose that this sequence plays the same role as the Zapruder film does in the essay: it illustrates the dire consequences of the denial of the cut. Indeed, there are a number of parallels between the Zapruder film and this sequence. Where in his essay Pasolini focused on the seemingly anonymous but actually highly—and disturbingly—subjective look of one person, Zapruder, in the sequence from *Salò* three spectators are involved, and their disturbingly subjective, unflinching looks are prosthetically enhanced not by a camera but by a pair of binoculars. The spectators, three of the four sadistic libertines who are at the center of the narrative, assume the apathetic posture of distanced and cruel objectivity characteristic of sadists, but the image they view is clearly marked as subjective insofar as it is visually opacified and distorted by the masking of its edges and central section, an indication of the shape of the (subjective) filtering device through which the scene is being viewed. The masking reveals that the scene is being shot from the exact position of the spectators, who are of course placed *behind* the binoculars. The object of the libertines' looks is as horrific as the one on which Zapruder focused: the ripping or laceration of flesh, not this time through an act of assassination but through the ritualistic torture and execution of the libertines' beautiful victims.

The intensified presence of the image of assassination, remarked by Pasolini, is paralleled in *Salò* by a suffocating nearness. Indeed, as one of the libertines turns the binoculars the wrong end around before looking through them, the spectator vainly hopes that the resulting reduction of the image will distance it and thus bring some relief from its overwhelming presence. But it does not. During the sequence sound is almost totally eliminated, which has the effect of exacerbating the feeling of closeness. Had the sound not been deadened, it would have drawn attention to the point source from which it emanated and would thus have challenged the hegemony of the visuals; that is, sound would have introduced a limit, a cut, in the field of vision and would have permitted some distance to open up between us and the image. Silence fastens us to the present tense of the image. Everything happens as if the external frame of the image, the masking device, were somehow a substitute for an internal, distancing cut. The frame does not split the world from within, but cuts it out from a black background and makes it appear as a fragment, a fetish.

The question now before us is this: what, if anything, does the content of these images have to do with the formal argument regarding the presence or absence of point of view or montage? What does the formal absence of montage

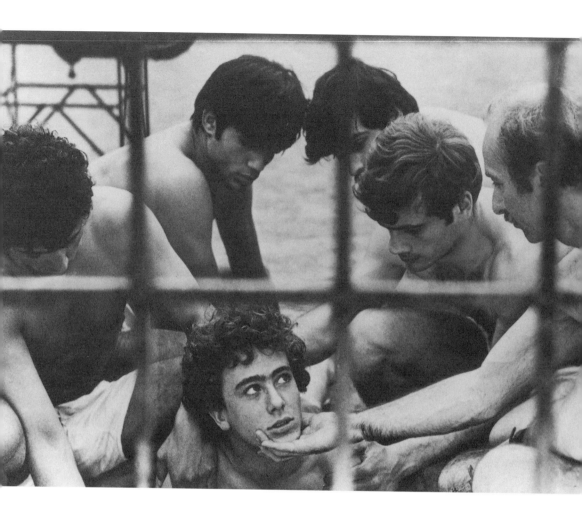

Figure 8.1 Pasolini, *Salò*. Courtesy The Museum of Modern Art (N.Y.)/Film Stills Archive.

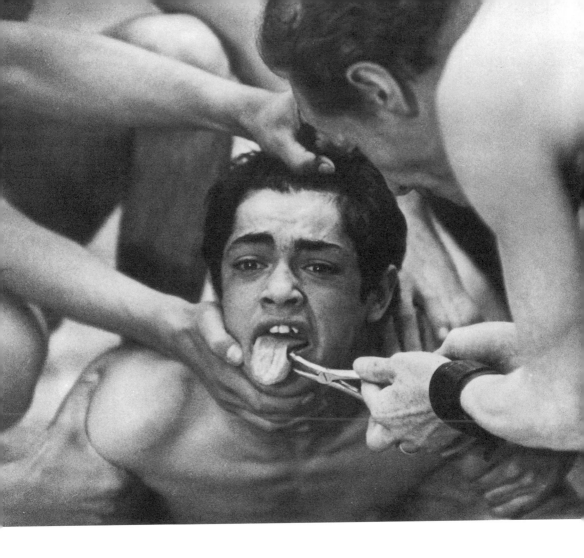

Figure 8.2 Pasolini, *Salò*. Courtesy The Museum of Modern Art (N.Y.)/Film Stills Archive.

(that is, an internal cut) have to do with the physical cutting of flesh? In Pasolini's essay a disconcerting imbalance exists between the seemingly limited, formal intent of the cinematic argument and the freighted content of the film chosen to illustrate it. It is almost as if the action recorded by the long take were beside, or in excess of, the formal point, and yet when Pasolini does summarize the action—"falling and dying, on the seat of a black presidential car, in the weak embrace," and so on—his unsentimental, slightly contemptuous tone betrays something other than neutrality. It seems to be *affected* by what it describes. By double-loading the content with an additional reference to *Salò*, I mean to foreground the actions on which these subjective shots are trained. The problem is to know how much to count the parallels between what happens in the Zapruder film and what happens in the sequence from *Salò*, because in the latter, where we witness the torture and execution of the victims, the acts that take place before our eyes are not just any acts, they are acts of *perversion*. Surely the same cannot be said of the act taking place before our eyes in Zapruder's infamous film?

Let me try to forestall at the outset any misunderstanding regarding my use of the charged term *perversion*. As Laplanche and Pontalis have warned, "It is difficult to comprehend the idea of perversion otherwise than by reference to a norm."[3] That is, it is difficult to understand perversion as anything but a deviation from the norms of sexual conduct. The problem with this, however, is that the supposed norm—which Freud summarized thus: typically, sexuality is "understood to be absent in childhood, to set in at the time of puberty in connection with the process of coming to maturity and to be revealed in the manifestation of an irresistible attraction exercised by one sex upon the other; while its aim is presumed to be sexual union, or . . . action leading in that direction"[4]—was almost immediately scrapped by Freudian theory, which located a *generalized* perversion in the heart of human sexuality and unearthed a fundamental absence of any sexual ratio between the sexes.

What meaning then can the *restricted* notion of perversion have in psychoanalysis? To answer this question one has first to stop thinking of sexuality as a relation between a subject and an other, or object-choice deemed to be either correct or incorrect, normal or deviant. Under this new stricture, for example, homosexuality would not automatically be classifiable as a perversion. The difference between neurosis and perversion does not only concern one's object-choice, or relation to a particular other, but also one's relation to the big Other or the

various laws and institutions governing social existence. It has often been observed that this structural definition brings the psychical categories of neurosis,
psychosis, and perversion closer to Heidegger's notion of *Existentialen,* formal conditions for the possibility of being-in-the-world, than to the clinical "patholo-
gies," which Freud inherited from an older psychology. Beyond psychoanalysis,
one should point to the fact that various works of political philosophy also invoke
the name of Sade in trying to name the emergence of a new mode of the subject's
relation to the world. Adorno and Horkheimer in *Dialectic of Enlightenment,* Hannah
Arendt in *Eichmann in Jerusalem,* and of course Lacan in "Kant with Sade" have all seriously considered the perversion of sadism not as an individual pathology in the
pre-Freudian sense, but as a type of relation on the same order and level as the
one Kant describes between the modern subject and its world. This is why it is "a
stupid thing to say" that Sade anticipates Freud by providing a kind of "catalogue
of perversions" (pathological and plural), for, the true value of the Sadean bedroom, which is to have clarified the perverse structure, makes it "the equal to
those places from which the schools of ancient philosophy took their name."[5] In
Lacan, Arendt, Horkeimer and Adorno, it is Kant's moral philosophy that is the
primary reference, and the question for each of these is: how does the apathy or
disinterestedness of the Kantian subject, and the transgressive indifference to
man-made laws associated with this apathy, differ from that form of apathy and
those types of transgressions found in sadism? Or: what, if anything, distinguishes
the free, ethical act from the sadist's cruel instrumentalization of others? Because
Kant saw the modern subject as "out of joint" with its world, or as structurally in
revolt against its laws and institutions, the question that keeps arising in these
texts—and in others that strive for a "fashionable look" by celebrating Sade as a
man of courage, as an ethical man[6]—is this: are not the transgressions of perversion a development, either dialectical or direct, of this modern stance of revolt or
"out-of-jointness"?

The first distinction to be made is between the *possibility* of rebelling that
is available to the Kantian subject with the *obligation* to rebel that weighs on the pervert. Through his flagrant violations of the prohibitions of bourgeois society,
Sade (who spent one-third of his life in prison) kept courting the gallows, but it
would be foolish to mistake these violations for ethical independence. Rather
than attempts to dismantle the law, Sade's acts of defiance were the means by
which he sought to make it perform its "proper" function, namely, to punish

him. What he wanted above all was for the law to assume its full strength and potency, and he wanted to test its force on his own skin.

The conflation of Kant with Sade, or of ethical action with perversion, is no doubt due, in large part, to a theoretical laxity on the question of transgression. Guy Rosolato made the point some time ago that to speak of transgression, "it is necessary first to imagine a contestation in the order and spirit of the law, a division in the heart of belief, a certain hesitation in credence, or even a revolt of pleasure."[7] For, it is only insofar as there has been a certain disqualification that a transformation or rebellion in the domain of the law is conceivable. There has to be a *fissure* in the law itself in order for transgression to get a foothold. If Freud can speak of the perversity of the drive as such, of a generalized perversion of the sexual instinct, it is because the law to which the subject is subjected is fissured, and it is this that permits the drive to develop precisely as an infringement of the laws of "civilized sexual morality."

THE OTHER, PROBABLY

From Pasolini's views on cinematic form, montage versus long take, to Kant versus Sade; let me remind you how we got to this point. "It is impossible to perceive reality as it happens," Pasolini tells us, "*if not from a single point of view,* and this point of view is always that of a perceiving subject"(3). As mentioned earlier, this is one of the main theses of Kant's philosophy: objective reality emerges in and through the perspective of an individual subject. In the subjective shot, however, cinematic form bears witness to another type of perceiving subject (coeval with the Kantian subject) for whom the world no longer has this same objectivity. From this we can deduce that there has been an alteration in the structure of the subject's relation to the law. For Pasolini this sort of subjective shot is best exemplified by the Zapruder film; I have proposed that *Salò* is an equally appropriate example, but I have left open the question of how far to take the comparison.

Since his focus is on the sort of look specific to the two types of film he wants to distinguish, we can approach the distinction Pasolini makes through the theory of the look and the gaze developed within film theory. The contribution of Lacan to this theory is well acknowledged, as is his reliance on Sartre's thoughts on "the look" (which is more or less equivalent to Lacan's *gaze*) in *Being and Nothingness.* In fact in this context it is the text of Sartre that most seductively invites our attention, for there the general elaboration of the phenomenon of the gaze is followed by some reflections on the function of the gaze in sadism.

The scene Lacan borrows from Sartre is well known, but let me recall it. A voyeur peering through a keyhole is absorbed in his own act of looking, until suddenly he is surprised by the rustling of branches behind him, or the sound of footsteps followed by silence. At this point the *look* of the voyeur is interrupted by the *gaze* that precipitates him as an object, a *body* capable of being hurt.[8] What is this gaze? The best way of approaching this question is to determine what problem the concept of the gaze is meant to solve. The problem, it turns out, is one raised by the very assumption from which we have been proceeding, that the world exists only in relation to me, as subject, and comes into being only through my perspective on it. Given this assumption, how then can I lay claim to any objectivity? How can I be sure that the world I see, and thus the one I inhabit, is not *merely my own private fantasy*? How can I be certain that others exist, that there is some objectivity to my world? It is to this series of questions that the gaze is offered as answer: I can be sure that others exist because I encounter a gaze. Now, Sartre is explicit about what he is *not* saying when he ascribes to the gaze this role of guarantor of objectivity. He is *not* saying that the gaze of the Other is the *formal condition of the possibility of my knowledge*; the gaze is not proof of the objectivity of my *cognitive knowledge* of the world. He plainly and repeatedly protests that the Other as gaze does not appear to me "as a unifying or regulative category of my experience" (360); that the gaze "does not serve as a regulative or constitutive concept" (367); that it is not a "purely formal notion which refers to an . . . omnipresent, infinite subject *for whom* I exist" (375); and so on. And yet film theory, which consistently confuses the gaze with a single point or eye totally outside and transcendent to the filmic space, a point from which the space is unified or mastered, chose from the beginning to understand the gaze in the precise manner against which Sartre warned. For film theory the gaze is a unifying or regulative category of my experience.

Kaja Silverman, to her credit, is the only film theorist, however, to have taken a serious look at the Sartrean source of Lacan's concept of the gaze. Nevertheless, I find myself in respectful disagreement with her reading on several points. Turning his own warnings against him, she accuses Sartre of theorizing the gaze as a "transcendent eye," and then proposes that the ahistorical structure he describes ought to be revised to include a historical dimension.[9] She then argues that the gaze be reconsidered as a preexisting "cultural screen" (168) or an "imaginary viewfinder" (197), which "frames us" (135) and "organizes what we see" (197). In other words, after taking the gaze precisely *as* a unifying and regulative category of experience, she then *historicizes* it by reducing the Kantian notion of the "conditions of possibility" of perception to a set of social conventions, or an "unconscious" social contract specific to a given culture or historical moment. To say that we are subject to a gaze is to say that we apprehend ourselves through a "cultural screen," which acts as a unifying framework or cognitive condition of experience. There is an animus motivating this revision, which stems from a misunderstanding regarding Sartre's use of the term *transcendent* to define the relation of the gaze to the visual field. His argument is *not* that the gaze is transcendent in the sense of being a cognitive condition of my experience (again, as he repeatedly says), but in the sense that *it cannot be attached to any object in my world,* despite the fact that it is met with *only* in the world. This is a very different proposal than the one he is accused of making. Although the gaze is not, in Sartre's view, an immanent part of my world, neither does it have an existence anywhere else. I stumble on it as a surplus object *in the world,* through what Lacan, interpreting Sartre, called a "failed encounter."

Let us take a closer look at this notion of encounter. The first thing to note is that the encounter prevents us from thinking "emptily" about the Other. Rather than conceiving the Other as transcendentally out of my reach and therefore as lacking any sensible content by which I might apprehend it, Sartre argues that the Other is revealed to me *directly* through a chance meeting. The infinitely receding horizon of experience on which idealist philosophers place the Other stops receding all at once: I stumble immediately on the gaze of the Other in a sensible form. And yet it is not the gaze that has a sensible form, for the gaze is not an object in the ordinary sense. While it is always met with among objects, is always "manifested in connection with the appearance of a sensible form," which can be seen (in the slight parting of curtains on a window in a horror film, for example), or heard (the creaking of a door), or smelled (an exotic perfume), the gaze itself would swiftly evaporate were any of these sensible disturbances to become the index of a determinate observer, that is, were the Other of the gaze to become a determinate person, a small other. The reference to a specific seer remains in suspense in the encounter with the Other's gaze. This is also why I disagree with Silverman's assessment that the gaze is the subject's "imaginary rival" (166). There is no reciprocity between the observing subject and the Other of the gaze whereby each could come to recognize the other. On this point Sartre is clear: "The Other [of the gaze] is inapprehensible; he flees me when I seek him and possesses me when I flee him" (529). The gaze looks at me, but I can never catch sight of it there where it looks; for there is no "there," no determinate lo-cation, no place whence it looks.

Let us attend more closely to the fact that the presence of the Other is *sensible* to me. On first approach this seems to accord with the claim that what I ap-prehend immediately through these experiences of the gaze is not that *"there is someone there*; it is that I am vulnerable, that I have a body which can be hurt." If the gaze is revealed to me, it is not insofar as I am a disembodied subject, through pure cognition; it is rather as embodied subject, through sensible indications, that I encounter the gaze of the Other. We must be careful, however, not to con-fuse the body with that biophysiological fiction constructed in the nineteenth century by the burgeoning "life sciences." According to these sciences, the body is an *object* that bumps up against other objects in the world through sense organs located at its surface. Unaccountably, however, it is not the body but "mind" or consciousness that is "bruised," as it were, by this mechanical notion of contact. Traces called *sensations* are formed in the mind, and from them one is supposed to be able to refer back to the particular external objects that caused them. This no-tion of sensation attempts to resolve the problem of perception by fiat. It posits the existence of the external world teleologically, on the basis of the fact that I am provided with sense organs that put me in touch with it; but in order to do so, it opens an unbridgeable gap between mind and body that completely undermines the solution it offers. Thus, the problem of perception—of how we can be sure it refers to an existence separate from itself—remains unsolved.

The sensible form—whether a pair of eyes peering through shutters, or the rustling of branches, or the sound of footsteps—that manifests the gaze is not a sensation, in the above sense, whose referent is a determinate object. If on hear-ing footsteps he were to turn around and catch someone looking at him, the voyeur would confront not the gaze but merely the eyes of a particular observer. Sartre begins his discussion of the gaze with an implied question: "Does the Other exist?" To this he gives a firm response, "Probably." One must be clear about the meaning of his reply. Sartre is not hedging or conjecturing, "Well, there is no way to be sure, but my guess is that he does." He replies without hesitation, "The Other exists probably." *Probably* describes not the chances of the Other's existence, but the manner of that existence: by chance, through the contingency of an en-counter. It is not possible, however, to proceed analytically from the contingency of this meeting to any cognitive knowledge of the Other. The Other is not the ob-ject of a possible cognition.

And yet Sartre does also speak of a certainty that attaches to our encounter with the Other's gaze. Of what can we be certain? That there is "some" Other, that there are "(some) consciousnesses for whom I exist" (374).[10] The term *some* has nothing to do with quantity, with plurality (which can only be attributed to objects); it is not meant to imply that some part of the Other makes itself known to me nor that some concrete number of others exist alongside me. As Sartre puts it, the Other one encounters in the experience of the gaze is "prenumerical" (375); that is, it is neither an empty, transcendent *One* that unifies and guarantees existence, nor is it a *concrete community of others,* whose shared notion of reality acts as its own guarantee. In other words, *the presence of others as such,* of which the encounter assures us, cannot be objectivized either as (1) something unifying and abstract, a formal condition of knowledge that will—as long as I divest myself of all my prejudices and particularities—ensure that what I see is objectively true, nor as (2) a "scientific" community that can confirm, on the basis of the norms and procedures we share, the validity of my perceptions. This definitively rules out the possibility that the gaze might be understood as a matter of social consensus or as a "cultural screen."

Here we have evidence of that objectivity for which we have been searching. But it is not what we expected to find. The gaze stamps my perception with a seal of *objectivity,* but this seal guarantees only that some others exists, not that what I see is "true" in the sense of being an adequate representation of a reality outside my point of view. Rather than an external confirmation of the clarity and truth of my perception, I encounter an obstacle to it. Perception stumbles. Again, Lacan's translation—the encounter is always a *missed* encounter—is helpful, and not least of all because it establishes an important link between Freud and Sartre, whose denial of the unconscious is notorious. In his essay "The Unconscious," Freud argued that the very phenomena that cloud consciousness—parapraxes, dreams, symptoms, foreign ideas, thought inhibitions, and so on—serve as incontrovertible evidence, direct *proof,* of the existence of the unconscious.[11] Freud then immediately warns that the unconscious should not be confused with that of a *second consciousness.* Thus: though parapraxes are indisputable proof of the existence of some Other (scene), to associate them with a determinate, second consciousness, would only imperil the notion of the unconscious by objectivizing (and thus destroying) its "prenumerical" reality. (The point here is not merely to use Freud to help us understand Sartre, but also to use Sartre to help avoid the traps into which post-Freudian conceptions of the unconscious all too frequently fall.)

This seal of objectivity, the sense of the presence of others as such, emerges not in a moment of *cognition* ("I know that others exist"), but in *a feeling of shame* that suffuses the body of the observer. This moment is commonly celebrated by visual theorists as one of deflation: pure, transcendent consciousness finds itself suddenly demoted to the status of a corporealized observer. Consciousness is shamed by an abrupt reminder that it is after all tethered to bodily vulnerability. This is a distortion of Sartre's point and smacks of a confusion of shame with the warm blush of social censure or disgrace. The voyeur is not caught off guard by a representative of social respectability in whose censorious eyes he falls condemned: for all your pretensions you are nothing but carnal being. He is caught by a gaze, it is good to remember, that cannot refer back to any specific norm of judgment because it refers to no determinate object. The shame that seeps through the body of the observer announces not a particular judgment, but the birth of the social as such. It therefore precedes the possibility of shame in the sociological or civic sense.

We know that Freud associated women, specifically, with the feeling of shame, but what this association implies is not generally thought through. Feminists routinely insist that if women are the particular repositories of this feeling it is because they see themselves through the eyes—or the "cultural viewfinder"—of their own society, which stigmatizes them as inferior in worth. A sociological rather than a psychoanalytic explanation, this mistakes the meaning of shame, which results not from "seeing oneself through the Other," as is supposed, but from "making oneself seen." Lacan draws this last distinction from Freud, who anticipated in his own way the argument Sartre makes about the feeling of shame.

Sartre's distinction depends on the difference he had already introduced between an objectivized Other, either a determinate individual or a countable number of them, and an "Other-as-subject," the prenumerical Other, once again. Shame results from looking at ourselves through the second, not the first, the "Other-as-subject" not the objectivized Other. Freud's argument is remarkably similar; it distinguishes the act of looking at oneself through the intermediary of an *alien object* from the act of looking at oneself through an *alien person.*[12] The first concerns that reflexive circuit by which one apprehends oneself in the categories of the culture to which one belongs or of someone one wishes to please, with the result that one thereby regards oneself as a known or knowable object. The second concerns a completely different kind of circuit, that of the active-passive drive, which turns around on itself. In this case, because I do not expose myself to the look of a determinate other, I do not receive a message back regarding my determinate identity. The reflexive circuit of the scopic drive does not produce a *knowable object;* it produces a *transgression of the principle of pleasure,* by forcing a hole in it. The scopic drive produces an exorbitant pleasure that disrupts the ego identity formed by the first circuit. Or: in the drive, the subject does not see itself by looking at itself through the Other, but rather, in Freud's words, *"Selbst ein Sexualglied beschauen* [the self is seen in its sexual member]."[13] It is this "seeing oneself in one's sexual member," in the exorbitant pleasure of the drive, that occasions the feeling of shame, of being seen by others as such.

Before examining further this question of shame, we must pause to take stock of the implications of Sartre's argument, which is after all not without resonance in the very field we are investigating. The structure Sartre describes, whereby we experience ourselves as visible in the world, informs, for example, the following observation made by Deleuze, specifically in relation to Pasolini:

> Can we not find this dividing-in-two, or this differentiation of the subject in language, in thought and in art? It is the *Cogito:* an empirical subject cannot be born into the world without simultaneously being reflected in a transcendental subject which thinks it and in which it thinks itself. And the *Cogito* of art: there is no subject which acts without another which watches it act, and which grasps it as acted. . . . But this dividing in two never goes to the limit. It is rather an oscillation of the person between two points of view on himself. . . . What, in all of this, relates to cinema? Why does Pasolini think that [in] the cinema [there is] an equivalent of free indirect discourse in the image?[14]

Pasolini had a long-standing interest in free indirect discourse, that narrative form which came into existence with the birth of the novel and was associated originally with women writers, such as Fanny Burney and Jane Austen, who is credited with perfecting it. To be brief, in free indirect discourse a character's thoughts and words are neither directly represented, or quoted, nor indirectly rendered by a distant report. Rather, between the character and the instance of narration there occurs "an exchange of linguistic ardors,"[15] wherein the narration itself either seems to adopt the lexical features of the character's discourse or lends to the character a type of speech she or he would not realistically employ. In the latter case think, for example, of *Madame Bovary,* in which Emma's banal ideas and insipid fantasies are often narrated in an elevated style that is clearly foreign to Emma. Or, to illustrate the former case, think of Yvonne Rainer's *Film about a Woman Who . . .*, when the narration reports the woman's feelings this way: "She wanted to bash his fucking face in." The adjective that attaches itself to the man's face does not present an objective description of it and thus cannot belong to a neutral observer, but borrows rather from the idiom of the woman who wanted to do the bashing. What we are given in both cases is the point of view of the character, Emma or the unnamed woman, yet this point of view, as per Pasolini's argument, is saved from being merely subjective by being rendered not directly but as though watched or reflected in a transcendental subject. Yet this observer never crystallizes into another character, into an actual, determinate viewer. As a result, though he seems to be omnipresent, capable of observing events the characters do not (but which are nevertheless critical to the presentation of their points of view) and penetrating even the innermost thoughts and feelings of each of the characters, this transcendental subject in which everything that is narrated seems to be reflected cannot be located anywhere specifically and thus remains *invisible.*

Pasolini referred to free indirect discourse as "reanimated speech" because in it we can discern "the purring of meditative thought, of grumbling, of regretting, of recrimination, etc."[16] Everything happens as if the characters, while fully immersed in their points of view or in their lives as such, simultaneously stood partially outside themselves, reflected in the gaze of another. The purring, grumbling, regretting, recrimination we hear running through the narrative results from our sense that every thought and action is being examined simultaneously from the point of some external gaze. And yet, as we noted, all we ever get are these moments of "linguistic ardor," these moments of "lexical anamorphosis" when the idiom strikes us as inappropriate either to the character or to the narration, or when dashes and exclamations points are interjected, thus spoiling the expected neutrality of the narration. The parallel to Sartre's argument here is precise. These moments of lexical disturbance are exactly equivalent to the rustling of branches, the parting of curtains, or the sounds of footsteps. Outside the novel or poetry, in film, such moments are to be found, Deleuze tells us, in an "'insistent' or 'obsessive' framing, which makes the camera await the entry of a character into the frame, wait for him to do and say something and then exit, while it continues to frame the space which has once again become empty."[17] In other words, these moments are to be found in what I called earlier *unattributable shots,* shots that cannot be linked to a specific observer. The point is this: these camera movements or shots, like the rustling of branches and so forth, are sensible indications of the *gaze* of the Other, but not of the Other as such, who never appears in the flesh, as a sensible presence. In all these instances, *we encounter the gaze rather than the Other, not as part of the Other. There is no bearer of the gaze, there is only the gaze,* and this, to speak like Deleuze, is the cogito of modern art. Objective reality is rendered novelistically and cinematically through the point of view of a character, which is reflected in "another consciousness." Yet there is no transcendental subject to be found, no omniscient God who sees everything; this is even the ineluctable fact on which point-of-view structure—and thus novelistic and cinematic narrative form—is founded. Point-of-view structure depends on there being no total view, no transcendental position from which an all would, if only in principle, come into view.

What, then, to return to our original and only partially answered question, is the gaze? It is that excess object, encountered as some disturbance within point of view, which makes visible the *emptiness* of the transcendental position, the *absence* of the transcendental subject. For, to be looked at from all sides by a nomadic gaze is to experience ourselves as visible in the world, as sunk within a perspective on which there can be another perspective, whereas to be visible to an all-seeing God would be to experience ourselves as part of some whole. In the first case, the other perspective threatens to demolish or overwhelm our own, while in the second this radical antagonism of perspectives gives way to the sense that God's view enlarges or rectifies our own. In this latter case we are no longer visible in the world, but fully visible only outside it.

Let us return to the relation Sartre establishes between the flush of shame and the birth of the social. This relation interests Lacan, who seeks to confirm it, we noted, through reference to "Instincts and Their Vicissitudes," where Freud posits that the original object of the scopic drive is the subject's own sexual organ. In the drive the subject actively makes himself seen in his sexual organ, actively undertakes to bring about the passivity he undergoes in being seen. Since shame is often associated with a feeling of sexual exposure or nakedness, one is likely to be satisfied with a hasty gloss of this description. More care is necessary, however, if we are to avoid the already mentioned error of interpreting shame as the sudden realization of the inescapability of the subject's body by that subject attempting to flee into pure consciousness. First, although the agent and object of the drive coincide in the same subject, they are not simultaneous. The Sartrean phrase "uneasy indetermination" (351) remains applicable as a description of the flickering relation the active and passive moments of the drive maintain toward each other. The subject feels himself to be seen without at any moment actually seeing himself. There is no transparency of the subject to himself; where he sees, he is not seen. A gap is thus opened up between the subject and himself, and it is to this opening that one can attribute our sense that there are (some) indeterminate others. Second, although shame is generally linked to sexual exposure, "having a sense of shame" also implies a kind of restraint, a certain veiling of oneself. Shame recognizes limits.

How are we to define the relation between exposure and veiling? The easiest solution would be to understand the latter as a response to the former, but I think this is wrong; I propose we think of the two as equivalent. It is not that feeling oneself vulnerable, unconcealed before a prying eye, one reacts by concealing oneself; rather that which is exposed by the gaze is a veiling. In his reading of *Antigone,* Lacan attempts to elaborate a notion of what he refers to as the limit of "the second death." It is to this limit that shame is witness, if not the exclusive one: for beauty also acknowledges this limit: Lacan focuses on the phenomenon of the beautiful while noting its parallels to the experience of shame. His analysis centers on the "unbearable splendor" the image of Antiogone assumes in the eyes of the Chorus, who observe her on the point of death and just after she delivers her long lament on all the joys of which her death sentence will deprive her. Commentators have often been scandalized by this fiery and passionate speech and her clinging to life at the last moment because it seems to them to be out of character. After all, they argue, she is as Creon aptly observed "a cold object to caress" and has disregarded he own self-interests up until this point.[18]

Compare Antigone's reaction to the imminent threat of death to the following one, cited by Giorgio Agamben from Robert Antelme's *The Human Race.* The passage relates an incident at the end of World War II, when on a march of prisoners from Buchenwald to Dachau, Nazi soldiers selected an Italian prisoner, apparently arbitrarily, to be shot on the spot. I quote the full citation:

The SS continues. *"Du komme hier!"* Another Italian steps out of the column, a student from Bologna. I know him. His face has turned pink. I look at him closely. I still have that pink before my eyes. He stands there at the side of the road. He doesn't know what to do with his hands. . . . He turned pink after the SS man said to him, *"Du komme hier!"* He must have glanced about him before he flushed; but yes, it was he who had been picked, and when he doubted it no longer, he turned pink. The SS who was looking for a man, any man, to kill, had found him. And having found him, he looked no further. He didn't ask himself: "Why him, instead of someone else?" And the Italian, having understood it was really him, accepted this chance selection. He didn't wonder: Why me, instead of someone else?[19]

The point is not to contrast the Italian soldier's acceptance of his cruel fate with Antigone's resisting lament. There is little doubt that Antigone knows and accepts fully the death to which she has been condemned. One must see her heated speech, rather, as equivalent to the flush of warm pink that warms and brightens the soldier's face. While the Greek heroine and the Italian solider are in these moments stripped completely of all illusions of a future, know themselves to be on the threshold of death, the very stripping away of all life and every illusion exposes a remainder, a kind of surplus of life beyond life or a final barrier between life and their ultimate annihilation, their fall into nothingness. Or: that which is exposed in these moments is what conceals the nothingness of death.

In the midst of her lament, Antigone compares herself to Niobe, that mythological figure whose unendurable grief at the loss of her entire family was preserved forever when she was turned to stone. Antigone is like Niobe in this sense: her unendurable suffering perpetuates itself even after she has surrendered all claims to life. We are now in a position to see that Sartre has to be revised. For whereas he argues that shame indicates we have a body that can be hurt, it is apparent from the cases of Antigone and the student from Bologna that shame gives evidence of a body that can be made to suffer unbearable pain—which is to say: a suffering that consciousness cannot own. Psychoanalysis calls this particular pain libidinal satisfaction or jouissance, which is a pleasure that cannot be absorbed by consciousness. Classicists tell us that Greek tragedy revolved around the display of the "beautiful death" of the hero or heroine. This does not mean that the Greeks sought some pleasure or comfort from knowing that they could, when necessary, stare death in the face without flinching. It is not death that is on display in these tragedies but the terrible image of immortal jouissance, the final barrier against death. This image must be opposed, of course, to the sort of image that idealization might produce. The idealized image and the image of the beautiful death both function as barriers that cause the spectator to respect the limits they define. But the idealized image makes us long for an unreachable plenitude beyond it, whereas the image of the beautiful death makes us despise the nothingness that lies beyond it.

ANXIETY AND THE GAZE

At one point Sartre refers to the affect attendant on the encounter with the gaze as one of *pure monition.* Freud would have called it anxiety. Because it does not issue from a determinate source or as a determinate warning, it is a blank threat or objectless fear. In attempting to trace the precise relation between anxiety and the gaze it is worthwhile to follow the reasoning of Leo Bersani, whose customary caution makes him one of the subtlest readers of Freud. In *Homos,* Bersani examines the Wolf Man case, in which the anxiety aroused by the threat of castration posed by the father is first theorized. What piques Bersani's suspicion is the Wolf Man's evident feelings for his father, which are far more compassionate and loving than one might have expected on the basis of the theory Freud drew from it. Yet no amount of evidence of the real relation between father and son is able, Bersani marvels, to deter Freud "from giving the father the dubious privilege of exercising his castration prerogative."[20] That is, "in spite of everything," in spite of the boy's *actual* or "accidental experience," Freud insists that the boy perceived his father as the bearer of a threat. Why? The only answer which is offered is that it *has to have been* the father since, if we look into the prehistory of man, we will find that it was unquestionably the father who practiced castration as a threat. As evidence goes, this is flimsy, so Bersani implies; Freud goes to preposterous lengths to preserve his theory, claiming in a last ditch effort to save it that it has to be so. On closer inspection, however, the theory Freud struggles to preserve is far more interesting than Bersani wants here to admit. The reference to prehistory, which appears so desperate at this point, does not recede in Freud's later work like some youthful error; on the contrary, it blossoms into one of the major inventions of psychoanalysis: the myth of the primal horde. From this myth we learn why the reference to the prehistorical father must be retained: although this father has been dead since the beginning of time, when his sons rose up to assassinate him, the *fact of his death* has not prevented the *necessity of his existence* from outliving him. (Here we encounter a harder fact, a more unbudgeable reality, than anything one might find in reality itself; we would be safe to call it *real.*) The sons thus take it upon themselves to keep the knowledge of his death from the father, for were he simply to die, to cease to have this permanent, dislodgeable place in the unconscious, reality itself would collapse. This does not mean that reality depends on keeping the primordial father alive; what must be retained is his empty place.

It would be hard to overlook the parallels between this description of the relation of the sons to the law of the dead father and Sartre's description of the voyeur's relation to the gaze. The fact of the Other's death is beyond dispute, and yet the necessity of his law and the real of his gaze survive his death. This law of the dead father must be, then, according to the logic of the gaze as presented by Sartre, neither immanent in the world—a law on the books, enforceable in courts—nor transcendent to it, a divine law. Yet we encounter the father and his law obliquely in his concrete, living representatives—earthly fathers, judges, police, and so on—which is not to say that either the father or his law are reducible to these mundane instances. These paternal figures are perceived as *only* the representatives, not the creators, of the law. The difficulty Bersani was attempting to locate must then be stated something like this: the boy's actual father cannot be the source of castration anxiety; the threat emanates, rather, from the gap or hiatus that opens up between the father and a law that is felt to exceed him. It is this noncoalescence of representative and creator that fissures symbolic law and eventually allows it to be transgressed. No man-made or cultural law constitutes the law as such, and this is what makes it susceptible to infringement.

The myth of the assassination of the father of absolute power accounts for a curious situation, a problematic clearly manifest in the modern world. We are confronted with the difficulty of knowing how to stand up to a father who is dead. How does one address oneself to a faceless law, one that—like the gaze—always approaches us, as in Sartre's scenario, *from behind*? These are the same questions posed by the emergence of the modern public sphere in which the gaze makes its always unexpected and phantomlike appearances. How does one put oneself on the public stage when one's audience is no longer out in front of us, but everywhere and nowhere? It is no coincidence that "publicity," the new sphere of social relations set up in modernity, immediately threatened "theatricality" (theatrical space and performance), which would eventually lose ground to those techniques of "absorption" identified by Michael Fried in late-eighteenth-century paintings,[21] but attributable also to novelistic narration and adopted, much later, by narrative cinema. In brief: at the end of the eighteenth century, the emergence of publicity was accompanied by the retraction from painting of the proscenium stage—and thus the turning away from a determinate, locatable audience—in favor of the construction of an internally coherent space (or, as I have argued, of a semicoherent space, riven by a split) in which characters would become completely "absorbed" and thus shun any acknowledgment of an extradiegetic audience. Characters would confine their attentions exclusively to the diegetic world that formed around them. It is important to recognize that the techniques of absorption did not sever the novel (and later film) from audience as such, but only from that older type of audience which had positioned itself in front of live, theatrical events. The novel still had to address itself to an audience, a public, but that public was, as Sartre described it, indeterminate. One of the most important devices employed by the novel to break with the theatrical form of audience and establish the diegetic space was the one on which Pasolini dwells in his "long take" essay: the insistent use of the unmarked present tense. The surrender of the present tense in favor of the "past present" (as Pasolini refers to it), the tense of narrative objectivity, had one clear function: to untie narration from the present of frontal address, of the "I stand before you here and now" that brings one's interlocutor into focus before one. The past present is more oblique, for it does not face a punctually locatable "there." Christian Metz, in his well-known essay "History/Discourse," makes note of this link between the unmarked past tense and the indeterminate address of objective narration, but he argues that this indeterminacy is the effect of an ideological operation designed to *disguise* the film's limited, particular point of view and *pretend* to historical objectivity.[22] Our disagreements with this reading have by now been sufficiently represented; they revolve around the fact that point of view is not the contrary of objectivity.

You will not find in Pasolini any mention of the law of the dead father, yet this reference permits me to introduce a critical qualification to his argument. Pasolini speaks of death rather than of the dead father. For him, as we saw, death interrupts the pure present in order to shroud it, retroactively, in meaning. Through the cut, death enters and converts meaningless contingency into sense. This argument makes death life's absolute master. If the cut were viewed, rather, not as an encounter with death, but with the gaze that marks the place left empty by the death of the father, the argument would make more sense. Whereas in Pasolini's account, death provides the possibility of transcending life's contingencies by converting life into meaning, in Freud's account it is the encounter with the gaze of the dead father that enables us to create new meanings, inasmuch as it forces a hole in the homeostatic principle of pleasure.

One more point needs to be made. The law of the dead father has so far seemed to be indeterminate, but psychoanalysis maintains that this law is the law of sexual difference. The law of sexual difference is a law of unconscious necessity, which is to say, it is a law that *founds* culture and is *not a cultural law*. This means that *this law, which mandates that each subject make a choice as to his or her own sexual identity, does not define or even permit a fixed identity so much as it defines the mode in which the subject will come to question and challenge his or her own identity and the cultural laws that attempt to fix it.* The law that founds culture is not a constituent part of the culture it founds and maintains an antinomic relation to the latter. And the subject—the neurotic subject, specifically—for whom this law is an unconscious necessity remains in a state of "uneasy indetermination" regarding the question of his own pleasure and sexual identity. In perversion, which will be examined next, the law of sexual difference is instead treated as an arbitrary law of culture.

THE OTHER, ABSOLUTELY

"'By and large,' the Duke warns his female slaves just before the orgies of sex, violence, and storytelling get under way in the *120 Days of Sodom,* 'offer your fronts very little to our sight; remember that this loathsome part, which only the alienation of her wits could have permitted Nature to create, is always the one we find most repugnant.' Sadean misogyny is based on the libertine's view of the female genitalia as a scandalous offense to reason."[23] In the perverse structure, the subject maintains a different relation to the Other; he disavows the lack in the Other the neurotic perceives. Since this lack is nowhere more visible than in the offensive perception of the missing maternal phallus—this perception is disavowed. Whereas repression institutes an antinomic relation (one has one or the other, not both simultaneously) between gaze and vision, desire and law, unconscious and conscious, disavowal holds onto conflicting terms simultaneously, at once denying and acknowledging the same idea. Octave Mannoni's well-known formula for perversion—"I know very well, but just the same . . ."—so successfully translates the peculiar simultaneity involved in disavowal that it has effectively blocked any further inquiry. It is as if this formula alone resolved all questions before we had a chance to pose them.

One needs to emphasize nevertheless that the antinomic structure of the *split subject* in neurosis is quite different from the *splitting of consciousness* in perversion. We are not speaking of the same split in both cases. On the contrary, perversion is the attempt to avoid the very status of subject, precisely by avoiding the split—

embodied in a whole series of antinomies—that characterize and unsettle the (neurotic) subject. Perversion seeks to ensure that gaze and vision, desire and law, conscious and unconscious no longer contradict each other but inhabit the same plane, and attempts to force them to coalesce. If the phrasing of Mannoni's formula can be held partially responsible for disguising this distinction between the two kinds of split it is because the formula tends to be read as pitting a *rebellious* belief (the fault no doubt of that impudent *but*) against a settled and normative knowledge. But this is far from an accurate description of perversion.

Let us start with the most naive approach to the topic of perversion possible, by holding up for inspection that simple and "obvious" phenomenological description (not of perversion in general, but of sadism, specifically) from which Horkheimer and Adorno operate. Sadism, this description assumes, expresses a will to dominate the other by instrumentalizing him, by treating him as a mere object to be exploited and tortured. Sartre wasted no time pointing out what is wrong with this definition: if he were in fact to instrumentalize or objectify the other, the sadist would only vitiate his own project. For, "the sadist does not seek to suppress the freedom of the one whom he tortures but to force this freedom freely to identify with the tortured flesh" (523). By inflicting pain the sadist does indeed aim, as Horkheimer and Adorno maintain, to produce in the other a certain objectification, an excess of corporeality, a suffering or sheer passivity of the body that would no longer be summonable to purposive action. The ultimate goal of the sadist, however, is not the simple scene of suffering he manages to stage, the sight of the other's helpless passivity. On the contrary, the sight that arouses the sadist's excitement is that of the other's *choosing to stop rising above the pain, to which he has up until now been subjected, and deciding instead to submerge himself in it.* The source of the sadist's, or the sadean libertine's, pleasure is the other's *free decision* to identify himself with the obscene, unutilizable facticity of his pain. For, at this moment, freedom and flesh, which have thus far appeared as antinomic, cease to be so; they come together all at once in a new "*synthesis* of the Other" (521). In terms of Sartre's overall argument this point could be restated thus: where in the encounter with the gaze, the Other who manifests himself to me is *neither* reducible to an actual, intramundane presence *nor* emptied completely to become a transcendent condition of possibility, in sadism the effort of torture is devoted to forcing the Other to be *both* an actual person *and* a transcendent condition of possibility. The sadist wants to trap freedom in flesh; to attach the gaze to a determinate, flesh-and-blood individual.

If psychoanalysis defines perversion primarily through the mechanism of disavowal, Sartre's theory of sadism gives us a precise picture of how disavowal behaves. Rather than holding the two opposing ideas apart, side by side, it attempts joins them to form a single entity, a new synthesis. This insight is confirmed in other ways by the phenomenon of perversion. Take another look at one of the most notorious cases of perversion, that of the Marquis de Sade. In this case we find a similar synthesis in the person of Madame de Montreuil, Sade's mother-in-law. For Sade, no gap, no antinomy existed between Madame de Montreuil, as representative of the law, and some inapprehensible yet necessary authority. Mother-in-law, *she was*, for Sade, *the law itself*: both idealized and obscene, infallible and contingent, at the same time. She was not, as the law of the dead father is for the neurotic, necessary but dead. In the testimony he gave at his notorious trial, Adolf Eichmann provided additional evidence of the perverse abolition of the gap between unconscious law and its mundane representative. Rather than a fallible stand-in for the law, Hitler was for Eichmann an infallible authority. Protesting that he himself had nothing against the Jews, Eichmann clearly and publicly acknowledged the arbitrariness of Hitler's edicts. They contained for him no necessary truth, yet he insisted that he had to obey them to the letter because they were the law. *Arbitrary, relative, and yet absolute in its power*; this is the Other of the pervert, the Other forged in the furnace of disavowal.

Toward this arbitrary, relative, and yet absolutely powerful authority, the pervert maintains an unquestioning relation. That is, he does not hesitate before the various figures of authority with whom he comes into contact; he does not try to puzzle out what they require of him. The style of the neurotic is one of hesitation: she tries to please figures of authority, to show proper respect, on the one hand, while questioning their legitimacy and taking precautions against or making allowances for their fallibility, on the other. For, unsure of the Other's desires and unsure therefore if this particular representative isn't actually a fraud, the neurotic ends up wavering in her allegiance to particular laws. It is not that she does not want to obey the law—it is just that she is a little vague about what it is. There is no such vagueness, no wavering in the pervert's relation to the law. This is why his relations to others have, as has often been noted, the character of *contracts* rather than *symbolic links*. Contracts spell things out clearly, they eliminate ambiguities. Their job is to replace symbolic uncertainty with perverse clarity, to spell out in words what desire only murmurs. A contractual agreement will always thus be more strict, more rigid than symbolic law. It is, in fact, precisely this quality of *rigidity* that Freud found most characteristic of perversion: "We . . . recognize more and more clearly that the essence of the perversions lies not in the extension of the sexual aim, not in the replacement of the genitals, not even always in the variant choice of the object, but solely in the exclusiveness with which these deviations are carried out."[24]

Deleuze's definition of perversion as a "black theology" emphasizes the way this characteristic rigidity concerns the pervert's relation to pleasure: in perversion, "pleasure ceases to motivate the will and is abjured, disavowed, 'renounced,' the better to be recovered as . . . a law."[25] As his relation to the Other assumes the form of a contract and the Other takes the form of an actual person, only crueler, "ferocious in his demands and invulnerable,"[26] the pervert (according to Lacan's characterization, which is surprisingly close to Deleuze's) surrenders his *right* to jouissance in order to assume it as a *duty* that he has contracted to carry out. Enjoyment becomes a service he performs for the Other.

A cloud of questions is beginning to form around these various characterizations, but other questions are beginning to evaporate. It is clearer now, for example, why perversion is so often confused with transgression. Why Sade is often mistaken for a revolutionary hero: a man of courage, a moral man. Kant taught us that the life of a coward is a life devoid of meaning; if we were not able, at least in principle, to refuse to bear false witness against our neighbor, say, even if it meant risking our own happiness, and ultimately our very life, then we could not consider ourselves reasonable. At some point we are obliged to put an end to our neurotic hesitation regarding the Other's desire and obey our own moral law. As Kant was formulating this lesson, Sade was thumbing his nose at social mores, without caring a fig about the consequences of his actions on his well-being. He seemed, through his flamboyantly nonneurotic disregard for the judgment of others, to be fashioning himself as the poster-boy for Kant's notion of freedom. Like the moral man, Sade visibly served a crueler, more inhumane law than the wavering neurotic could ever conceive. Yet Sade's ruthless mother-in-law and Eichmann's Hitler, as (only) some have been able to see, are grotesque caricatures of that categorical imperative which forces Kant's split subject to surrender his indecision.

Pasolini's *Salò* could fittingly be described as an attempt to expose just such a perversion of the moral imperative. The film's prologue—which features a road sign for Marzabotto, the northern Italian town where spontaneous acts of resistance precipitated an infamous and large-scale massacre by the Fascists—is filled with (neo)realistically rendered action set against a natural, outdoor setting. This prologue is abruptly bracketed, however, by the rest of the film, which takes place completely indoors, in the interior, rationalist spaces of an Italian Bauhaus villa, confiscated from some "rich Jew" (to quote one of the libertines). The threshold of this transition into the interior is defined by a scene in which the four libertines are shown signing a contract, thus signaling that this change of locations will see the replacement of the realistic setting structured through symbolic relations by a counterworld in which contractual ties are all that bind. This transition is also, significantly, marked by a change in cinematic style, from the alternating chase montage of the opening sequence to the extremely long long takes of the rest. As we enter the interior we leave behind the problematic of the spontaneous political act in order to focus on the specific act of artistic creation. Pasolini chooses to expose the literary inventions of the four female narrators as they are enacted by the libertines as caricatures of the creative act.

In this sense, *Salò* is Pasolini's own "Kant with Sade." The film rummages the ruins to which the sadist reduces not only Kant's practical reason but also his aesthetic judgment. It is an icily gorgeous mess; but what strikes the eye especially is how static and repetitive it all is. The balanced compositions, emphasized by the geometric pattern of the floor tiles, remove every bit of dynamism from the image. Cutting, as mentioned, is minimal in this almost essayistic longtake (rather than montage) film. It is as if the act of creation had jammed, had frozen on these aestheticized scenes, and the acts of torture were violent attempts to unfreeze it. Instead of a *drive to create* and a *research,* such as one finds when jouissance bores a hole through the homeostatic pleasure of the ego, here in this perverse world we have simply a *state of certainty* and *display.*

The act of aesthetic judgment is isolated and parodied in a darkly humorous sequence where the four libertine-executioners devise what they call "the most beautiful ass" contest in order to determine which of their victims possesses the finest example of this nearly featureless feature. In a dimly lit scene, the judges soberly scrutinize rows of virtually indistinguishable bare bottoms before delivering their final judgment. Here it seems that the anticapitalist critique to which Pasolini was committed throughout his life led him to discern a curious point of convergence between the notion of aesthetic judgment and the perverse practices of the sadist: both set out, in effect, to annul the capitalist logic of the marketplace. This logic is, of course, that of universal equivalency: everything can be exchanged. Kant and Sade both disdain not only this idea of equivalency but, additionally, the compassionate attitude it requires us to adopt toward our fellows. And each assumes instead a stance of principled apathy. If we find in the form of the human body an *ideal of beauty,* this is not because it moves us to sympathy or arouses in us an identificatory pleasure but because, Kant says, we find in it a sensible indication of a purposefulness that resists appropriation, or use, by ends external to reason. Mocking this very notion of an ideal of beauty by focusing on only one ignoble body part, Pasolini's feudalistic libertine lords nevertheless maintain the scene of judgment as a search for a kind of use value that would have no truck with exchange, that could ultimately resist the taint of market relations. Yet, instead of a Kantian "purposefulness without purpose," these libertines discover in their *ideal ass* not only the complete absence of any occasion for sympathy or compassion, but a use befitting the ends of their debauchery. The radical act of judgment tears this one ass from the relations of equivalency that would otherwise link it (through resemblance) not only to all the others on display, but to the sadists (through sympathy) as well. This one ass becomes an object of pure use. Moreover, the beautiful body serves a different function for these libertines than the one we attributed to the beautiful death in Greek tragedy and the beautiful image of Antigone. While still representing a barrier against death, it now serves as support for the infinite and unreserved torture of the victims.

To detect in the superficial resemblances between perversion and ethical action or creation is one thing, to understand their structure is another. And so it is to this question of structure that we once more return, prepared now to face the storm cloud of questions we chose earlier to push quietly aside. First, a short summary. We set out to establish that a fundamental difference separating the neurotic from the pervert is that the former cannot directly confront the Other, but remains exposed rather to an indeterminate public, whereas the latter is able to "face-off" against the Other. But when we further characterized the Other of perversion first via Sartre's discussion, then through remarks made by Lacan regarding Madame de Montreuil, we refrained from observing that in Sartre's account the pervert subjects the Other to torture, whereas in Lacan's he subjects himself to the Other's. Lacan's theoretical innovation was to argue that the pervert is the *servant* of the Other. But what happens to the topic of torture if this is so? It would be simple to rid ourselves of this problem by answering that the pervert tortures small others in order to fulfill his duty to the big Other. But this answer does not satisfy us, since it does not sufficiently correspond to the facts nor to the direction in which Freud's late theory seemed to be heading.

Let us look at the theory first. In his exposition of the structure of the fetish, Freud proposes the same sort of synthesis that we detected in the pervert's Other: a rather pedestrian object, ready-to-hand, but one with absolute, exclusive power to arouse enjoyment. The special durability of the fetish, the tenacity with which the fetishist holds onto and reveres it, is attributed to the fact that the fetish is "doubly derived from contrary ideas."[27] And yet this double derivation gives rise not merely to the special reverance but also to the hostility with which the fetishist approaches his fetish. To illustrate this point Freud cites as example "the Chinese custom of mutilating the female foot and then revering it like a fetish after it has been mutilated," which makes it seem, he says, "as though the Chinese male wants to thank the woman for having submitted to being castrated."[28]

The notion of a splitting of consciousness returns in this question of the pervert's relation to the Other. This relation offers a way out of our theoretical quandry regarding the issue of torture. The pervert is *both* the servant who reveres the Other *and* his torturer. This relation should not be mistaken for ambivalence, or the "uneasy indetermination" that characterizes the neurotic's relation to the Other. Freud gives us a clue as to how to understand this curious relation when he speculates that the Chinese fetishist may in fact be revering the Other for submitting to his hostility, or thanking the Other for submitting to torture. Lacan's intervention suggests that it is the other way around; the Other thanks, or is expected to thank, the pervert for torturing him. Or perhaps: the pervert reveres the Other precisely *by* torturing him. The point of introducing these contortions into Freud's phrasing is to propose that the pervert's own activity, the torture he imposes, cannot be subjectivized, but is experienced by the pervert as imposed on him by the ineluctable will of the Other. It is this interpretation that prevents the perverse splitting of consciousness from being conflated with wavering or hesitation. For, it is not that some part of the pervert's experience is split off into the unconscious, but rather that some part, while still remaining conscious, fails to be subjectivized.

This thesis also helps clarify the phenomenon of perverse apathy. "The intense hatred which is no longer psychologically experienced by the [pervert] is transposed onto (or materialised/embodied in) [the Other, or] the 'objective' ideological system which legitimises [his] activity—[he] can afford to be indifferent, since it is the 'objective' ideological apparatus itself that hates on [his] behalf."[29] And, to make a slightly different point, to say that the pervert seeks to fulfill a duty to the Other is not to imply that the pervert, in carrying out this duty, seeks the Other's validation, or permission, or sanction. These all form part of the neurotic's quest to discover the Other's desire; but if the pervert makes himself an instrument of the Other, he does so without assuming the affects of docility and servility that identify the neurotic relation.

The pervert is a pure, pathos-less instrument of the Other's will. Let us not forget, however, that we have just put forward the curious idea that this will is experienced by the pervert as a command to subject the Other to torture. Clinical evidence shows that the pervert is one who constantly seeks out respectable people, "people sufficiently engaged, inscribed in the social structure,"[30] not as mere delegates but as actual, infallible instances of the law. *The purpose of this association is the humiliation or debauchery of the law—not, however, in order to unseat this fallible law, to transgress it and replace it with one's own autonomous law, but in order better to revere it.* If the pervert looks for legal authorities to bear witness to obscene acts and thus to reveal their complicity in the very scenes that would seduce them from their virtue, to confess their jouissance, this is not to mortify the law simply, but through this mortification to purify the law of the arbitrary and contingent, to purge it of flesh. In Rosolato's still valid thesis, the pervert's active search for the jouissance of the fallen flesh, for every manner of sexual debauchery, aims primarily at exhausting their attractions in order finally to attain the revelatory illumination of certainty and thus to be able to follow the law as an ineluctable path.[31] Thus the "worst pervert," as Jacques-Alain Miller has argued, is not the most obscene or the most flagrantly transgressive figure you have met in literature or life, but the one who is the most righteous, the savage moralist who sees himself as a mere instrument of the law.[32] "One more effort," was Sade's *moralistic* rallying cry, if you would be republicans!

"Kennedy, dying, expresses himself in his final action: falling and dying, on the seat of a black presidential car, in the weak embrace of his American petit-bourgeois wife." This is the Zapruder film: "a gun shot, more gun shots, a body falls, a car stops, a woman screams, the crowd shouts . . ." (4). A subjective long take, the film expresses itself, as Pasolini says, in the "extreme language of action," that is, in "nonsymbolic signs" that attempt, like the language of perversion in general, to replace the symbolic with signs that would strike the senses immediately and would not leave a more lasting mark in a network of differential relations. A language

that would exhaust itself in the present. Public ceremony has indeed been converted into a private home movie insofar as the gap between eye and gaze that opens vision to the presence of others as such has vanished. The difference between eye and gaze collapses, or as Lacan once put it, "the contemplative eye" is confused "with the eye [gaze] with which God [the Other] looks at [us]."[33] We are no longer in the presence of "some" (indeterminate) other consciousnesses, of a public with which we maintain a relation of "uneasy indetermination," but of an infallible law with which we maintain a relation that leaves no room for doubt. It is the coincidence of eye and gaze that creates the tightly constricted space we observe here and in *Salò;* one is made to look through the eyes of the Other, from which we can take no distance. The possibility of another, contravening look, always left open in the point-of-view structure, is for structural reasons blocked off. Yet, if the subjective shot doubles with certainty the Other's gaze, it does not afford a view that could be described as pellucid or omniscient, but one, on the contrary, that is stained with obscene enjoyment, with the subjective markings—blurring, shadowing, and the like—of an arbitrary vision.

One wonders if Pasolini did not catch a glimpse in this footage of the assassination of America's premiere legal authority, the tearing of his flesh, of a perverse relation to the law—a relation in which law is no longer regarded as necessary but fallible (because it has to be represented by particular policies and persons), but is viewed instead as an infallible contingency. In the latter case, the punishing and humiliation of the law's representative would aim not at installing a new law, but at preserving the certainty of the law's truth and would thus replace the autonomy of the citizen-subject with a determination to carry out the duty spelled out by a heteronomous edict.

Depicting Zapruder as a mere servant of history, as surrendering the opportunity to choose an angle on the events he witnesses, Pasolini's formal argument moves clearly in the direction of this political insight. It is as if in his brief essay Pasolini had been able not only to see the perverse structure of the Zapruder film but to foresee a time when an American President and his petit-bourgeois wife would be hounded by an apathetic independent prosecutor who, eschewing any title to a point of view of his own, would come to serve as a humble yet unwavering instrument of "the rule of law." A prosecutor who would carry out his officially mandated duty by hunting down and publishing, for the legal record, volumes and volumes of it, every evidence of the sexual weaknesses of the law's own flesh, and who would force the law to confess its jouissance in the most intimate detail, in front of a camera. If it could be claimed that this prosecutor were an example of the worst sort of perversion, it would not be because one detected a secret "lust in his heart," but because one could not help observing in him a certain barrenness of desire. Nor would it be because he sought to institute a revolutionary new order, to overthrow the law, but because he wanted to purify it. One more effort, Republicans, if you would rid the sacred Oval Office of sexual debauchery!

INTRODUCTION: **IMAGINE THERE'S NO WOMAN**

1. Jacques Lacan, "Kant with Sade," trans. James Swenson, *October* 51 (winter 1989), p. 57. In an enlightening seminar presentation, later published as an essay, "A Discussion of Lacan's 'Kant with Sade'" (*Reading Seminars I and II: Lacan's Return to Freud,* ed. Richard Felstein, Bruce Fink, Maire Jaanus [New York: SUNY Press, 1996]), Jacques-Alain Miller first drew our attention to the importance of père Ubu's maxim.

2. Gottlob Frege, *The Foundations of Arithmetic,* trans. J. L. Austin, Evanston: Northwestern University Press: 1980, pp. iv, v.

3. Alain Badiou, "Frege," trans. Sam Gillespie and Justin Clemens, *Umbr(a) 1* (2000), p. 104. This essay informs this whole section of my introduction. Jacques-Alain Miller also gives an illuminating and, for the most part, compatible analysis of Russell's paradox in the May 7, 14, and 21 sessions of his 1985/1986 unpublished seminar, "*Extimité.*"

4. Jacques Lacan, *Seminar XI: The Four Fundamental Concepts of Psycho-Analysis,* trans. Alan Sheridan, Jacques-Alain Miller, ed. (London: Hogarth Press and the Institute of Psycho-Analysis, 1977), p. 106.

5. In *Kant and the Exact Sciences* (Cambridge, MA: Harvard University Press, 1992), Michael Friedman argues in a completely different mode that Kant was hampered by a lack of set-theoretical notions, which had not yet been formulated when he wrote.

6.   Miller, *Reading Seminars I and II*, p. 228.

7.   Lacan, "Kant with Sade," p. 57.

8.   Lacan, *Seminar XI*, p. 106.

9.   Jacques Lacan, *Encore: On Feminine Sexuality, The Limits of Love and Knowledge* (S XX), ed. Jacques-Alain Miller, Bruce Fink, trans. (New York and London: Norton, 1998), p.11.

10.   Sigmund Freud, *Civilization and its Discontents, The Standard Edition of the Complete Psychological Works of Sigmund Freud* (SE), trans. James Strachey (London: Hogarth Press and the Institute of Psychoanalysis, 1961), 21:83.

11.   The list of artists and description of the fate of their work is from Benjamin Buchloh, "Statement," in *The Destruction of Tilted Arc: Documents,* Clara Weyergraf and Martha Buskirk, eds. (Cambridge, MA : MIT Press, 1991), p. 92.

I   THE TOMB OF PERSEVERANCE

1.   Jean-Pierre Vernant, "Greek Tragedy: Problems of Interpretation," in *The Structuralist Controversy,* ed. Richard Macksey and Eugenio Donato (Baltimore and London: Johns Hopkins University Press, 1972), pp. 278 and 288.

2.   Ibid., pp. 278–279.

3.   Note that anachronism formed part of the very substance of Athenian tragedy; as Vernant remarks, "the surprising fact, often pointed out, is that there are more archaisms in Greek tragedy than, for example, in the epic" (ibid., p. 283). Although the Chrous, which was made up of Athenian citizens, responded to dramatic situations remarkably similar to their own, they did so in a lyrical, elevated language that appeared antiquated in comparison with normal speech. Contrarily, the dramatic protagonists of the tragedies represented

legendary figures from the past, but who spoke in the rhythms and idiom of the current day. This curious anachronistic stuff of tragedy is precisely what the films of Pier Paolo Pasolini and Jean-Marie Straub and Danièle Huillet attempt to redeploy.

4.   A history of the relation of the German Idealists to Sophocles' *Antigone* can be found in George Steiner, *Antigones* (Oxford: Clarendon, 1984).

5.   G. W. F. Hegel, *Aesthetics: Lectures on Fine Art,* trans. T. M. Knox (Oxford: Clarendon, 1975), p. 464.

6.   G. W. F. Hegel, *The Phenomenology of Spirit,* trans. A. V. Miller (Oxford: Clarendon, 1977), para. 468; all subsequent references to this work will be to this edition and will be indicated in the text by paragraph numbers.

7.   Sophocles, *Antigone,* ed. and trans. Hugh Lloyd-Jones (Cambridge: Harvard/ Loeb Classical Library, 1994), p. 45.

8.   Jacques Lacan, *Seminar VII: The Ethics of Psychoanalysis (SVII),* ed. Jacques-Alain Miller, trans. Dennis Porter (London: Routledge, 1992), p. 88; further references to this seminar will be made in the body of the text.

9.   Sigmund Freud, "Civilization and Its Discontents," *The Standard Edition of the Complete Psychological Works of Sigmund Freud* (SE), vol. 21, trans. James Strachey (London: Hogarth, 1957), p. 80n. Mary Ann Doane, in her fascinating essay "Sublimation and the Psychoanalysis of the Aesthetic" (*Femmes Fatales* [New York and London: Routledge, 1991]), also highlights this footnote.

10.   Jacques Lacan, *The Four Fundamental Concepts of Psycho-Analysis* (SXI), ed. Jacques-Alain Miller, trans. Alan Sheridan (London: Hogarth Press, 1977), pp. 210–215.

11.   Sigmund Freud, "The Ego and the Id," SE,19:58.

12.   Claude Lefort, "The Death of Immortality?" (L), in *Democracy and Political Theory* (Minneapolis: Minnesota Press, 1988), p. 256; further references to this essay will be indicated in the text.

13. Hans Blumenberg, *The Legitimacy of the Modern Age* (B), trans. Robert M. Wallace (Cambridge, MA: MIT Press, 1983), p. 443; further references to this work will be made in the text.

14. An examination of the Blumenbergian concept of the "reoccupation of positions" would be a good way to explore the contrast with Lefort further. My own sense is that Blumenberg's notion is a functionalist one, but I will not argue that here.

15. In "What Is an Author?" (*Language, Counter-Memory, Practice,* ed. and trans. Donald Bouchard and Sherry Simon [Ithaca: Cornell University Press, 1977]), Michel Foucault reserves for two authors, Marx and Freud, this singular and immortal status. One might answer the essay's question this way: an author is a writer who, for us, does not die, to whose text we continue to return and whose place is not occupied by any intellectual successor.

16. Immanuel Kant, *Critique of Practical Reason,* trans. Mary Gregor (Cambridge: Cambridge University Press, 1997), pp. 102–103.

17. See Lewis White Beck, *A Commentary on Kant's Critique of Practical Reason* (Chicago: University of Chicago Press, 1960), pp. 270–271; and Alenka Zupancic, "Kant with Don Juan and Sade," in *Radical Evil,* ed. Joan Copjec (London and New York: Verso, 1996), pp. 118–119.

18. Aristotle, *Economics,* 1343b24; quoted by Hannah Arendt in *The Human Condition* (Chicago: University of Chicago Press, 1958), p. 19.

19. Walter Benjamin, "Critique of Violence," *Illuminations,* ed. Peter Demetz, trans. Edmund Jephcott (New York and London: Harcourt Brace Jovanovich, 1978), pp. 298–299; Benjamin then adds, in order to forestall any ahistorical objection: "The antiquity of all religious commandments against murder is no counterargument, because these are based on other ideas than the modern theorem."

20. Giorgio Agamben, *Homo Sacer: Sovereign Power and Bare Life,* trans. Daniel Heller-Roazen (Stanford: Stanford University Press, 1998), p. 3; further references to this source will be marked in the text.

21.   Ibid., p. 5.

22.   Michel Foucault, *The Birth of the Clinic*, trans. A. M. Sheridan Smith (New York: Vintage, 1975), p. 145.

23.   Benjamin, "Critique of Violence," p. 299.

24.   Agamben, *Homo Sacer*, p. 88.

25.   Ibid., p. 182.

26.   Ibid., p. 187.

27.   Ibid., pp. 181–182.

28.   Alain Badiou, "Being by Numbers," Lauren Sedofsky interview with Badiou, *Artforum,* October 1994, p. 87. Badiou further summarizes his own mathematical and resolutely atheistic project by stating, "The philosophical destiny of atheism, in a radical sense, lies in the interplay between the question of being and the question of infinity. . . . Mathematics secularizes infinity in the clearest way, by formalizing it. The thesis that mathematics is ontological has the double-negative virtue of disconnecting philosophy from the question of being and freeing it from the theme of finitude." The covertly theological theme of the "finitude of man," epitomized by the Heideggerian phrase "being-towards-death" and vaunted by deconstruction, is rigorously challenged by Badiou, who remains faithful (in his carefully theorized sense of this term) to Lacan on this issue.

29.   Phillippe Ariès's *Essais sur l'histoire de la mort en Occident, du Moyen Age à nos jours* (Paris: Seuil, 1975) is one of the sources on which Lefort draws for his analysis of immortality in the modern era.

30.   Sigmund Freud, "Instincts and Their Vicissitudes," SE, 14 : 125.

31.   The contrast is never stated this starkly. Instead, instinct is described as an innate, biological "knowledge"/pressure toward sexual reproduction, whereas the drive is said to be a kind of derailment of this trajectory; drive then becomes

a kind of failed instinct. This description is misleading because it (1) allows a normative viewpoint to take hold, even as it attempts to counter it; (2) obscures the true aim of the drive, which is away from rather than toward the empirical world; (3) muddies the conceptualization of human sexuality; and (4) effaces the double paradox of the death drive. My restatement of the contrast is a strategic intervention designed to help rectify these problems.

32. Sigmund Freud, *Beyond the Pleasure Principle*, SE, 18:121–122; further references to this work are indicated in the text.

33. Plato, *Timaeus*, 33b–d.

34. See the essay by Gilles Deleuze, "The Idea of Genesis in Kant's Aesthetics," *Angelaki*, vol. 5, no. 3 (December 2000).

35. Freud, *Project for a Scientific Psychology*, SE, 1:331.

36. Freud, *Three Essays on the Theory of Sexuality*, SE, 7:222.

37. Alenka Zupančič has brilliantly developed and illustrated this Lacanian argument in "On Love as Comedy" (Lacanian Ink, 20 [2002]); there she makes use of Deleuze's phrase "minimal difference" to describe the splitting of appearance from itself. I am indebted to her fine analysis.

38. Leo Steinberg, "Jasper Johns: The First Seven Years of His Art," in *Other Criteria* (New York: Oxford, 1972).

39. Freud, *The Ego and the Id*, SE, 19: 56.

2 NARCISSISM, APPROACHED OBLIQUELY

1. Plato, *Timaeus* (Cambridge: Loeb Classical Library, 1986), 33b–d.

2. Quoted in David Krell, *Contagion: Sexuality, Disease, and Death in German Idealism and Romanticism* (Bloomington: Indiana University Press, 1998).

3.   Jacques Lacan, *Seminar VII: The Ethics of Psychoanalysis,* ed. Jacques-Alain Miller, trans. Dennis Porter (London: Tavistock/Routledge, 1992), p. 93. Subsequent citations from this seminar will appear in the text with the number of the seminar and the page reference.

4.   I borrow this distinction from Jean-Claude Milner, *Le triple du plaisir* (Paris: Verdier, 1997).

5.   Lacan, *Seminar XI: The Four Fundamental Concepts of Psychoanalysis,* ed. Jacques-Alain Miller, trans. Alan Sheridan (London: Hogarth Press and the Institute of Psycho-Analysis, 1977), p. 198. Subsequent citations will refer to the seminar by number in the body of the text.

6.   Gilles Deleuze, *Cinema I: The Movement-Image,* trans. Hugh Tomlinson and Barbara Habberjam (Minneapolis: University of Minnesota Press, 1986), pp. 95–96.

7.   Sigmund Freud, *Three Essays on the Theory of Sexuality, The Standard Edition of the Complete Psychological Works of Sigmund Freud* (SE), trans. James Strachey (London: Hogarth Press and the Institute of Psycho-Analysis, 1957), 7:207.

8.   Freud, "On Narcissism: An Introduction," SE, 14: 80. This important argument is advanced by Leo Bersani in "Erotic Assumptions: Narcissism and Sublimation in Freud," *The Culture of Redemption* (Cambridge: Harvard University Press, 1990). Bersani's essay will be referred to subsequently as "Erotic," followed by a page number in the text.

9.   Freud, "The Unconscious," SE, 14:177.

10.   Jean Laplanche, "To Situate Sublimation," *October 28* (spring 1984), p. 9.

12.   Michel Foucault, "What Is an Author?" in *Language, Counter-Memory, Practice: Selected Essays and Interviews,* ed. Donald Bouchard, trans. Donald Bouchard and Sherry Simon (Ithaca: Cornell University Press, 1977), p. 117.

12.   Bersani, "Sociality and Sexuality," *Critical Inquiry,* vol. 26, no.4 (summer 2000).

13.   Freud, "Psycho-analytic Notes on an Autobiographical Account of a Case of Paranoia," SE, 12:34.

14.   Mikkel Borch-Jacobsen, "Ecco Ego," in *The Freudian Subject,* trans. Catherine Porter (Stanford: Stanford University Press, 1988), p. 113; hereafter, "Ecco," followed by a page number.

15.   Lacan, *Seminar XX: On Feminine Sexuality, the Limits of Love and Knowledge,* ed. Jacques-Alain Miller, trans. Bruce Fink (New York and London: W. W. Norton, 1998), p. 47.

16.   Alain Badiou, "What Is Love?" trans. Justin Clemens in *Umbr(a) 1* (1996), special issue ed., Sam Gillespie and Sigi Jottkandt, p. 44.

17.   Ibid., p. 53.

18.   Judith Williamson, "Images of 'Woman'—the Photographs of Cindy Sherman," *Screen,* vol. 24, no. 6 (Nov.–Dec. 1983), p. 104. Despite my contrary views, still a very useful essay.

19.   Béla Balázs, *Theory of the Film: Character and Growth of a New Art,* trans. Edith Bone (New York: Dover, 1970), p. 136; quoted in Deleuze, *Cinema I,* p. 102.

20.   Deleuze, *Cinema I,* p. 95.

21.   For analyses of Lacan's argument, see chapter 8 of Alenka Zupančič's superb *Ethics of the Read: Kant, Lacan* (London and New York: Verso Press, 2000) and Slavoj Žižek's insightful comments in various locations, but particularly in *The Fragile Absolute—or, Why Is the Christian Legacy Worth Fighting For?* (London and New York: Verso Press, 2000), pp. 143–160.

3 MOSES THE EGYPTIAN AND THE BIG BLACK MAMMY OF THE ANTEBELLUM SOUTH

1. Dan Cameron, "Kara Walker: Rubbing History the Wrong Way," *On Paper*, vol. 2 (Sept./Oct. 1997), p. 11.

2. Kara Walker, "The Emancipation Approximation," *Heart Quarterly*, vol. 3, no. 4 (spring 2000), p. 25.

3. Kara Walker, "The Big Black Mammy of the Antebellum South Is the Embodiment of History," in *Kara Walker*, The Renaissance Society at The University of Chicago, Jan. 12–Feb. 23, 1997, not paginated.

4. James Hannaham, "The Shadow Knows: An Hysterical Tragedy of One Young Negress and Her Art," *New Histories* (Boston: The Institute of Contemporary Art, 1996), p. 177.

5. Jacques Lacan, *Le seminaire XVIII: L'envers de la psychanalyse* (Paris: Seuil), p. 128.

6. Freud, *Moses and Monotheism*, SE, 23:129.

7. Freud, *Totem and Taboo*, SE, 13:xv.

8. These are the words Lacan uses to describe the pure life instinct from which we are separated but which is represented by the object a. See Lacan, *Seminar XI: The Four Fundamental Concepts of Psycho-Analysis*, ed. Jacques-Alain Miller, trans. Alan Sheridan (London: Hogarth Press and the Institute of Psycho-Analysis, 1977), pp. 197–198.

9. William Faulkner, *The Sound and the Fury*, p. 6.

10. Gilles Deleuze, "Foldings, or the Inside of Thought (Subjectivation)," in *Foucault*, trans. Sean Hand (Minneapolis: University of Minnesota Press, 1988), p. 95.

11. I borrow the description of the uncanny as a parasitte from Jean-Claude Milner. See his essay, "The Doctrine of Science," in *Umbr(a) 1* (2000), special is-

sue editor, Theresa Giron. This essay was translated by Oliver Feltham from Milner's *L'oeuvre claire: Lacan, la science, la philosophie* (Paris: Seuil, 1995).

12.   Walker uses this phrase in her interview with Jerry Saltz, "Kara Walker, Ill-Will and Desire," *Flash Art International,* no. 191 (Nov./Dec. 1996), 84.

13.   See Liz Armstrong's interview with Kara Walker in *No Place (Like Home)* (Minneapolis: Walker Art Center, 1997), p. 108.

14.   Freud, "Observations on Transference Love," SE, 12:167.

15.   Deleuze, "Foldings," p. 98.

16.   Michelle Montrelay, "Inquiry into Femininity," in *The Woman in Question,* ed. Parveen Adams and Elizabeth Cowie (Cambridge, MA: MIT Press, 1990), p. 262.

17.   Thierry de Duve, *Voici: 100 ans d'art contemporain* (Brussels: Ludion/Flamarion, 2000). De Duve also curated the exhibition that this catalog accompanies.

18.   Freud, "The Uncanny," SE, 17:242.

4 THE INVENTION OF CRYING AND THE ANTITHEATRICS OF THE ACT

1.   Quoted from Diderot by Michael Fried in *Absorption and Theatricality: Painting and Beholder in the Age of Diderot* (Berkeley: University of California Press, 1980), p. 78.

2.   Peter Brooks, *The Melodramatic Imagination: Balzac, Henry James, Melodrama, and the Mode of Excess* (New Haven: Yale University Press, 1976), p. 16.

3.   Fried, *Absorption and Theatricality,* p. 95.

4.   Jacques Lacan, *Seminar XI: The Four Fundamental Concepts of Psycho-Analysis,* ed. Jacques-Alain Miller, trans. Alan Sheridan (London: Hogarth Press and the Institute of Psycho-Analysis, 1977), p. 75.

5. Ibid.

6. Ibid,

7. Ibid.

8. Fried, *Absorption and Theatricality*, p. 97.

9. Ibid., p. 96.

10. See my "Sex and the Euthanasia of Reason," in *Read My Desire: Lacan against the Historicists* (Cambridge, MA: MIT Press, 1994).

11. Brooks, *The Melodramatic Imagination*, p. 5.

12. See Roland Barthes, "The World of Wrestling," in *Mythologies* (New York: Hill and Wang, 1972).

13. One thinks particularly of Linda William's fine essay, "Something Else Besides a Mother: *Stella Dallas* and the Maternal Melodrama," in Christine Gledhill, ed., *Home Is Where the Heart Is* (London: BFI, 1987).

14. See, for this argument, William Rothman's perceptive essay, "Pathos and Transfiguration in the Face of the Camera: A Reading of *Stella Dallas*," in *The "I" of the Camera* (Cambridge, MA: Harvard University Press, 1988).

15. Jacques Lacan, *Seminaire VIII: Le transfert* (Paris: Seuil, 1991), p. 289.

16. See Catherine Millot, "Parodoxes du surmoir," in *Nobodaddy: L'hystérie dans le siècle* (Paris: Point hors ligne, 1988); this entire book lucidly states the relation of the hysteric to the problem of limits.

17. Freud, "Psychoanalytic Notes upon an Autobiographical Case of Paranoia," SE, 12:49.

18. This phrase actually comes from Kant's *Anthropology from a Pragmatic Point of View* (The Hague: Nijhoff, 1974); it is quoted by Jacob Rogozinski in "The Gift of the World," in *Of the Sublime: Presence in Question* (Buffalo: State University of New York, 1993) 153.

19. I also treat the concept of shame below, in chapter 8.

20. For a discussion of melodrama's tears as a product of the encounter that is missed, see Steven Neale, "Melodrama and Tears," *Screen*, vol. 27, no. 6 (Nov.– Dec. 1986).

5 EVIL IN THE TIME OF THE (IN)FINITE WORLD

1. Immanuel Kant, *Religion within the Limits of Reason Alone*, trans. Theodore M. Greene and Hoyt H. Hudson (New York: Harper and Row, 1960), pp. 28–29. Further references will be to this translation and will be indicated in the text by page number only.

2. *Religion within . . .* was first published in 1793; the volume of essays I edited under the title *Radical Evil* was published by Verso Press in 1996. See also Kant, *Religion within the Boundaries of Mere Reason*, trans. and ed. Allen Wood and George Di Giovanni (Cambridge: Cambridge University Press, 1998), the recent retranslation of Kant's 1793 text.

3. Jean-Luc Nancy, in his informative and intelligent book, *The Experience of Freedom* (trans. Bridget McDonald [Stanford: Stanford University Press, 1933]), makes this argument; Jacques Derrida refers in a footnote in *Given Time 1: Counterfeit Money* (trans. Peggy Kamuf [Chicago: Chicago University Press, 1994]) to a "satanic *cruelty* that Kant does not want to acknowledge," p. 166; and Slavoj Žižek, a colleague with whom I usually agree, refers in several places to Kant's inability to admit the fact of diabolical evil. Finally, Alenka Zupančič, in *Ethics of the Real* (London and New York: Verso Press, 2000), a book published after the first version of this chapter appeared, offers a compelling vindication of the position from which I am setting my own apart. I address explicitly one of her points later in this chapter.

4.   The primary source of my information about the history of the concept of evil and Kant's contribution to it is Olivier Reboul's indispensable book, *Kant et le problème du mal* (Montreal: les presses de l'universite de Montreal, 1971).

5.   Freud, *Totem and Taboo*, SE, 13:68.

6.   Gilles Deleuze, *Coldness and Cruelty* (New York: Zone Books, 1991), p. 81.

7.   Phillipe Lacoue-Labarthe and Jean-Luc Nancy, "The Nazi Myth," *Critical Inquiry*, vol. 16, no. 2 (winter 1990), p. 307.

8.   Jacques Lacan, *Seminar XI: The Four Fundamental Concepts of Psycho-Analysis*, ed. Jacques-Alain Miller, trans. Alan Sheridan (London: Hogarth Press and the Institute of Psycho-Analysis, 1977), p. 275.

9.   In his powerful and polemical book, *Ethics: An Essay on the Understanding of Evil* (London and New York: Verso Press, 2001), Alain Badiou foregrounds the relation between an ethics founded on the pursuit of happiness and this modern contempt for life.

10.   Freud, *Moses and Monotheism*, SE, 23: 128.

6 SOUR JUSTICE, OR LIBERALIST ENVY

1.   Cited in Melanie Klein, *Envy and Gratitude: The Writings of Melanie Klein*, ed. Roger Money-Kyrle (London: Hogarth Press and the Institute of Psycho-Analysis, 1975), p. 182.

2.   Peter Shabad, "The Evil Eye of Envy: Parental Possessiveness and the Rivalry for a New Beginning," in *Gender and Envy*, ed. Nancy Burke (New York and London: Routledge, 1998), p. 255.

3.   Klein, *Envy and Gratitude*, p. 182.

4.   Kristen Thompson's argument, in "Closure within a Dream: point-of-View in *Laura*" (*Film Reader 3* [1978]), as her title suggests, is that the whole last section of the film, from the reappearance of Laura until the film's end, is marked by an un-motivated tracking shot as MacPherson's dream.

5.   John Rawls, *A Theory of Justice* (Cambridge, MA: Harvard University Press, 1971). References to this book will be made in the body of the text.

6.   Sigmund Freud, *Group Psychology and the Analysis of the Ego, The Standard Edition of the Complete Psycho-logical Works of Sigmund Freud,* ed. James Strachey (London: Hogarth Press and the Institute of Psycho-Analysis, 1953–1974), XVIII, pp. 120–121.

7.   Ibid.

8.   Saint Augustine, *The Confessions,* trans. Maria Boulding, O.S.B. (New York: Random House, 1997), Book I. Jacques Lacan, in *The Four Fundamental Concepts of Psycho-Analysis* (ed. Jacques-Alain Miller, trans. Alan Sheridan [London: Hogarth Press and Institute of Psycho-Analysis, 1977], p. 116), makes the suggestion that one of the siblings might be older than the other and thus uninterested in mother's milk, but St. Augustine hints at this possibility himself when he writes, "What then was my sin at that age? Was it perhaps that I cried so greedily for those breasts? Certainly if I behaved like that now, *greedy not for breast, of course, but for food more suitable to my age,* I would provoke derision" (p. 9, my emphasis).

9.   Freud, *Group Psychology,* p. 121.

10.   John Forrester, "Psychoanalysis and the History of the Passions: The Strange Destiny of Envy," in *Freud and the Passions,* ed. John O'Neil (University Park: Penn. State University Press, 1996).

11.   Jacques Lacan, *The Ethics of Psychoanalysis,* Book VII, ed. Jacques-Alain Miller, trans. Dennis Porter (New York and London: Routledge, 1992), p. 228.

12.   Robert Penn Warren, *All the King's Men* (New York: Harcourt Brace, 1996), p. 73.

13.   Lacan, *The Ethics of Psychoanalysis*, p. 187.

14.   Immanuel Kant, *Critique of Judgment*, trans. Werner S. Pluhar (Indianapolis and Cambridge: Hackett, 1987), para. 59.

15.   Elaine Scarry, *On Beauty and Being Just* (Princeton: Princeton University Press, 1999), p. 112. Further references to this book will appear in the body of the text.

16.   Immanuel Kant, *Religion within the Limits of Reason Alone*, trans. Theodore Greene and Hoyt Hudson (New York: Harper and Row, 1960), p. 4.

17.   Dieter Henrich, *Aesthetic Judgment and the Moral Image of the World* (Stanford: Stanford University Press, 1992).

18.   Alain Badiou, "Philosophie et politique," *Conditions* (Paris: Seuil, 1992), p. 247.

19.   Jacques Lacan, "Logical Time and the Assertion of Anticipated Certitude," *Newsletter of the Freudian Field*, vol. 2 (1988).

7   **THE STRUT OF VISION**

1.   Since the publication of several essays on the Freudian/Lacanian notion of the drive, in *Reading Seminar XI: The Four Fundamental concepts of Psychoanalysis*, ed. Richard Feldstein, Bruce Fink, Maire Jaanus (Albany: SUNY Press, 1995), and the publication of Jean Laplanche's *Seduction, Translation, Drives*, ed. John Fletcher and Martin Stanton (London: ICA, 1992), this situation has improved.

2.   I am thinking here of Althusser's argument that the enslavement of positivism to empirical "fact" is what renders it an *abstract* science. See the essays by Tom Gunning, "Phantom Images and Modern Manifestations: Spirit Photography, Magic Theater, Trick Films, and Photography's Uncanny" (in *Fugitive Images: From Photography to Video*, ed. Patrice Petro, Bloomington and Indianapolis: Indiana University Press, 1995) and Alenka Zupančič, "Philosophers' Blind Bluff" (in *Gaze and Voice as Love Objects*, ed. Renata Salecl and Slavoj Žižek, Durham and Lon-

don: Duke University Press, 1996) for the hilarious details of positivism's self-entanglements.

3. In *The Origin of Perspective* (Cambridge, MA: MIT Press, 1995), Hubert Damisch points out that light passed into the perspective apparatus not through a "pinhole" exactly, but through a lentil-shaped opening that could better accommodate the physical shape of the observer's eye. Damisch's book offers a welcome antidote to historicist analyses of Renaissance perspective.

4. Jonathan Crary, *Techniques of the Observer: On Vision and Modernity in the Nineteenth Century* (Cambridge, MA: MIT Press, 1990), p. 47.

5. Sigmund Freud, "Instincts and their Vicissitudes," *The Standard Edition of the Complete Psychological Works of Sigmund Freud,* trans. James Strachey (London: Hogarth Press and the Institute of Psycho-Analysis, 1957), vol. XIV, p. 118.

6. Jacques Lacan, *Seminar XI: The Four Fundamental Concepts of Psycho-Analysis,* ed. Jacques-Alain Miller, trans. Alan Sheridan (London: Hogarth Press and the Institute of Psycho-Analysis, 1977), p. 22.

7. In *The Visible and the Invisible* (ed. Claude Lefort, trans. Alphonso Lingis [Evanston: Northwestern University Press, 1968]), Merleau-Ponty admonishes, "We have to reject the age-old assumptions that put the body in the world and the seer in the body, or, conversely, the world and the body in the seer as in a box," p. 138.

8. Jacques Lacan, *Seminar XIII: L'objet de la psychanalyse* (unpublished seminar), May 4, 1966. I would like to thank Cormac Gallagher for allowing me to consult his unpublished English translation of this seminar. Further references to *Seminar XIII* will be to the date of the oral transmission.

9. Freud, SE XIV: 121–122.

10. An excellent, nonreductive introduction to the notion of infinity is provided by Mary Tiles, *The Philosophy of Set Theory: An Introduction to Cantor's Paradise* (London: Blackwell, 1989).

11.   See Jean-Claude Milner's definitive discussion of this relation between quantification and Quality in *Le triple du plaisir* (Paris: Verdier, 1997).

12.   Tiles, *The Philosophy of Set Theory*; I have also relied on Rudy Rucker, *Infinity and the Mind: The Science and Philosophy of the Infinite* (Boston, Basel, Stuttgart: Birkhauser, 1982), and Shaughan Lavine, *Understanding the Infinite* (Cambridge, MA: Harvard University Press, 1994) in this section.

13.   J. V. Field, *The Invention of Infinity: Mathematics and Art in the Renaissance* (Oxford: Oxford University Press, 1997), p. 192. Damisch also cites this title, which he translates slightly differently: "*Universal Method for Putting Real Objects or Objects for Which Specifications Are Available into Perspective, Such That Their Proportions, Measurements, and Distancing Are Correct, without Respect to an Point outside the Field in Question*" (p. 50), to make the same point.

14.   Lacan, S XIII, May 4, 1966; emphasis mine.

15.   Lacan displaces the Euclidean phenomenon of "infinite extension," which makes no room for any notion of the body, with that of human embodiment here; but Frege's consequential set-theoretical redefinition of extension, the class to which objects belong, does not seem to be far from his mind. That is, the word *extension* operates in this section on several levels.

16.   See Victor Tausk, "On the Origin of the Influencing Machine in Schizophrenia," *Psychoanalytic Quarterly* (1933); this paper was first read and discussed at the Vienna Psychoanalytic Society in January 1918 and was published in German the following year.

17.   Jacques Lacan, *Seminar VII: The Ethics of Psychoanalysis,* ed. Jacques-Alain Miller, trans. Dennis Porter (London: Routledge, 1992), p. 30.

18.   Merleau-Ponty, *The Visible and the Invisible*, p. 263.

19.   Damisch, *The Origin of Perspective*, p. 91.

8 WHAT ZAPRUDER SAW

1. Pier Paolo Pasolini, "Observations on the Long Take," *October* 13 (summer 1980), p. 3. All further references to this essay will be given in the text.

2. See Slavoj Žižek's argument regarding Hitchock's *The Birds* in *Looking Awry* (Cambridge, MA: MIT Press, 1991), pp. 96–97.

3. Jean Laplanche and J. B. Pontalis, *The Language of Psychoanalysis*, trans. Donald Nicholson-Smith (New York: Norton, 1973), p. 306.

4. Sigmund Freud, *Three Essays on the Theory of Sexuality, The Standard Edition of the Complete Psychological Works of Sigmund Freud*, trans. Alix Strachey (London: Hogarth Press and the Institute of Psycho-Analysis, 1957), 7:135.

5. Jacques Lacan, "Kant with Sade," trans. James Swenson, *October* 51 (winter 1989), p. 55. See also Max Horkheimer and Theodor Adorno, *Dialectic of Enlightenment,* Johan Cumming, trans. (New York: Seabury Press, 1972), pp. 81–119; Hannah Arendt, *Eichmann in Jerusalem: A Report on the Banality of Evil* (New York: Viking, 1963).

6. Lacan, "Kant with Sade," p. 65.

7. Guy Rosolato, *Essais sur le symbolique* (Paris: Gallimard, 1969), p. 172; Rosolato's discussion of perversion remains to date one of the most cogent.

8. Jean-Paul Sartre, *Being and Nothingness,* trans. Hazel Barnes (New York: Washington Square Press, 1992), p. 347; further references to this work will be given in the text. I would like to acknowledge the excellent analysis of Sartre's theory of the gaze, particularly as it compares to Lacan's, which has been undertaken by Kirsten Hyldgaard. Unfortunately, only an abbreviated version of this analysis is available in English, as "The Subject as an Ill-Timed Accident," in the journal *(a),* vol. 1 (fall 2000). My conversations with Hyldgaard in Aarhus were influential in developing many of my thoughts on these matters.

9.   Kaja Silverman, *The Threshold of the Visible World* (New York and London: Routledge, 1996); future references to this book will be made in the text.

10.   In *Encore: On Feminine Sexuality, The Limits of Love and Knowledge* (ed. Jacques-Alain Miller, trans. Bruce Fink [New York: Norton, 1998]), Lacan's formulation "There is some One [*Y a d' l'Un*]" appears to borrow from Sartre.

11.   Freud, "The Unconscious," SE, 14:170.

12.   Jacques Lacan, Seminar XI: *The Four Fundamental Concept of Psycho-Analysis*, ed. Jacques-Alain Miller, trans. Alan Sheridan (London: Hogarth Press and the Institute of Psycho-Analysis, 1973), p. 194.

13.   Ibid.

14.   Gilles Deleuze, *Cinema I: Movement-Image*, trans. Hugh Tomlinson and Barbara Habberjam (Minneapolis: University of Minnesota Press, 1988), p. 74.

15.   Pier Paolo Pasolini, "Comments on Free Indirect Discourse," in *Heretical Empiricism*, trans. Ben Lawton and Louise K. Barnett (Bloomington: Indiana University Press, 1988), p. 87.

16.   Ibid., p. 85; see also Pasolini's "The Cinema of Poetry" in the same volume.

17.   Deleuze, *Cinema I*, p. 74.

18.   Jacques Lacan, *Seminar VII: The Ethics of Psychoanalysis*, ed. Jacques-Alain Miller, trans. Dennis Porter (London: Routledge, 1992), p. 280.

19.   Giordio Agamben, *The Remnants of Auschwitz: The Witness and the Archive*, trans. Daniel Heller-Roazen (New York: Zone Books, 1999), p. 103.

20.   Leo Bersani, *Homos* (Cambridge, MA: Harvard University Press, 1995), pp. 110–111.

21.   See Michael Fried, *Absorption and Theatricality: Painter and Beholder in the Age of Diderot* (Chicago: Chicago University Press, 1980), where this thesis regarding the work's

abandonment of its theatrical disposition in relation to an audience in favor of an immersion in its own fictive space is made through a detailed scrutiny of late eighteenth-century paintings and the writings of Diderot.

22.   Christian Metz, "Story/Discourse (A Note on Two Kinds of Voyeurism)," in *The Imaginary Signifier* (Bloomington: Indiana University Press, 1982).

23.   Leo Bersani and Ulysse Dutoit, "Merd Alors," *October* 13 (summer 1980), p. 24; this essay is a fine analysis of Pasolini's *Salò*.

24.   Freud, *Introductory Lectures on Psycho-Analysis,* SE, 16:322.

25.   Gilles Deleuze, *Coldness and Cruelty,* in *Masochism* (New York: Zone Books, 1991), p. 120.

26.   Rosolato, *Essais,* p. 175.

27.   Freud, "Fetishism," SE, 21:157.

28.   Ibid.

29.   Ibid.

30.   Slavoj Žižek, "The Concentration-Camp Father," in *Trauma and Memory: Cross-Cultural Perspectives,* ed. Franz Kaltenbeck and Peter Weibel (Vienna: Passagen Verlag, 2000), p. 168. An earlier version of this chapter also appeared in that volume.

31.   Jean Clavreul, "The Perverse Couple," in *Returning to Freud,* ed. and trans. Stuart Schneiderman (New Haven and London: Yale University Press, 1980), p. 227.

32.   Rosolato, *Essais,* p. 176.

33.   Jacques-Alain Miller, "On Perversion," in Reading Seminars I and II, ed. Richard Feldstein, Bruce Fink, Maire Jaanus (Albany: SUNY Press, 1996).